classic vegetarian

cookery

arto der haroutunian

GRUB STREET | LONDON

Acknowledgements

My grateful thanks to all the authors, editors, translators and publishers from whose works I have quoted (see Bibliography). If, unwittingly, some have not been mentioned — my deepest apologies.

Thanks are due also to all those whose advice and help was sought in the preparation of this book.

I am particularly grateful to the following people for their help and suggestions: the proprietors of 'Amee Supermarket' in Manchester, Mr Kantilal and Mr Ashok D. Vara; Mr Nori Shibahara of Mina-Japan restaurant, Manchester; Ms Lea Marjatta Nuutila; Mr Hamedan Saad Gisher; Mrs Rosette Ouzounian; Ms Joy Minto; Mr Mohammad Waheed and Mrs Shaheen Parveen Waheed; Mr Jerayr Azirian of 'Azir's Delicatessen' in Manchester; Mr Fadly Glada Shenouda.

Note: All recipes serve 6 people unless otherwise stated. Quantities of salt specified here are those required in authentic recipes and can be adjusted according to personal taste.

Published in 2011 by
Grub Street, 4 Rainham Close, London SW11 6SS
Email: food@grubstreet.co.uk
www.grubstreet.co.uk

Text copyright © Arto der Haroutunian 1985, 2011
Copyright this edition © Grub Street 2011

Formatting by Eclipse. roy.eclipse@btopenworld.com
Jacket design by Lizzie Ballantyne

ISBN 978-1-908117-01-4

A CIP catalogue for this book is available from the British Library

First published by Ebury Press in 1985 as *Classic Vegetable Cookery*

Printed and bound in Great Britain by MPG Books Ltd, Bodmin, Cornwall. This book is printed on FSC (Forest Stewardship Council) paper

contents

introduction

'The person who constantly eats vegetables can do everything'
Chinese proverb

With hindsight I now realise how fortunate I was to have spent my childhood and early teens in that part of the world we call 'the Fertile Crescent' or the Middle East. Fortunate, not so much for the educational and material advantages, but for the simple, peaceful (then), almost biblical way of life. I was brought up in two major towns — Aleppo and Beirut, where the pace of life was as calm and assured as that of a camel. Indeed, both towns belonged to the camel, the sheep, the goat — not forgetting the mule and the ox. Throughout there existed a natural harmony which, alas, was abruptly shattered when I set foot in Britain one rainy, foggy August day. That was well over 30 years ago and by now I have become acclimatised to all the vagaries of Nature except one — the limitations of her fruit and vegetable products. I admit I was spoilt.

Our house in Beirut was an island surrounded by apple, orange, cherry, chestnut, tangerine, palm and banana trees. We hardly ever bought any oranges, but simply picked them from the trees. Occasionally we bought a 22 kg (50 lb) sack of the famed 'Antilias' oranges (better known in Britain as Jaffas) from neighbouring orchards for a few pence. My family went through at least two such sacks a week and no-one blinked an eye. Imagine my consternation when, upon our arrival at our new home in Manchester, we (my younger brother and I) found no sackful of oranges in the kitchen. There was nothing but potatoes, onions, cabbages and leeks. These were not unknown to me, but who in their right mind could go on eating potatoes day after day when such vegetables as aubergines, okra, courgettes, kohlrabi, spinach and peppers were the everyday vegetables of his 'old' country?

Since food plays a major role in the life of a Middle Easterner, my life suddenly became dull and unappetising.

My mother, excellent cook that she was, tried to enliven our beleaguered diet with all kinds of innovations and substitutions. Relations and family friends from Paris, Aleppo, Beirut and Cyprus would send us Christmas packages filled with dried fruits, vegetables such as green peppers, courgettes and okra, apricot paste (amardin), goat's cheese, sumac powder, herbs and spices to alleviate the siege mentality that had enveloped our very souls.

I recall (much to my chagrin and amusement) how, during those early years, I went to sleep in tears, longing for the fresh mulberries and blood-red pomegranates of our

Beirut garden. With hindsight, I now realise how fortunate I was to have spent the formative years of my life in the part of the world that was the orchard of our Western civilisation. For, from a very early age, I ate, enjoyed and appreciated many of Nature's wonderful products unconsciously.

Today in Britain, however, all the variety of Nature is ours for the buying. At the local Indian grocery a box full of sweet potatoes from the West Indies is flanked by chayotes and pawpaws from Brazil; silky smooth aubergines from Kenya or Spain or Israel are shelved next to twisted karelas (bitter gourds) and there are other gourds of different shapes and sizes, some weighing up to 22 kg (50 lb). There are boxes of pickling cucumbers from Holland, tindoras (tiny cucumber-shaped vegetables not much larger than radishes) from Bangladesh, Far Eastern white radishes, courgettes from Italy, yams from Africa and kohlrabi, beets and spinach from Greece. Then there are the chillies — small, bitter, hot, pungent, large, green or red from all parts of the globe; and those delicious fruits: guavas, mangoes, pineapples, grapes, fresh dates, watermelons — the list could go on and on — which have made me, belatedly, realise how fortunate I am to be living where I do. Indeed, I can most assuredly affirm that no other part of the world has such a wealth of choice. The reasons are obvious. Our climate, with its shortcomings, has forced us to import extensively, thus the world has become our oyster. The immigrants, too, have brought with them the foods that sustained them at home and these are now becoming commonplace on our supermarket shelves.

LEARNING ABOUT 'NEW' VEGETABLES

'But what do you do with it?' My local Indian greengrocer smiles a sad but understanding smile and goes on to explain most patiently how to prepare the 'drumstick' I am pointing at. 'It's very tasty,' he says, his eyes gleaming under the neon lights, and I know I will not be disappointed.

To all my questions he or his assistant, and several times his wife, who comes rushing out from her kitchen, give precise details of the many ways they have been cooking this or that 'unknown' vegetable for centuries in their part of the world.

I understand that longing in their eyes or on the edges of their lips as they expound the diverse qualities of the vegetable under discussion; a few years ago I, too, would lovingly describe to my classmates, as we played in the school yard, what a palm tree, a banana or a watermelon looked and tasted like and would feel a pang of longing for the sun-drenched orchards of my childhood.

This book is about vegetables: the known, the little known and the few still unknown to the British. This is also a vegetarian book. In essence it is an excuse on my part to exalt the many qualities in vegetables. It is vegetarian because vegetables are at their best when treated as they are without the addition of meat, fish or poultry.

The recipes in this collection hail from every corner of the world and are 'classics' in their own right. Some will undoubtedly be known to you, others are still confined to their native regions. I have not adapted any recipe to rechristen it as 'vegetarian'. Hence several well-loved dishes have consciously been omitted — because they may have included rice or other grains, or pastas, or rashers of bacon. What is left is a rich, wholesome repertoire of fascinating recipes reflecting man's tireless drive to create food that flatters his palate, fills his stomach and satisfies his bodily needs.

THE INFLUENCE OF RELIGION ON FOOD

In this overtly secular society of ours we appear to have forgotten how much our spiritual and religious beliefs have influenced not only our moral and cultural attitudes, but also the development of our food.

The numerous olive oil-based dishes of Greece, Turkey and the rest of the Middle East (particularly the Coptic and Ethiopian Orthodox Churches) were first and foremost developed to satisfy a religious dogma which affirmed that a good Christian must fast for 40 days during Lent when no meat, poultry, fish or any other animal products shall enter his body.

In Southeast Asia and the Far East vegetarian diets have been used for centuries by those whose philosophy and religion (Hinduism, Jainism, Buddhism, Zen-Buddhism and their offshoots) sanction the right of animals to live, seeing their killing as sinful unless the animal is harmful to humans. Indeed the first (some say the best) vegetable dishes of India, China and Japan are still found in Buddhist monasteries.

Today, in the West, it is not so much religion but rather a wish to nurture their health which has prompted a great many people to eat more and more vegetables. There is a very definite trend towards eating less meat and other fatty foods. People are reducing their meat consumption in a simple but valid pursuit of better health and a more equitable ecological balance. Doctors have carried out numerous studies on this subject and have arrived at a simple conclusion — vegetarians in general appear to be healthier than non-vegetarians; their bodies are leaner, their blood pressure and serum cholesterol levels lower.

Economy, too, plays a major role in this transformation. It is becoming more and more expensive to live on a meat diet. The nutrition supplied by 450 g (1 lb) of meat costs eight to nine times the nutritive value in plant foods the animals need to be fed on, and with a world fast approaching the 7,000,000,000th human inhabitant it is able to support only a small minority with the privilege of eating meat as their staple food.

DIET FOR THE FUTURE

I believe we have no choice but to eat more vegetables in the future. I do not think we will all become vegetarians but I am sure we will consume more vegetables, fruits and nuts, many of which are still unknown to us and as yet unavailable in our corner shops.

What is already there, however, is a magnificent array of all the goodness of Nature brought 'at great expense and with a great deal of trouble' from all corners of the world for us to indulge in, in the pursuit of our earthly pleasures.

soups

Soup, from the French *soupe*, meaning a broth or a bouillon made with various vegetables and/or meat and often incorporating pulses, grains and fruits, is today subdivided into two main categories — clear soup and thick soup. Clear soup is a consommé with diverse garnishes, while a thick soup is either puréed or thickened with cream, yogurt, roux or some other liaising element such as rice, bread or eggs.

For thousands of years soup was, and in certain societies still is, the basic food of the people. The North African harira soups or the Caucasian *abour* or *chorbas*, ranging from very light yogurt or fruit-based soups to the many substantial ones which are eaten as entire meals, are very typical of those of Central Europe, Africa and the American continents.

Man's first breakthrough in evolving a culinary tradition may have commenced with the technology of grilling the flesh of animals he so ruthlessly hunted, but the art of cooking was undoubtedly born when he threw chunks of meat, vegetables and herbs into a large container, covered them with water and created the first broth or stew.

Few people in Britain and North America make their own soup any more, preferring the '57' and more varieties commercially available; the more's the pity, for a 'good cook is soon perceived by her ability in preparing broth'. In Europe and the rest of the world soups are still prepared at home and still form part of the basic diet.

There is nothing as nourishing and appetising as a large bowl of home-made soup, whether served at the start of a meal, as is the custom in Europe, throughout the course of a meal, as in China, or often at the end of the meal, as in certain Middle Eastern lands.

A basic component of soups is the stock, which is usually prepared with a meat (often bones), chicken or fish base. Obviously for vegetarians — in the strictest sense of the word — the most difficult thing is to arrive at an acceptable stock. To achieve this one must cook the vegetables slowly in order to extract all the mineral salts. If you then wish to thicken the soup use a roux, which is a mixture of butter and flour cooked together (see Glossary).

For a vegetable stock use the recipe in the Glossary. With certain soups I have suggested using water, with others ingredients such as yogurt, milk, cream, coconut milk or miso — the choice is yours.

FLAVOUR, TEXTURE AND COLOUR

There are three important points to consider when making a soup — flavour, texture and colour.

Flavour is usually subdivided into two categories — 'warm' or 'cool'. The first applies to soups where spices are generously used. The second to those that include fruit juices, yogurt or cream and fresh herbs.

Texture has come to play a more important role than in the past as thick, rich soups, such as those from Africa, the Middle East and Central Europe, have given way to the French-inspired consommés.

Colour of course is of supreme importance. The elegant light green of a watercress soup patterned with a few streaks of milk-white yogurt, or the rich, ruby red of a Ukrainian borsch, the green of a thick pea soup or the light blue-green of an avocado soup sprinkled with paprika or cumin will enhance the dining table and make the contents of the tureen more appetising.

asparagus soup

Asparagus was loved by the ancient Egyptians and the Romans, and was highly prized by the khalifs of Baghdad of the '1001 Nights' fame. It makes an excellent soup and there are several variations. The recipe below is an Anglo-French standard.

450 g (1 lb) fresh asparagus
600 ml (1 pint) water
50 g (2 oz) butter
50 g (2 oz) flour
600 ml (1 pint) milk
5 ml (1 teaspoon) salt
1.25 ml ($^1/_4$ teaspoon) black pepper
1.25 ml ($^1/_4$ teaspoon) nutmeg

Garnish
30 ml (2 tablespoons) finely chopped parsley or chervil

1 Wash the asparagus, cut off the tips and reserve. Cut the stalks into 2.5 cm (1 inch) pieces, place in a saucepan, cover with the water and bring to the boil. Lower the heat, cover the pan and simmer for 30 minutes. Remove the stalks with a slotted spoon and discard. Add the reserved tips to the water, cover then simmer for 10 minutes. Strain, reserving both the tips and the cooking water.

2 Melt the butter in a large saucepan, add the flour and cook for 3-4 minutes, stirring constantly with a wooden spoon. Mix the milk and cooking liquid together and make up to 1.1 litres (2 pints) with water if necessary.

Gradually mix this into the roux, stirring constantly to prevent lumps forming. Slowly bring to the boil and simmer for 2-3 minutes, still stirring all the time.

3 Season with the salt, pepper and nutmeg, add the reserved asparagus tips and simmer for a further 2-3 minutes. Serve garnished with the parsley or chervil.

VARIATION: The famed POTAGE CRÈME D'ASPERGES D'ARGENTEUIL makes use of the best-known French asparagus variety — Argenteuil. This soup is related to the one above, but is much thicker and richer, incorporating both cream and béchamel sauce. Use the tips of 450 g (1 lb) white asparagus, blanched. Simmer them in 50 g (2 oz) melted butter, covered, for 10-15 minutes. Add 1.1 litres (2 pints) béchamel sauce (see Glossary) and simmer over a low heat for about 10 minutes, stirring occasionally to prevent sticking. Either pass the mixture through a sieve, rubbing through as much asparagus as possible, or process in a blender until smooth. Return to the pan and dilute to the thickness you require with milk. Season with 7.5 ml (1$^1/_2$ teaspoons) salt and 2.5 ml ($^1/_2$ teaspoon) black pepper and bring gently back to the boil. Just before serving stir in 450 ml ($^3/_4$ pint) cream.

Serve garnished with freshly chopped parsley or chervil and with croutons, fried lightly in butter or vegetable oil.

lo sun — chuk matong

asparagus and bamboo shoot soup

A popular soup from the Hopeh and Shantung regions of northeast China. It is typical of the numerous vegetable-based soups that are simple and delicately flavoured.

There are many varieties of bamboo shoots (*chuk sun*), each with its own characteristic flavour and sweetness. Fresh shoots are lightly sweet in taste with a crunchy texture. Originally a north Chinese vegetable popular in the cuisines of Shanghai, Peking and Nanking, bamboo shoots now appear in Cantonese-owned restaurants — although not, I understand, on Cantonese dining tables. You can buy both canned and dried bamboo shoots from Chinese food shops.

45 ml (3 tablespoons) oil
4–5 spring onions, thinly sliced
450 g (1 lb) asparagus, tough root ends discarded, cut into 2.5 cm (1 inch) pieces
225 g (8 oz) canned bamboo shoots, cut into 1 cm ($^1/_2$ inch) cubes
2.3 litres (4 pints) vegetable stock (see Glossary)
30 ml (2 tablespoons) soy sauce
7.5 ml (1$^1/_2$ teaspoons) salt
2.5 ml ($^1/_2$ teaspoon) black pepper
1.25 ml ($^1/_4$ teaspoon) ground ginger
30 ml (2 tablespoons) dry sherry
5 ml (1 teaspoon) sesame oil

1 Heat the oil in a large saucepan, add the spring onions and asparagus and sauté for 2–3 minutes. Add the cubed bamboo shoots and cook, stirring frequently, for a further 2 minutes. Stir in the stock, soy sauce, salt, pepper and ginger and bring to the boil. Lower the heat, cover the pan and simmer for 1$^1/_4$–1$^1/_2$ hours.

2 Remove from the heat, stir in the sherry and sesame oil and serve.

azokod abour

aubergine and chickpea soup

Aubergine, the 'Queen of vegetables' as one Persian poet of the twelfth century penned, is the vegetable of Middle Eastern cuisines.

It is particularly at its best in Armenian-Turkish cookery, from where this recipe originates.

Traditionally sour (unripe) grapes were used. If you have a vine in your garden use the unripe grapes, but if not, I suggest an excellent alternative, sumac, which is the berry of a small shrub that grows wild in northern Iran, the Caucasus and Turkey. The berry, reddish in colour, is powdered and then used in soups and stews.

It has a sharp lemony flavour and can be bought in many Greek and Middle Eastern shops.

45 ml (3 tablespoons) oil
2 garlic cloves, crushed
450 g (1 lb) aubergines, cut into 1 cm (¹/₂ inch) cubes
50 g (2 oz) chickpeas, soaked overnight in cold water,
drained, cooked in boiling water until tender and drained
50 g (2 oz) whole lentils, washed
1.7 litres (3 pints) water or vegetable stock (see Glossary)
4 large tomatoes, blanched, peeled and chopped
juice of 1 large lemon
10 ml (2 teaspoons) sumac powder or
30 ml (2 more tablespoons) lemon juice
7.5 ml (1¹/₂ teaspoons) salt
10 ml (2 teaspoons) dried mint

1 Heat the oil in a large saucepan, add the garlic and fry for 1 minute. Add the aubergine cubes and fry, turning frequently for 2-3 minutes. Add the drained chickpeas and lentils to the pan with the water or stock and bring to the boil. Lower the heat, cover the pan and simmer for 20 minutes.

2 Add the tomatoes, lemon juice and sumac and simmer for a further 45 minutes or until the lentils and chickpeas are really tender. If necessary, add a little more water or stock to maintain about 1.4-1.7 litres (2¹/₂-3 pints) of liquid.

3 Stir in the salt and mint, simmer for a few more minutes and serve.

sopa de aguacate

avocado soup

Avocado is a remarkable fruit-vegetable, one of Nature's many gifts that arrived in the Old World from the New — to be more precise from South America. Avocado was known in Britain as far back as the seventeenth century, but it was only a few decades ago that it appeared on a regular basis in our high street greengrocers. Since then it has become standard fare, not only in restaurants and hotels all over Britain and Europe but, more importantly, in our homes.

Avocados make a fine soup. This one is of South American origin, though I hasten to add that there are many excellent avocado soups in North American and Israeli cuisines — all of recent vintage. Serve it cold.

2 ripe avocados, peeled and stoned
1 garlic clove, crushed
5 ml (1 teaspoon) salt
1.25 ml ($^1/_4$ teaspoon) black pepper
1.25 ml ($^1/_4$ teaspoon) allspice
15 ml (1 tablespoon) lemon juice
900 ml (1$^1/_2$ pints) milk

Garnish
2 tablespoons finely chopped mint or chives

1 Chop the avocado flesh and place in a blender with the garlic, salt, pepper, allspice and lemon juice and blend to a thick pulp. If necessary add a little of the milk to help it blend smoothly. Turn into a large bowl and stir in the milk.

2 Chill for at least 1 hour and then serve garnished with the mint or chives.

bean soups

'Hunger makes raw beans into almonds'
German proverb

A quick glance at your local supermarket shelves will convince you of three facts. First, that we have come a long way from the day when Esau sold his inheritance for a bowl of lentil soup — since there was nothing else available — second, that many beans from the *Leguminosae* family crossed the Atlantic after the conquest of the New World and, third, that there are now so many beans available, both fresh and dried, that one is momentarily at a loss to know what to do with them.

The solution is simple. Study the cuisines of the Mediterranean coastline (north and south), the Middle East and the Indian subcontinent. They have, more than any others, mastered the art of bean cookery.

Your supermarket shelves are filled to the brim with broad beans, butter beans, haricot beans, flageolet beans, runner beans, french beans, black beans, black-eyed beans, kidney beans, Adzuki (Japanese) beans, chickpeas, different-coloured lentils, mung beans, Egyptian brown beans (*ful*), pinto beans, soya beans and many others — all full of colour, texture and, above all, goodness.

Next to cereals, beans are the most important of human foods. The protein content of some varieties is higher than that of any other vegetable and can be substituted for animal protein in human nutrition.

For further information on beans see the Glossary.

sopa de frigoles negros

black bean soup

The first bean soup I have chosen is from the Caribbean — from the island of Cuba, famed for her middle-aged revolutionaries, sugar-cane plantations and dark-haired maidens between whose ivory thighs it is rumoured that the flavoursome Havana cigars are rolled. The soup is full of flavour too.

30 ml (2 tablespoons) oil
1 onion, chopped
2 garlic cloves, crushed
1 celery stick with its leaves, chopped
225 g (8 oz) dried black beans, soaked overnight
in cold water and drained
2.3 litres (4 pints) water or vegetable stock (see Glossary)
10 ml (2 tablespoons) salt
1.25 ml ($1/_4$ teaspoon) black pepper
2.5 ml ($1/_2$ teaspoon) cayenne pepper
juice of 1 large lemon
45 ml (3 tablespoons) dry sherry

Garnish
2 hard-boiled eggs, chopped

1 Heat the oil in a large saucepan. Add the onion, garlic and celery and fry, stirring frequently, for 3–4 minutes. Add the beans and water or stock and bring to the boil. Lower the heat, cover the pan and simmer for about 1$1/_2$ hours or until the beans are tender.

2 With a slotted spoon, remove about half of the beans and place in a blender. Add a little of the cooking liquid and process to a smooth purée. Return this to the whole beans in the saucepan, season with the salt, black pepper and cayenne pepper and simmer for a further 10 minutes, stirring constantly.

3 Stir in the lemon juice and sherry and serve garnished with the chopped eggs.

VARIATION: In Mexico 125 g (4 oz) tomato purée is stirred into the soup with the lemon juice and then it is garnished with grated cheese.

fasoulada

greek bean soup

'One may chatter long before the soup boils'
German saying

This is the national soup of Greece and is also popular throughout Turkey, Kurdistan and Armenia. It is simple and wholesome. The greatest honour a host can confer is to offer his guests a bowl of hot fasoulada with crusty Greek bread and some olives, sliced celery, radishes and cucumber. When preparing this soup do use good-quality olive oil — it will enhance the taste.

120 ml (8 tablespoons) olive oil
1 leek, chopped
2 carrots, chopped
1 small onion, finely chopped
2 celery sticks, chopped
1 garlic clove, crushed
225 g (8 oz) haricot beans, soaked overnight
in cold water and drained
1.7 litres (3 pints) water
25 ml (1 heaped tablespoon) tomato purée
7.5 ml (1^1/$_2$ teaspoons) salt
2.5 ml (^{1}/$_2$ teaspoon) black pepper
2.5 ml (^{1}/$_2$ teaspoon) paprika
30 ml (2 tablespoons) finely chopped parsley

Garnish
Lemon wedges

1 Heat the oil in a large saucepan, add the leek, carrots, onion, celery and garlic and fry for 3–4 minutes. Stir in the beans, water and tomato purée and bring to the boil. Lower the heat, cover the pan and simmer for about 1 hour or until the beans are tender.

2 Stir in the remaining ingredients and simmer for a further 5 minutes. Serve with lemon wedges, as many people like to stir a little lemon juice into the soup.

kong na-mool kook

bean sprout soup

A classic from Korea. This is the vegetarian version. Koreans in general love to include small quantities of meat in their soup whether needed or not.

30 ml (2 tablespoons) oil
6 spring onions, thinly sliced. Slice green tops and set aside
1 celery stick, thinly sliced
1 garlic clove, thinly sliced
7.5 ml (1^1/$_2$ teaspoons) salt
2.5 ml (^{1}/$_2$ teaspoon) black pepper
1.25 ml (^{1}/$_4$ teaspoon) sugar
15 ml (1 level tablespoon) prepared sesame seeds (*see* Glossary)
120 ml (8 tablespoons) soy sauce
450 g (1 lb) fresh bean sprouts
2.3 litres (4 pints) water

1 Heat the oil in a large saucepan, add the spring onions, celery and garlic and fry until soft. Add the salt, pepper, sugar, prepared sesame seeds and half the soy sauce and fry for 3–4 minutes. Add the bean sprouts and fry for a further 2–3 minutes, stirring frequently.

2 Stir in the remaining soy sauce and the water and bring to the boil. Lower the heat, cover the pan and simmer for about 8–10 minutes or until the bean sprouts are tender.

3 Stir in the chopped green spring onion tops and simmer for 5 more minutes.

vartabedi abour

lentil soup

A classic Armenian soup which is also popular in southern Turkey and parts of Syria. The name derives from the story of a young priest who was poor and had little time so he devised this nourishing but simple soup to keep his body alive — his soul, no doubt, was in safe hands.

Use any kind of whole lentils. They come in varying colours of grey, green, yellow and reddish-brown. Lentils have been known and cultivated in the Middle East for centuries, while India is the world's largest producer of this most nutritional pulse.

175 g (6 oz) whole lentils, rinsed
2.8 litres (5 pints) water
50 g (2 oz) long grain rice, washed thoroughly
under cold running water and drained
125 g (4 oz) macaroni or spaghetti, broken into 2.5 cm (1 inch) pieces
50 ml (2 fl oz) oil
1 large onion, finely chopped
7.5 ml (1^1/$_2$ teaspoons) salt
1.25 ml (^{1}/$_4$ teaspoon) black pepper
2.5 ml (^{1}/$_2$ teaspoon) cumin

Garnish
2.5–5 ml (^{1}/$_2$–1 teaspoon) chilli powder
lemon juice

1 Place the lentils and water in a large saucepan and bring to the boil. Lower the heat, cover the pan and simmer for 20 minutes. Add the rice and simmer for a further 10 minutes. Finally, add the macaroni or spaghetti and simmer for another 8–10 minutes or until all the ingredients are tender.

2 Meanwhile, heat the oil in a small pan, add the onion and fry until golden. Stir into the soup and then season with the salt, pepper and cumin. Taste and adjust seasoning, if necessary.

3 Serve garnished with a little chilli powder and a few drops of lemon juice.

dhal rasam

pepper water with lentils

A regional speciality from southern India. Pepper water — *rasam* — is always served with a meal, either as a soup or as a sauce accompaniment to a main course. *Dhal rasam*, however, is treated strictly as a soup.

75 g (3 oz) whole brown or green lentils, washed
2 medium onions, quartered
1.7 litres (3 pints) water
2 cloves
10–12 black peppercorns
7.5 ml (1^1/$_2$ teaspoons) salt
2.5 ml (^{1}/$_2$ teaspoon) ground cumin
1.25 ml (^{1}/$_4$ teaspoon) ground coriander
30 ml (2 tablespoons) ghee (see Glossary) or butter
juice of 1 small lemon
300 ml (^{1}/$_2$ pint) coconut milk (see Glossary)

1 Put the lentils in a large saucepan with 1 onion, the water, cloves, peppercorns, salt, cumin and coriander. Bring to the boil, lower the heat, cover the pan and simmer for 45–60 minutes or until the lentils are very tender.

2 Pour the mixture into a sieve placed over a large pan and rub through as much of the lentils and onion as possible with a wooden spoon. Discard the residue.

3 Return the liquid to the saucepan.

4 Heat the ghee or butter in a small pan. Thinly slice the remaining onion quarters and add to the fat. Fry until golden and then pour into the soup. Stir in the lemon juice and coconut milk and bring back to the boil. Simmer for 3–5 minutes and serve.

ash-e shol ghalamcar

chickpea and herb soup

This soup is a meal in itself. It is thick, tasty and wholesome. It is traditionally served when a person is off on a long journey such as a pilgrimage to the holy cities of Mecca and Medina. Made in large quantities it is distributed to neighbours and relations.

15 ml (1 tablespoon) ghee (*see* Glossary) or butter
1 large onion, sliced
5 ml (1 teaspoon) turmeric
75 g (3 oz) chickpeas, soaked overnight in cold water and drained
40 g (1¹/₂ oz) pinto or red kidney beans,
soaked in cold water for 4 hours and drained
2.8 litres (5 pints) water
60 ml (4 tablespoons) finely chopped parsley
125 g (4 oz) fresh spinach, coarse stems discarded, rinsed thoroughly and chopped
1 leek, chopped and washed
40 g (1¹/₂ oz) whole lentils, washed
75 g (3 oz) long grain rice, washed thoroughly
under cold running water and drained
10 ml (2 teaspoons) salt
1.25 ml (¹/₄ teaspoon) black pepper
15 ml (1 tablespoon) flour
150 ml (¹/₄ pint) yogurt

Garnish
15 ml (1 tablespoon) ghee (see Glossary) or butter
45 ml (3 tablespoons) chopped fresh mint or 1 tablespoon dried mint

1 Melt the ghee or butter in a large saucepan, add the onion and fry until soft. Stir in the turmeric, chickpeas, pinto or kidney beans and the water. Bring to the boil, lower the heat, cover the pan and simmer for 1 hour.

2 Add the parsley, spinach, leek and lentils and simmer, covered, for a further 20 minutes. Then stir in the rice, salt and pepper and simmer for 20 more minutes.

3 Mix the flour and yogurt together in a small bowl until smooth and then stir into the soup. Simmer for 2–3 minutes.

4 Meanwhile melt the ghee or butter in a small pan and fry the mint for 2 minutes. Sprinkle over the soup and serve immediately.

VARIATION: In Afghanistan 225 g (8 oz) of shredded cabbage is also often added to this soup.

sopa de garbanzos
chickpea soup

The chickpea, native to Asia, is particularly popular in Indian, Middle Eastern and North African cookery. It is small, hazelnut shaped and light golden in colour. This recipe from southern Spain is very reminiscent of Moroccan and Middle Eastern soups and the connection is obvious — the centuries-long occupation of Spain by the Moors and Arabs. Compare this soup with its variation from Iran. The simple Spanish recipe contrasts strongly with the rich and filling one from Khuzistan.

250 g (9 oz) chickpeas, soaked in cold water overnight and drained
50 g (2 oz) butter
1 medium onion, chopped
2 medium carrots, peeled and diced
15 ml (1 tablespoon) lemon juice
1 bay leaf
7.5 ml (1$^1/_2$ teaspoons) salt
1.25 ml ($^1/_4$ teaspoon) black pepper

Garnish
30 ml (2 tablespoons) finely chopped mint or parsley
croutons

1 Place the chickpeas in a large saucepan with plenty of water and bring to the boil. Lower the heat, cover the pan and simmer for 1–1$^1/_2$ hours or until tender. Add more boiling water if necessary. When tender drain the chickpeas and reserve the cooking liquid, making it up to 1.7 litres (3 pints) with water.

2 Melt half the butter in the saucepan, add the onion and carrots and fry for about 5 minutes or until soft. Add the chickpeas, cooking liquid and remaining ingredients and bring to the boil. Lower the heat, cover the pan and simmer for 30 minutes. Discard the bay leaf and set the soup aside to cool.

3 Transfer the contents of the pan to a blender and process to a smooth purée. Return to the saucepan and bring back to the boil. Stir in the remaining butter and, if necessary, add a little more water until you have the consistency you require. Taste and add a little more salt if you wish.

4 Serve in individual bowls garnished with a little chopped mint or parsley and a few croutons.

borsch kievsky
kiev-style beetroot soup

There are countless beetroot soups in the world, but the truly classic ones come from Central Europe or, to be more accurate, the Ukraine. In Russia, 'first course' on menus means soup, and soup with a capital S implies one of the scores of variations on beetroot. Although borsch includes other ingredients such as potatoes, marrow, carrot, apple, turnip, all kinds of pulses, peppers and sweetcorn, the main one is the red beet, 'borsch' in old Slavic, hence the name of the soup which is traditionally served with soured cream and buckwheat or pancakes.

I have included several recipes of this magnificent soup, the first of which is from Kiev, the capital of the Ukraine.

Traditionally the liquid used is either stock and beetroot *rassol* — the liquid in which beetroot is preserved — or stock and *kvass*.

50 g (2 oz) mushrooms, wiped clean and sliced
225 g (8 oz) carrots, peeled and sliced
350 g (12 oz) white cabbage, finely shredded
2 large tomatoes, blanched, peeled and chopped
1 parsley root or parsnip, peeled and sliced
2.3 litres (4 pints) *kvass* (see Glossary), vegetable stock or water
450 g (1 lb) cooked beetroot
10 ml (2 teaspoons) salt
2.5 ml ($^1/_2$ teaspoon) black pepper
1 bay leaf
25 g (1 oz) butter
1 onion, thinly sliced

Soured Cream Sauce
2 egg yolks
150 ml ($^1/_4$ pint) soured cream

Garnish
30 ml (2 tablespoons) finely chopped parsley

1 Put the mushrooms, carrots, cabbage, tomatoes and parsley root or parsnip into a large saucepan with the *kvass*, stock or water and bring to the boil. Lower the heat, cover the pan and simmer for 20 minutes.

2 Peel and grate the beetroot and add to the pan together with the salt, black pepper and bay leaf. Cover and cook for a further 20 minutes.

3 Meanwhile, melt the butter in a frying pan, add the onion and fry, stirring frequently, until soft and golden. Add to the soup, stir well and continue to cook until all the vegetables are tender.

4 Prepare the sauce by mixing the egg yolks and cream together thoroughly in a small bowl.

5 To serve ladle the soup into individual bowls, spoon some of the sauce into each one and swirl gently. Sprinkle with a little parsley.

postnyee borsch

borsch with apples

This soup belongs to the rich tradition of the Russian Orthodox Church's Lent cuisine, a cuisine which, incidentally, is as yet little known in the rest of Europe.

In this recipe the leaves of the young beetroots are used as well as the roots. If you cannot obtain them, use spinach instead.

225 g (8 oz) mushrooms, chopped
2 raw beetroots, peeled and chopped
225 g (8 oz) young beetroot leaves or spinach,
washed thoroughly and coarsely chopped
1 large onion, chopped
1 turnip, peeled and chopped
1 swede, peeled and chopped
2 large cooking apples, peeled
2 celery sticks, chopped
1 garlic clove, crushed
10 ml (2 teaspoons) salt
2.5 ml ($^1/_2$ teaspoon) white pepper
15 ml (1 tablespoon) chopped fresh dill or 5 ml (1 teaspoon) dried dillweed
2.3 litres (4 pints) water
45 ml (3 tablespoons) chopped parsley
juice of 1 lemon

Garnish
150 ml ($^1/_4$ pint) soured cream

1 Place all the ingredients except the parsley and lemon juice in a large saucepan and bring to the boil. Lower the heat, cover the pan and simmer for about 45 minutes or until all the ingredients are tender. Add a little more water, if necessary.

2 Stir in the parsley and lemon juice and simmer for 10 more minutes.

3 Serve in individual bowls with a tablespoon of the soured cream swirled into each.

shchi

russian cabbage soup

'Having a good wife and rich cabbage soup, other seek not'
Russian saying

Shchi is the classic Russian cabbage soup and it has numerous variations. The most essential ingredient is sauerkraut (*kislye shchi*). Ordinary fresh cabbage just will not do. Sauerkraut can be bought in bottles and jars, but if you wish to make your own — and home-made is always superior to the commercial rivals — I suggest you follow carefully the simplified method on page 244.

50 g (2 oz) dried mushrooms or 175 g (6 oz) fresh mushrooms, cleaned and sliced
2.3 litres (4 pints) water
450 g (1 lb) sauerkraut, drained and shredded finely
3 large potatoes, peeled and cut into 2 cm ($^3/_4$ inch) cubes
5 ml (1 teaspoon) sugar
2 bay leaves
4 peppercorns
25 g (1 oz) butter
1 carrot, peeled and thinly sliced
1 small parsnip, peeled and thinly sliced
1 celery stick, chopped
1 onion, chopped

Garnish
150 ml ($^1/_4$ pint) soured cream, optional
30 ml (2 tablespoons) finely chopped parsley or dill

1 Place the mushrooms in a large saucepan with the water and bring to the boil. Lower the heat, cover the pan and simmer for 15 minutes.

2 Pour half of the stock into another pan, add the sauerkraut and simmer for 15 minutes.

3 Meanwhile, place the potatoes, sugar, bay leaves and peppercorns in the pan with the mushrooms and also simmer for 15 minutes.

4 Melt the butter in a frying pan and sauté the carrot, parsnip, celery and onion for 5 minutes. Transfer the sautéed vegetables to the pan with the mushrooms and potatoes. Add the contents of the sauerkraut pan. Stir well and continue to simmer until all the vegetables are tender.

5 Serve in individual bowls garnished with a little soured cream, if using, and fresh parsley or dill.

mehudehra

albanian garlic soup

'Do not plant garlic with the great'
(don't have dealings with powerful personages)
Albanian saying

If you like garlic this soup is for you. The quantity of garlic can be increased if you wish, but I think 6 cloves should be sufficient. This soup is best eaten soon after it is cooked. If it is left to stand the pasta absorbs the liquid.

30 ml (2 tablespoons) butter or margarine
6 garlic cloves, crushed
10 ml (2 teaspoons) paprika
1.7 litres (3 pints) water or vegetable stock (see Glossary)
75 g (3 oz) vermicelli, broken into 2.5 cm (1 inch) pieces
7.5 ml (1^1/$_2$ teaspoons) salt
1.25 ml (^{1}/$_4$ teaspoon) black pepper
5 ml (1 teaspoon) dried mint

Garnish
30 ml (2 tablespoons) finely chopped parsley or coriander

1 Heat the fat in a large saucepan. Add the garlic and fry over gentle heat for 2–3 minutes. Stir in the paprika and water or stock and bring to the boil.

2 Add the vermicelli, salt and pepper and simmer for 10 minutes. Stir in the mint and simmer for a further 2 minutes.

3 Serve in individual bowls sprinkled with the parsley or coriander.

caldo verde

portuguese cabbage soup

This is the best-known Portuguese soup and it is named after the dark green couve cabbage which, early in this century, was highly esteemed in Britain. Unfortunately it is now very difficult to find — a pity since it is a delicious cabbage with large, broad, ribbed leaves. The alternative I suggest, reluctantly, is the ordinary, readily available green cabbage.

Traditionally *caldo verde* is eaten with the dark rye and wheat flour bread called *pão de broa*. Sometimes 2–3 tablespoons olive oil is substituted for the cream.

1.7 litres (3 pints) water or vegetable stock (see Glossary)
1 onion, peeled and cut into rings
450 g (1 lb) potatoes, peeled and sliced
5 ml (1 tablespoon) salt
2.5 ml (1/2 teaspoon) black pepper
30–45 ml (2–3 tablespoons) single cream
350 g (12 oz) couve or other green cabbage, very finely shredded

1 Bring the water or stock to the boil in a large saucepan, add the onion and potatoes, salt and pepper. Lower the heat, cover the pan and simmer for about 25–30 minutes or until the vegetables are tender.

2 Remove the vegetables and either pass through a sieve or process in a blender. Return the purée to the stock in the saucepan and stir in the cream.

3. Meanwhile, bring a large saucepan half filled with lightly salted water to the boil, add the cabbage and cook, uncovered, for 5–6 minutes. Strain into a colander and stir into the vegetable purée. If the soup is too thick for your taste stir in a little more water. Adjust the seasoning if necessary.

4 Bring the soup just back to the boil and serve.

karalabeleves

magyar-style kohlrabi soup

This recipe from Budapest is part of that rich Austro-Hungarian cuisine which dominated the nineteenth-century European social banquets, but which is now all but forgotten.

The recipe is simple and tasty. Italians add rice to the soup while the Albanians add pasta. I like this lighter version, although I prefer natural yogurt to soured cream.

Serve with croutons and bread. Hungarians would use *daragaluskas*, which are semolina or potato dumplings.

700 g (1^1/$_2$ lb) young kohlrabi
50 g (2 oz) butter or margarine
7.5 ml (1^1/$_2$ teaspoons) salt
2.5 ml (^{1}/$_2$ teaspoon) black pepper
25 ml (1^1/$_2$ tablespoons) plain flour
1.7 litres (3 pints) water or vegetable stock (see Glossary)
30 ml (2 tablespoons) finely chopped coriander or parsley

Garnish
150 ml (^{1}/$_4$ pint) soured cream or yogurt
15 ml (1 tablespoon) paprika
croutons or dumplings, optional

1 Trim and peel the kohlrabi and then slice very thinly.

2 Melt the butter or margarine in a large pan, add the kohlrabi slices, salt and pepper and fry, stirring frequently, for 5–10 minutes or until the vegetables have softened. Sprinkle in the flour and fry, stirring constantly, for a further 2 minutes. Gradually stir in the liquid and bring to the boil. Lower the heat, cover the pan and simmer for 15–20 minutes or until the kohlrabi are tender.

3 Stir in the coriander or parsley and simmer for a further 2 minutes.

4 Serve in individual bowls with a little soured cream or yogurt swirled into each and sprinkled with paprika. Add croutons or dumplings if you wish.

zuppa di finocchio

fennel soup

A very popular soup from northern Italy, the home of the fennel root. This delicious soup evokes a faint aniseed flavour. Serve it with bread for, as the Italian adage goes, 'All soup is baked bread'.

50 g (2 oz) butter
1 large onion, finely chopped
3 fennel bulbs (about 350 g/12 oz), trimmed and thinly sliced
1.4 litres (2^1/$_2$ pints) water or vegetable stock (see Glossary)
10 ml (2 teaspoons) salt
2.5 ml (^{1}/$_2$ teaspoon) black pepper
300 ml (^{1}/$_2$ pint) milk

Garnish
90 ml (6 tablespoons) single cream or yogurt
30 ml (2 tablespoons) roasted pine kernels or chopped pistachios
30 ml (2 tablespoons) finely chopped parsley

1 Melt the butter in a large saucepan, add the onion and fry for 3 minutes until soft. Add the fennel and fry, stirring constantly, for a further 4–5 minutes. Pour in the stock or water, season with the salt and pepper and bring to the boil. Lower the heat, cover the pan and simmer for 25–30 minutes or until the fennel is tender. Set aside to cool.

2 Purée the mixture by passing through a sieve or processing in a blender. Return the soup to the pan and stir in the milk. Bring to the boil and simmer for 2 minutes.

3 To serve, pour into individual bowls, swirl 15 ml (1 tablespoon) of cream or yogurt into each bowl and sprinkle with a few nuts and a little chopped parsley.

tai sen tong

leek soup

The Chinese serve their soups at the beginning, in the middle or at the end of a meal. The principal function of Chinese soups is to provide a savoury liquid to go with rice and therefore they tend to be light and rather watery, similar to Indian soups, but most unlike those of the Middle East and Central Europe.

Leeks are much used in the Chinese cuisine and the recipe below is a typical example of these soups. You can prepare in much the same way soups from spinach, cucumber, cress, mushrooms, celery or lettuce.

30 ml (2 tablespoons) butter or margarine
1 garlic clove, crushed
15 ml (1 tablespoon) dried mushrooms,
soaked in warm water for 30 minutes and drained
350 g (12 oz) leeks, trimmed, thinly sliced and washed very thoroughly
1.7 litres (3 pints) water or vegetable stock (see Glossary)
15 ml (1 tablespoon) soy sauce
7.5 ml (1^1/$_2$ teaspoons) salt
1.25 ml (^{1}/$_4$ teaspoon) black pepper

1 Melt the butter or margarine in a large saucepan, add the garlic and mushrooms and fry, stirring constantly, for 1 minute. Add the sliced leeks and fry, still stirring constantly, for 2 more minutes. Pour in the water or stock, soy sauce, salt and pepper and bring to the boil. Lower the heat, cover the pan and simmer for 10–12 minutes.

2 Serve in individual bowls with a little extra soy sauce if desired.

VARIATION: Vermicelli-type noodles are often added to the soup as well as thinly sliced carrots.

cream of tomato soup

Tomatoes make excellent soups and there is a very rich repertoire available.

25 g (1 oz) butter
1 celery stick, finely chopped
1 medium carrot, peeled and thinly sliced
1 small onion, finely chopped
30 ml (2 tablespoons) flour
700 g (1^1/$_2$ lb) ripe tomatoes, blanched, peeled and quartered
1.1 litres (2 pints) water or vegetable stock (see Glossary)
bouquet garni
5 ml (1 teaspoon) salt
1.25 ml (^{1}/$_4$ teaspoon) black pepper
30–45 ml (2–3 tablespoons) single cream

Garnish
30 ml (2 tablespoons) finely chopped basil, parsley or coriander
croutons

1 Melt the butter in a large saucepan, add the celery, carrot and onion and fry, stirring frequently, for 3–4 minutes. Sprinkle with the flour and cook, stirring constantly, for 1 minute. Add the tomatoes, water or stock and bouquet garni and bring to the boil. Lower the heat, cover the pan and simmer for 30 minutes.

2 Remove and discard the bouquet garni. Either pass the contents of the pan through a sieve or purée in a blender. Return to the saucepan and stir in the salt, pepper and cream. Simmer for a further 5 minutes over a low heat.

3 Serve in individual bowls garnished with the herbs and croutons.

VARIATION: If you wish you can eliminate all other vegetables and increase the amount of tomatoes to 900 g (2 lb). Add 1 tablespoon tomato purée and proceed as with the recipe above. Garnish with 50 g (2 oz) of grated cheese of your choice.

soupe a l'oignon

french onion soup

What a pleasure, what a pleasure,
What a great delight to me.
From the cheese and from the onions
And the helmet to be free.
For I can't enjoy a battle,
But I love to pass my days
With my wine and boon companions
Round the merry, merry blaze.
The Complete Plays of Aristophanes

Aristophanes may not have cared much for cheese and onion, but this great classic, which contains both ingredients, has stood the test of time. Perhaps the ancients were far too busy writing comedies/tragedies to be bothered with the versatility of *Allium sepa*, which was so beloved by the Prophet Mohammad.

50 g (2 oz) butter
700 g (1¹/₂ lb) onions, sliced into thin rounds and separated into rings
30 ml (2 tablespoons) flour
1.7 litres (3 pints) water
7.5 ml (1¹/₂ teaspoons) salt

Garnish
6 large, thick slices bread cut into rounds
175 g (6 oz) cheese, Emmenthal or Gruyère, grated

1 Heat the butter in a large saucepan, add the onions, cover the pan and fry gently, stirring occasionally, for 20–30 minutes or until the onions are soft and golden.

2 Stir in the flour and cook gently for 2 minutes. Gradually add the water, stirring constantly, until it comes to the boil and thickens slightly. Season with the salt, cover the pan and simmer gently for about 30 minutes or until the onions are tender. Taste and adjust seasoning, if necessary.

3 Toast the bread. Ladle the soup into 6 individual bowls and add a slice of toast to each. Sprinkle each slice generously with cheese, stand the bowls on a baking tray and place in a 230°C (450°F) mark 8 oven for 5 minutes. Remove carefully and serve immediately.

eshkaneh

iranian onion soup

As a contrast to the classic French onion soup, here is one from western Iran. It is a more aromatic soup and is typical of the ancient cuisine of Persia. Serve it with bread and a bowl of fresh herbs such as tarragon, mint, basil or spring onions.

Do not be put off by the strong smell of onions, but remember what the French say — 'He who deals in onions no longer smells them.'

60 ml (4 tablespoons) butter
3 onions, thinly sliced
30 ml (2 tablespoons) flour
1.7 litres (3 pints) water
7.5 ml (1$^{1}/_{2}$ teaspoons) salt
5 ml (1 level teaspoon) black pepper
5 ml (1 teaspoon) turmeric
juice of 2 lemons or 1 lime
30 ml (2 tablespoons) sugar
15 ml (1 tablespoon) dried mint
2.5 ml ($^{1}/_{2}$ teaspoon) cinnamon
2 eggs

1 Melt the butter in a large saucepan, add the onions and fry for several minutes until soft and golden.

2 Place the flour in a small bowl and mix to a smooth paste with a tablespoon or two of water. Stir into the fried onions. Slowly stir in the water, salt, black pepper and turmeric and bring to the boil. Lower the heat, cover the pan and simmer for 30 minutes.

3 Stir in the lemon or lime juice and the sugar and simmer for a further 10 minutes. Just before removing from the heat stir in the mint and cinnamon.

4 When ready to serve break the eggs into a bowl, beat thoroughly, stir into the soup and serve immediately.

sunshine soup

cold pumpkin soup

'Only a pumpkin is a head without cares'
Italian proverb

Pumpkin is much used in soups throughout the world, particularly in South America, the Caribbean, France and the Middle East. It is puréed or cooked in small chunks with or without other vegetables. I have chosen this West Indian soup because it is unusual. It is served cold while most pumpkin soups are eaten hot.

You can substitute other vegetables such as gourds or marrows for the pumpkin. This is a refreshing and tasty soup. Serve with bread.

900 g (2 lb) pumpkin, peeled and seeded
10 ml (2 teaspoons) salt
3 large tomatoes, blanched, peeled and chopped
2 medium onions, finely chopped
60 ml (4 tablespoons) finely chopped parsley
5 cm (2 inch) piece cinnamon stick
5 ml (1 teaspoon) paprika
450 ml ($^3/_4$ pint) water or vegetable stock (see Glossary)
150 ml ($^1/_2$ pint) single cream

Garnish
30 ml (2 tablespoons) finely chopped coriander, parsley or mint

1 Cut the pumpkin flesh into 2.5 cm (1 inch) cubes and place in a saucepan half filled with water. Add the salt, bring to the boil, cover the pan and simmer for 15 minutes.

2 Drain off the water and add the tomatoes, onions and parsley to the pumpkin in the pan. Add the water or stock, the cinnamon stick and the paprika and bring to the boil. Lower the heat, cover the pan and simmer for 30 minutes. Remove from the heat and set aside to cool.

3 Discard the cinnamon stick and purée the mixture by rubbing through a sieve or processing in a blender. Taste and adjust seasoning, if necessary.

4 When completely cold stir in half the cream and refrigerate until ready to serve. Pour into individual bowls, swirl a little of the remaining cream into each and sprinkle with the herb.

po tsai tou fu keng
spinach and bean curd soup

Use spinach if possible or callaloo, as the Caribbean islanders do, or Swiss chard.

700 g (1¹/₂ lb) spinach, coarse outer leaves and stems discarded
75 ml (5 tablespoons) oil
5 ml (1 teaspoon) sugar
10 ml (2 teaspoons) salt
4-5 standard-sized bean curds (see Glossary) — about 5 x 2.5 cm (2 x 1 inch)
1.1 litres (2 pints) water
45 ml (3 level tablespoons) cornflour mixed to a smooth paste
with 150 ml (¹/₄ pint) water
30-45 ml (2-3 tablespoons) soy sauce

1 Wash the spinach thoroughly under cold running water and then pat dry. Chop coarsely.

2 Heat a wok or heavy saucepan until very hot. Add the oil and swirl around the pan. Add the spinach and stir-fry for 2-3 minutes or until the spinach wilts. Add the sugar and salt and mix well. Remove the spinach and transfer to a saucepan. Discard any liquid in the wok.

3 Cut the bean curds into 1 cm (¹/₂ inch) cubes and add to the spinach. Pour in the water and bring to the boil. Lower the heat and simmer for 5 minutes. Add a few tablespoons of the hot cooking liquid to the cornflour paste and stir well. Pour into the spinach and stir constantly until the soup thickens. Simmer for a further 10 minutes. Just before serving stir in the soy sauce. Taste and add more salt, if necessary.

spanakli çorba

spinach soup

In contrast, this is a typical Balkan-Middle Eastern spinach soup which is tasty, colourful and filling. The recipe is from the European part of Turkey.

Use fresh spinach or the famed Egyptian melokhia leaves if available. Occasionally fresh ones can be found, but if not substitute dried melokhia leaves, which can be bought in some Indian and Middle Eastern shops.

You can use burghul (cracked wheat) or vermicelli in place of the rice.

700 g (1½ lb) spinach, coarse leaves and stems discarded
50 g (2 oz) butter or margarine
1 large onion, finely chopped
45 ml (3 tablespoons) tomato purée
75 g (3 oz) long grain rice, washed thoroughly under
cold running water and drained
2 litres (3½ pints) water
10 ml (2 teaspoons) salt
2.5 ml (½ teaspoon) black pepper
5 ml (1 teaspoon) paprika
1.25 ml (¼ teaspoon) chilli powder
2.5 ml (½ teaspoon) dillweed
300 ml (½ pint) yogurt
1 large egg
juice of 1 large lemon

Garnish
2 hard-boiled eggs, coarsely chopped
30 ml (2 tablespoons) finely chopped parsley, coriander or tarragon

1 Wash the spinach very carefully under cold running water and then drain thoroughly. Chop coarsely.

2 Melt the butter or margarine in a large saucepan, add the onion and fry, stirring frequently, until soft. Stir in the tomato purée, rice, spinach and water. Season with the salt, black pepper, paprika, chilli powder and dillweed. Stir well and bring to the boil. Lower the heat, cover the pan and simmer for 15 minutes.

3 Mix the yogurt and egg together in a bowl until well blended. Add several tablespoons of the hot stock and stir well. Pour this into the soup, reduce the heat and simmer for a further 2–3 minutes. Remove from the heat and stir in the lemon juice and chopped eggs. Sprinkle with the herb and serve immediately.

minestra

yugoslav-style minestrone

30 ml (2 tablespoons) butter or margarine
1 onion, coarsely chopped
2 garlic cloves, crushed
1 leek, halved lengthways and cut into 1 cm ($^1/_2$ inch) pieces
1 carrot, peeled and thinly sliced crossways
1 small kohlrabi, peeled and cut into 1 cm ($^1/_2$ inch) cubes
2 small courgettes, thinly sliced crossways
2 tomatoes, blanched, peeled and coarsely chopped
125 g (4 oz) french beans or mangetout, stringed and
cut into 2 cm ($^3/_4$ inch) pieces
2.3 litres (4 pints) water
10 ml (2 teaspoons) salt
75 g (3 oz) long grain rice, washed thoroughly under
cold running water and drained
15 ml (1 tablespoon) finely chopped parsley

Garnish
grated Parmesan cheese

1 Melt the butter or margarine in a large saucepan, add the onion and garlic and fry, stirring frequently, until soft. Add all the prepared vegetables and fry for 2–3 minutes, stirring occasionally, to coat with the butter.

2 Add the water and salt and bring to the boil. Lower the heat, cover the pan and simmer for 20–30 minutes.

3 Stir in the rice and parsley and simmer, covered, for a further 15–20 minutes. Serve immediately with Parmesan cheese.

minestrone

mixed vegetable soup

The only time my father did not need to dip his bread into a soup was when my mother prepared 'her version' of this great Italian soup. I have stressed 'her version' because there are countless variations of this soup throughout the length and breadth of not only Italy, but also southern Europe and the Balkans, from where I have included a Dalmatian favourite called Minestra.

The Italian version is a standard one, popular in many trattorias and pizzarias. Incidentally, minestrone simply means 'thick soup'.

75 g (3 oz) haricot beans, soaked overnight in cold water and drained
75 g (3 oz) spaghetti, broken into 5–7.5 cm (2–3 inch) lengths
60 ml (4 tablespoons) oil
2 carrots, peeled and cut into 1 cm (¹/₂ inch) cubes
1 celery stick, cut into 1 cm (¹/₂ inch) pieces
1 small onion, finely chopped
2 medium potatoes, peeled and cut into 1 cm (¹/₂ inch) cubes
3 medium tomatoes, blanched, peeled and coarsely chopped
1.7 litres (3 pints) water
2 bay leaves
1 garlic clove, crushed
10 ml (2 teaspoons) salt

Garnish
30 ml (2 tablespoons) finely chopped parsley
grated Parmesan cheese

1 Half fill a saucepan with water and bring to the boil. Add the beans, lower the heat, cover the pan and cook for 1 hour or until tender. Add a little more boiling water, if necessary. Drain.

2 In another saucepan bring some lightly salted water to the boil, add the spaghetti and simmer for 8–10 minutes or until just tender. Drain.

3 Meanwhile, heat the oil in a large saucepan, add the carrots, celery and onion and fry, stirring frequently, for 5 minutes. Add the potatoes and tomatoes and fry, still stirring frequently, for a further 2–3 minutes. Pour in the water and add the bay leaves, garlic and salt. Bring to the boil then lower the heat, cover the pan and simmer for about 20 minutes or until the vegetables are tender.

4 Add the cooked beans and spaghetti and cook for a further 10–15 minutes. Serve in individual bowls garnished with the parsley and cheese.

VARIATION: Instead of spaghetti you can use any other Italian noodles or pastas.

gazpacho

chilled tomato soup

2 garlic cloves, halved
1 red pepper, seeded and coarsely chopped
900 g (2 lb) tomatoes, blanched, peeled, seeded and chopped
1 onion, coarsely chopped
75 ml (5 tablespoons) oil
30 ml (2 tablespoons) vinegar
175 g (6 oz) fresh white breadcrumbs
2.5 ml ($\frac{1}{2}$ teaspoon) ground cumin
900 ml ($1\frac{1}{2}$ pints) water
7.5 ml ($1\frac{1}{2}$ teaspoons) salt
2.5 ml ($\frac{1}{2}$ teaspoon) black pepper

Garnish
A mixture of finely chopped green pepper,
cucumber. onion and seeded tomatoes
croutons, optional

1 Place the garlic, red pepper, tomatoes, onion, oil and vinegar in a blender and process until smooth. Pour into a large bowl and stir in the breadcrumbs and cumin. Chill for several hours.

2 Just before serving stir in the water and season to taste with salt and black pepper.

3 To serve, spoon the soup into individual bowls and garnish generously with the chopped vegetables. If you wish you can also add a few freshly fried croutons.

mulligatawny

curry-flavoured vegetable soup

My late father often used to pronounce with a great deal of glee as he dunked thick chunks of bread into his soup 'Soup is only an excuse for eating bread'.

In some recipes 150 ml ($^1/_4$ pint) coconut milk (see Glossary) is stirred into the soup just before serving.

50 g (2 oz) ghee (see Glossary) or butter
2 carrots, peeled and diced
2 leeks, trimmed and diced
1 turnip, peeled and diced
4 celery slicks, trimmed end diced
1 large bay leaf
1 large onion, peeled and diced
1.7 litres (3 pints) water
25 g (1 oz) white beans, soaked and cooked until tender
1 apple, peeled and diced
1 garlic clove, thinly sliced
seeds of 2 cardamom pods, crushed
25 g (1 oz) sultanas
10 ml (2 teaspoons) curry powder
10 ml (2 teaspoons) flour
10 ml (2 teaspoons) salt
15 ml (1 tablespoon) tamarind pulp (see Glossary) or 2 tablespoons lemon juice

1 Melt half the ghee or butter in a large saucepan, add the carrots, leeks, turnip, celery, bay leaf and half the onion and sauté, stirring frequently, for 8–10 minutes.

2 Add half the water, cover and simmer until the vegetables are very tender. Add the beans.

3 Meanwhile, heat the remaining ghee or butter in a frying pan, add the rest of the onion, the apple, garlic and cardamom seeds and fry, stirring frequently, until the onion is soft and golden. Stir in the sultanas and remove from the heat. Sprinkle the curry powder, flour and salt into the pan and stir well. Return the pan to the heat and gradually stir in the remaining water. Bring to the boil slowly, stirring constantly, until the mixture has thickened slightly. Pour this mixture into the large saucepan. Continue to simmer over a low heat for 10–15 minutes. Stir in the tamarind pulp or lemon juice just before serving.

lo po tong

turnip soup

If the man who turnips cries,
Cry not when his father dies,
'Tis a proof that he would rather
Have a turnip than his father.
Anecdotes of the late Samuel Johnson, 1786

In Europe turnips are little used in soups, but not so in the Far East, where this Cantonese recipe originates.

30 ml (2 tablespoons) dried mushrooms, soaked
in 200 ml (1/3 pint) warm water for 30 minutes
30 ml (2 tablespoons) butter
450 g (1 lb) turnips, peeled and cut diagonally into 1 cm (1/2 inch) slices
1.7 litres (3 pints) water or Chinese vegetable stock (see Glossary)
45 ml (3 tablespoons) soy sauce
30 ml (2 tablespoons) mirin (see Glossary) or dry sherry
10 ml (2 teaspoons) salt
1.25 ml (1/4 teaspoon) black pepper
5 ml (1 teaspoon) grated fresh ginger

1 Drain the mushrooms and remove and discard the stalks. Chop caps coarsely.

2 Melt the butter in a large saucepan, add the mushrooms and turnip slices and fry, stirring constantly, for 2 minutes. Add the water or stock and the soy sauce and bring to the boil. Boil vigorously for 2–3 minutes, then lower the heat and stir in the remaining ingredients. Simmer, covered, for about 1 hour.

3 Serve piping hot in individual bowls.

hin gha

burmese strong soup

'Of soup and love, the first is the best'
English saying

In Burma there is *hin* (soup), and of *hin* there are two main kinds — *hin cho* (mild soup) and *chin hin* (sour soup). But *hin gha* is the strong one and by far the most intriguing to our Western palate.

Most vegetables are suitable for the preparation of *hin*. The more popular ones are courgettes (peeled and cut crossways), pumpkin (diced), aubergines (peeled and thinly sliced crossways), cauliflower (each floret sliced lengthways), cabbage (thinly shredded) and okra (topped, tailed and sliced diagonally). In short, any vegetable that is available or that you particularly like.

1.4 litres (2¹/₂ pints) water or vegetable stock (see Glossary)
1 large onion, thinly sliced
4 peppercorns
3 garlic cloves, thinly sliced
1.25 ml (¹/₄ teaspoon) black pepper
2.5 ml (¹/₂ teaspoon) turmeric
2.5 ml (¹/₂ teaspoon) salt
450 g (1 lb) mixed vegetables of your choice, sliced

1 Place the water or stock in a large saucepan and bring to the boil. Add the onion, peppercorns, garlic, black pepper, turmeric and salt and simmer for 5 minutes.

2 Add the vegetables, cover the pan and simmer until just tender. Taste and adjust seasoning, if necessary. Serve hot.

corba ot bamja

okra soup

Canned okra will not do for this soup, so unless you can find small, fresh okra do not attempt this unusual Bulgarian recipe. This really tasty soup is best served with bread.

45 ml (3 tablespoons) oil
1 onion, finely chopped
1 garlic clove, crushed
10 ml (2 teaspoons) flour
5 ml (1 teaspoon) paprika
7.5 ml (1$^{1}/_{2}$ teaspoons) salt
1.25 ml ($^{1}/_{4}$ teaspoon) black pepper
1.7 litres (3 pints) water or vegetable stock (see Glossary)
450 g (1 lb) okra, washed and stems trimmed, but do not cut into the pods
3 large tomatoes, blanched, peeled and chopped
150 ml ($^{1}/_{4}$ pint) yogurt
1 egg

Garnish
5 ml (1 teaspoon) paprika
30 ml (2 tablespoons) finely chopped parsley

1 Heat the oil in a large saucepan, add the onion and garlic and fry, stirring frequently, for about 3 minutes. Sprinkle in the flour, paprika, salt and pepper and fry, stirring constantly, for 2 more minutes. Gradually stir in the water or stock and bring to the boil. Simmer for 5 minutes and then add the okra and tomatoes. Cook gently for about 10 minutes. Do not overcook or the okra will start to disintegrate and become a bit slimy.

2 Meanwhile, in a small bowl mix together thoroughly the yogurt and egg. At the end of the 10 minutes stir this gently into the soup, reduce the heat to very low and simmer for a further 2–3 minutes. Remove from the heat and serve in individual bowls garnished with a little paprika and parsley.

appetisers and dips

One can eat vegetables raw (as in salads), boiled, fried or baked. In northern Europe, including the British Isles, vegetables are, more often than not, simply boiled and served. As we go farther south vegetables are boiled and then served with several types of sauces, while in the Mediterranean and Middle Eastern lands vegetables are normally cooked in oil.

All along the Mediterranean coastline, including North Africa and the Middle East, deep-fried vegetables are very popular whether they are fried plain, dipped in seasoned egg or in a batter.

Traditionally, olive oil was used for frying, but you can experiment with any oil of your choice.

Another popular method of preparing vegetables as appetisers is the one called *à la grecque*, which is a French expression (in reality it has nothing to do with Greece) where the vegetable is cooked in water mixed with a little oil, lemon juice, salt, coriander seeds, peppercorns and a bouquet garni. When cooked the vegetables are left to cool in the cooking liquid and served cold.

More interesting still are the dishes where the vegetables are served with all kinds of sauces and dressings such as mayonnaise, soured cream, sauce tartare, walnut oil dressing, etc.

Let us then do a quick tour through the hors d'oeuvres, appetisers and dips of the various cuisines.

vegetables with vinaigrette dressing

Almost all vegetables can be served in this way, although artichokes, broccoli, fennel, leeks and kohlrabi are particularly good.

chou-rave vinaigrette

kohlrabi vinaigrette

Here the vegetables are not boiled in water, but simmered in oil and mustard. Turnips and celeriac can also be prepared in this way.

6 medium kohlrabi, trimmed and peeled
90 ml (6 tablespoons) olive oil
juice of 1 large lemon
15 ml (1 tablespoon) Dijon mustard
45 ml (3 tablespoons) finely chopped parsley

1 Slice the kohlrabi thinly and place in a large saucepan. Add the oil, cover the pan and simmer for 20 minutes, stirring occasionally.

2 Stir in the lemon juice, mustard and parsley and simmer for a further 1–2 minutes. Serve hot or cold.

artichauts à la vinaigrette

artichokes with vinaigrette sauce

6 globe artichokes, prepared (see Glossary)
vinaigrette sauce (see page 228)

Garnish
30 ml (2 tablespoons) finely chopped parsley

1 Half fill a large saucepan with lightly salted water and bring to the boil. Add the artichokes, bases downwards, and simmer, turning each one occasionally, for 15–20 minutes or until the bases are tender and the leaves pull out easily. Remove with a slotted spoon and drain upside down in a colander. Set aside to cool.

2 Meanwhile, prepare the vinaigrette sauce according to instructions.

3 Arrange the artichokes in individual bowls and spoon the vinaigrette sauce evenly over them. Sprinkle with the parsley and serve.

VARIATION: Baby leeks are delicious prepared in this way. First, trim away the roots and any damaged or discoloured leaves and then run under a cold tap. Poach in lightly salted, boiling water until just tender, about 10 minutes. Remove with a slotted spoon and drain well. Set aside to cool. Arrange the leeks on a serving dish, spoon over the prepared vinaigrette, sprinkle with chopped parsley, and if you like, some chopped boiled egg, and serve.

fried vegetables

Some vegetables, such as artichokes, asparagus and celery, are first blanched in lightly salted water and then dipped in a light batter and fried in oil. Other vegetables, for example aubergines, courgettes, marrows, cardoons and salsify, are first cooked in a court bouillon (see below), then dipped in batter and fried.

cardons frits

fried cardoons

900 g (2 lb) cardoons, coarse hard stems removed
1 lemon, halved
oil, for frying

Court Bouillon
1.1 litres (2 pints) water
30–45 ml (2–3 tablespoons) olive oil
juice of $1/2$ lemon
10 ml (2 teaspoons) salt

Bouquet garni
3–4 coriander seeds
4 peppercorns

Marinade
120 ml (8 tablespoons) olive oil
juice of 1 large lemon
45 ml (3 tablespoons) finely chopped parsley

Batter
225 g (8 oz) plain flour, sifted
60 ml (4 tablespoons) melted butter
2 eggs
2.5 ml ($1/2$ teaspoon) salt

1 Remove the stalks of the cardoon and cut into 7.5 cm (3 inch) pieces, trimming off any stringy bits. Rub the cut edges with lemon to prevent discoloration. Drop into a large pan containing the court-bouillon ingredients. Bring to the boil and cook for 2 minutes, stirring frequently. Lower the heat, cover the pan and simmer for $1^1/2$ hours.

2 Drain in a colander and leave for 1–2 minutes to steam dry.

3 Mix the marinade ingredients together in a large shallow dish, add the cardoon pieces and turn carefully until well coated. Set aside for 30 minutes.

4 Meanwhile, prepare the batter by mixing the flour, butter, eggs and salt together in a bowl. Gradually add enough water, stirring constantly, to make a medium-thick batter.

5 Heat a good depth of oil in a frying pan. Dip each portion of cardoon in the batter and then fry for a few minutes, turning once, until golden. Remove with a slotted spoon, drain on kitchen paper and keep warm while you fry the remaining pieces. Serve warm with salads, pickles and chutneys.

dabgevadz tetum

fried vegetable marrows

Courgettes, gourds and pumpkins are equally good if prepared in this way.

Serve with bread and yogurt.

900 g (2 lb) vegetable marrow, peeled, seeded and halved lengthways
3 eggs, beaten
oil, for frying

Garnish
30 ml (2 tablespoons) finely chopped parsley
30 ml (2 tablespoons) finely chopped fresh mint, fried in a little oil

1 Slice the marrow thinly — the thinner the better as, like courgettes, marrow slices will absorb more oil the thicker they are.

2 Dip each slice in the beaten egg and fry in hot oil for a few minutes, turning once, until golden and tender. Remove, drain on kitchen paper and keep warm while you fry the remaining slices in the same way.

3 Arrange on a large serving plate, sprinkle with the parsley and the mint.

havuj tavasi

fried carrots

Serve with plain yogurt, Georgian Walnut and Coriander Sauce (see page 235) or, as is often the custom in Turkey, with a Yogurt and Garlic Sauce (see page 234).

Other vegetables can be prepared in this way, for example sliced potatoes, turnips and onions.

900 g (2 lb) medium carrots, peeled and cut crossways into 0.5 cm ($^1/_4$ inch) slices
oil, for deep-frying

Beer Batter
225 g (8 oz) plain flour
7.5 ml (1$^1/_2$ teaspoons) salt
about 450 ml ($^3/_4$ pint) beer

1 Half fill a saucepan with lightly salted water and bring to the boil. Add the carrot slices and simmer for 5–7 minutes or until just tender. Drain and allow to steam dry in a colander.

2 Meanwhile, sift the flour and salt into a large bowl and gradually mix in enough of the beer to make a smooth, thick batter.

3 Heat oil in a deep-frying pan. Dip the carrot slices in the batter and fry in batches for several minutes until golden and crisp. Remove with a slotted spoon, drain on kitchen paper and keep warm while you fry the remaining slices in the same way.

4 Serve with one of the suggested sauces.

mixed appetisers

Vegetables, whether boiled or fried, are usually served as a first course or, as is often the case, as part of a buffet.

This method of eating, where a large array of food is laid out in apparent abundance on small trays and dishes, is called *mezzeh* in the Middle East. Its nearest equivalent is *fritto misto* in Italian, *tapas* in Spanish and *zakuski* in Russian.

Mezzeh is perhaps the great achievement of the Middle Eastern cuisines, for it is here that thousands of years of tradition and culture are best reflected. On the *mezzeh* table you will find all the culinary creations from the days of the Pharaohs, through the Greek merchant states to the Arab and Turkish empires. The Spanish *tapas*, which are at their best in Andalusia, are undoubtedly in the tradition of the Arab-Moorish culture that flourished there for centuries. *Tapas* are small snacks which one has with a glass of sherry or wine and usually consist of some olives, salads, cheese, hard-boiled eggs in mayonnaise, raw vegetables — radishes, onions, spring onions and nuts.

I have not, of course, included the many meat- and fish-based dishes, but these, too, may well grace a *tapas*.

The Italian *fritto misto* is a complete meal in its own right. It usually comprises meats and various vegetables either fried in fat or butter. They are often served, like the Middle Eastern *mezzeh*, as a first course or a buffet.

The Russian *zakuski* was once served in a room separate from the dining room. It usually consisted of salted and pickled fruits, mushrooms and vegetables and was then followed by innumerable hot or cold dishes, which would inevitably include fish, poultry and sausages.

praz cu mascine

leeks with olives and onions

Makes an excellent appetiser when served cold with bread.

6 leeks, roots trimmed and coarse outer leaves discarded
60 ml (4 tablespoons) oil
200 ml (1/3 pint) water or dry white wine
30 ml (2 tablespoons) butter or margarine
3 large onions, sliced into thin rings
10–12 black olives, stoned
5 ml (1 teaspoon) salt
2.5 ml (1/2 teaspoon) chilli powder
10 ml (2 teaspoons) paprika

Garnish
30–45 ml (2–3 tablespoons) finely chopped parsley

1 Cut the leeks into 2.5 cm (1 inch) pieces and then wash very thoroughly under cold running water to remove all sand and dirt.

2 Heat the oil in a large saucepan, add the pieces of leek and fry, turning frequently, for 5 minutes. Add the water or wine and bring to the boil. Lower the heat, cover the pan and simmer for about 15 minutes or until the leeks are tender.

3 Meanwhile, melt the butter or margarine in a large frying pan, add the onion rings and fry, stirring frequently, until soft and golden. Set aside to cool.

4 When the leeks are tender stir in the olives, salt, chilli pepper and paprika and set aside to cool.

5 To serve arrange the leeks on a large plate and garnish with the fried onions. Sprinkle with the parsley and serve.

radiska na smetaniu

radishes in soured cream

For this simple recipe you can use soured cream, as is the Russian way, or yogurt or a vinaigrette sauce (see page 228).

Cucumbers, cooked beetroot and cooked potatoes can also be served in this way.

You can use ordinary red radishes or the much larger long white variety, which can be found in Indo-Pakistani greengrocers.

450 g (1 lb) radishes, scraped and cut into thin slices
salt
2 large hard-boiled eggs, separated
150 ml (¼ pint) soured cream
5 ml (1 level teaspoon) salt

Garnish
pinch paprika

1 Place the radish slices in a colander, sprinkle with a little salt and leave to rest for 30 minutes. Rinse quickly and pat dry.

2 Meanwhile, mash the egg yolks and chop the whites finely.

3 Place the radish slices in a bowl and mix in the mashed yolks. Stir in the soured cream and salt until well blended and then stir in the chopped egg whites. Spoon into a serving bowl and sprinkle with the paprika. Serve immediately.

kabli channa

chickpeas with ginger and vegetables

'Old ginger is the sharpest'
Chinese proverb

The Indian subcontinent makes a great use of chickpeas and this simple earthy pea is cooked whole, mashed or turned into flour (*besan*) with which many tasty sweets and breads are made.

This rich aromatic dish can be eaten as an appetiser or as an accompaniment to other dishes.

Serve with bread — pita or preferably naan or chapati.

350 g (12 oz) chickpeas, soaked overnight in cold water and drained
90 ml (3 fl oz) oil
1 large onion, thinly sliced
2 garlic cloves, crushed
5 cm (2 inch) piece fresh ginger, peeled and thinly sliced
10 ml (2 teaspoons) salt
5 ml (1 teaspoon) turmeric
5 ml (1 teaspoon) ground cumin
2.5 ml ($^1/_2$ teaspoon) cayenne pepper
3 tomatoes, blanched, peeled and chopped
1 green pepper, thinly sliced
juice of 2 lemons

Garnish
5 ml (1 teaspoon) garam masala (see Glossary)
45 ml (3 tablespoons) finely chopped coriander or parsley

1 Half fill a saucepan with water and bring to the boil. Add the chickpeas and cook for 1–1$^1/_2$ hours or until tender, adding more boiling water if necessary. Drain, reserving 450 ml ($^3/_4$ pint) of the cooking liquid.

2 Heat the oil in a large saucepan, add the onion and fry, stirring frequently, for 3 minutes. Add the garlic and ginger and fry for 2 more minutes. Sprinkle in the salt, turmeric, cumin and cayenne pepper and fry for 2–3 more minutes, stirring constantly.

3 Stir in the tomatoes and green pepper and cook for 5 minutes. Stir in the chickpeas, reserved liquid and lemon juice and bring to the boil. Lower the heat, cover the pan and simmer for about 20 minutes. Uncover and cook for a further 10 minutes.

4 Transfer to a serving dish, sprinkle with the garam masala and coriander or parsley and serve hot or cold.

pawpaw and avocado salad

This is a colourful and flavoursome appetiser that will surprise and delight your guests. This recipe is from Polynesia.

1 large ripe avocado, peeled and stoned
juice of 1 large lemon or 1 lime
2 ripe pawpaws, peeled
120 ml (4 fl oz) fresh orange or grapefruit juice
30 ml (2 tablespoons) oil
15 ml (1 tablespoon) Tabasco sauce
1.25 ml ($^1/_4$ teaspoon) nutmeg

Garnish
chopped toasted almonds or pistachios

1 Either cut the avocado into 1 cm ($^1/_2$ inch) cubes or use a melon-ball scoop to scoop out the flesh. Drop immediately into a bowl containing the lemon or lime juice and toss well.

2 Halve the pawpaws and scoop out and discard the seeds. Slice into thin segments and add to the bowl. Add the remaining ingredients, stir gently and refrigerate until needed.

3 To serve, spoon into individual dishes and garnish with the chopped nuts.

kiopulu

aubergine and pepper spread

'An aproned wife has no time to be bad'
Bulgarian proverb

Sometimes also called *Zelen Haviar* (green caviar), it is similar to numerous other spreads that are found throughout the Balkans, Middle East, Caucasus and North India. Armenians like to add thinly sliced onions to the mixture. Kiopulu is served as an accompaniment to a roast or kebabs, but it is also marvellous when served as an appetiser with bread and a glass of *raki* or *ouzo*.

3 medium aubergines (about 700 g/1¹/₂ lb)
2 large green peppers
2 large tomatoes, blanched, peeled and finely chopped
45 ml (3 tablespoons) olive oil
30 ml (2 tablespoons) red wine vinegar
45 ml (3 tablespoons) finely chopped parsley
2.5 ml (¹/₂ teaspoon) chilli powder
1 garlic clove, crushed
5 ml (1 teaspoon) salt
1.25 ml (¹/₄ teaspoon) black pepper

Garnish
lettuce leaves
6–8 thin slices green pepper
black olives

1 Make 2 or 3 slits in each aubergine and place in a hot oven or under a hot grill. Cook until the skins are black and the flesh feels soft when poked with a finger. When cool enough to handle, peel the aubergines, scraping off and reserving any flesh that comes away with the skin. Set the flesh aside.

2 Meanwhile, cook the peppers alongside the aubergines, turning them occasionally, until the skins are evenly browned and wrinkled. When cool enough to handle, peel off the thin brown skins. Quarter the peppers and discard the seeds.

3 Place the aubergine flesh and pepper quarters in a bowl and mash with a fork. Add all the remaining ingredients and continue to mash until the mixture is reduced to a pulp. Refrigerate.

4 Serve on a bed of lettuce leaves and decorate with the pepper slices and olives.

imam bayildi

aubergines stuffed with peppers, tomatoes and onions

Turkey is rich in *mezzeh*-type dishes. Perhaps the most outstanding of all is the one that made the priest faint, *imam bayildi*. This recipe appears throughout Turkey, Armenia and the Balkans. It is a classic of the Ottoman cuisine. I eat this beautiful dish accompanied only by bread. It makes a marvellous appetiser.

6 small-medium aubergines, washed and dried. Leave stalks on
salt
90 ml (6 tablespoons) olive oil
3 onions, thinly sliced
2 large green peppers, seeded and thinly sliced
2 large garlic cloves, coarsely chopped
3 large ripe tomatoes, sliced
45 ml (3 tablespoons) tomato purée
2.5 ml (1/2 teaspoon) cayenne pepper
5 ml (1 teaspoon) allspice
45 ml (3 tablespoons) finely chopped parsley
180 ml (12 tablespoons) cooking oil
about 450 ml (3/4 pint) water

Garnish
chopped parsley

1 Make a slit about 5 cm (2 inches) long down one side of each aubergine. Salt the insides and set aside for 15 minutes.

2 Meanwhile, heat the olive oil in a large saucepan, add the onions, green peppers and garlic and fry gently until the onion is soft but not brown. Add the sliced tomatoes, tomato purée, 10 ml (2 teaspoons) salt, cayenne pepper and allspice and cook for 5 minutes, stirring occasionally. Stir in the chopped parsley, remove from the heat and set aside.

3 Rinse out the aubergines under cold running water and pat dry.

4 Heat the cooking oil in a large frying pan and add the aubergines, a few at a time, and fry gently, turning several times, until the flesh begins to soften. Take care not to spoil the shape. Remove the aubergines from the pan with a slotted spoon and arrange side by side in an ovenproof dish, slits uppermost. Carefully prise open the slits and spoon some of the onion mixture into each aubergine.

5 Add the water to any remaining onion mixture, stir and pour over the aubergines. Bake in a 190°C (370° F) mark 5 oven for about 1 hour. Remove and set aside to cool. Chill until ready to serve.

6 To serve, either transfer them to one large dish or, allowing one per person, arrange them on small individual plates and garnish with the parsley.

mutabbal

aubergine dip with tahini

Syrians have an equally famed aubergine dish where the flesh of the vegetable is mixed with tahini and spices. Throughout Syria, Lebanon, Palestine and Israel this dip appears on restaurant menus. It is served with pita bread and pickles.

3 large aubergines
3 garlic cloves, crushed
5 ml (1 teaspoon) salt
50–90 ml (2–3 fl oz) tahini paste (see Glossary)
juice of 2 lemons
5 ml (1 teaspoon) chilli powder
5 ml (1 teaspoon) ground cumin
15 ml (1 tablespoon) olive oil

Garnish
30 ml (2 tablespoons) finely chopped parsley
a few black olives

1 Make 2 or 3 slits in each aubergine and then cook over charcoal, under a hot grill or in a hot oven until the skins are black and the flesh feels soft when poked with a finger. When cool enough to handle, peel the aubergines, scraping off and reserving any flesh that comes away with the skin. Put the flesh in a large bowl and mash with a fork.

2 Add the garlic and salt and continue to mash or pound the mixture until it is reduced to a pulp. Add the tahini, lemon juice and chilli powder and stir thoroughly. Spoon the mixture on to a large plate, smooth it over with the back of a spoon and sprinkle with the cumin. Dribble the olive oil over the top and garnish with the parsley and olives.

chalda loubia khadra

green beans with almonds

North African cuisine is related to both that of the Middle East and of southern Europe as this recipe from Algeria shows.

700 g (1¹/₂ lb) french beans, topped and tailed and
cut into 5 cm (2 inch) pieces
45 ml (3 tablespoons) finely chopped parsley
150 ml (¹/₄ pint) vinaigrette sauce (see page 228)
5 ml (1 teaspoon) ground cumin
4 hard-boiled eggs, thinly sliced
50 g (2 oz) slivered almonds, toasted until golden
black olives

1 Cook the beans in lightly salted boiling water for 8–10 minutes or until just tender. Drain and leave to cool.

2 Place the parsley, dressing and cumin in a large bowl and mix well. Add the beans and toss gently. Pile into the centre of a shallow dish. Arrange the sliced eggs around the edge, scatter the almonds and black olives over the top and serve.

berenjena a la acapulco

aubergine acapulco style

The African slaves took with them into captivity their beloved yam. It is now a well-established crop in the Americas. But the New World was much richer than Africa in agriculture, science and religion. The food of the slaves was mixed with that of the native Americans and received its finishing touches from the new ruling white races.

The results of this admixture is best reflected in South America and Mexico, where some of the most attractive and flavoursome dishes are produced. A fine example is the Arab aubergine, which arrived in the New World via Spain.

4 medium aubergines
50 g (2 oz) fresh breadcrumbs
125 g (4 oz) cheese (Cheddar, mozzarella or Gouda), grated
125 g (4 oz) butter or margarine, melted
1.25 ml ($^1/_4$ teaspoon) cayenne pepper
5 ml (1 teaspoon) paprika
1.25 ml ($^1/_4$ teaspoon) black pepper
2.5 ml ($^1/_2$ teaspoon) salt
350 g (12 oz) mushrooms, wiped clean and thinly sliced
about 450 ml ($^3/_4$ pint) Tomato Sauce (see page 232)

1 Half fill a large saucepan with salted water and bring to the boil. Add the aubergines and simmer for 10 minutes. Drain and set aside until cool enough to handle. Cut the aubergines into quarters lengthways, peel each quarter and then cut the flesh crossways into 2.5 cm (1 inch) pieces.

2 Mix the breadcrumbs and grated cheese together in a small bowl.

3 Lightly grease a large ovenproof dish with a little of the melted butter or margarine. Arrange half the aubergine pieces over the base and pour half the melted fat evenly over them. Sprinkle with half the spices and seasoning. Lay half the sliced mushrooms over the top and cover evenly with half the tomato sauce. Sprinkle half the breadcrumb mixture over the top. Layer the remaining ingredients in the same order.

4 Place in a 180°C (350°F) mark 4 oven and bake for about 45–60 minutes or until the topping is golden. Serve immediately.

frijoles antojitos

caribbean bean dip

Cubans love chillies, but they also adore beans and in this recipe they mix both to create a rich, wholesome dip.

Serve with salted biscuits or pita bread or with *fritos* — crisp fried tortillas.

Some people like to substitute the water with single cream or yogurt.

350 g (12 oz) red kidney beans, cooked (see Glossary)
175 g (6 oz) cream cheese, feta (see Glossary) or cottage cheese
2.5 ml ($\frac{1}{2}$ teaspoon) curry powder
2.5 ml ($\frac{1}{2}$ teaspoon) oregano
5 ml (1 level teaspoon) chilli powder
1 garlic clove, crushed
10 ml (2 teaspoons) salt
1 small onion, finely chopped
5 ml (1 level teaspoon) ground coriander
2.5 ml ($\frac{1}{2}$ teaspoon) ground cumin
$\frac{1}{2}$ celery stalk, finely chopped
30–45 ml (2–3 tablespoons) lime or lemon juice
60 ml (4 tablespoons) tomato juice
water

1 Mix all the ingredients together and purée in a blender, adding sufficient water to ease the process and produce a 'dipping' consistency.

2 Refrigerate for 1–2 hours before serving.

californian spinach pâté

Spinach is not in great favour in North America inspite of Popeye the Sailor Man and his Olive Oyl. However, this magnificent recipe for spinach pâté is an exception.

The new Californian school of experimental cookery has, I believe, concocted many trivial dishes — usually adaptations of traditional ones from all over the world, but some are worthy of more recognition. This recipe is simply delicious, especially if you like spinach. However, note the basic similarity between this recipe and the one on the following page.

Serve with toast and pickles.

700 g (1¹/₂ lb) fresh spinach, coarse and discoloured leaves and stems discarded
25 g (1 oz) butter or margarine
1 small onion, finely chopped
2 medium carrots, peeled and finely chopped
150 ml (¹/₄ pint) single cream
10 ml (2 teaspoons) salt
2.5 ml (¹/₂ teaspoon) mace
5 ml (1 teaspoon) paprika
2.5 ml (¹/₂ teaspoon) chilli powder
2 large eggs, beaten

Garnish
15–30 ml (1–2 tablespoons) finely chopped coriander or tarragon

1 Wash the spinach very thoroughly under cold running water, pat dry and chop finely.

2 Melt the butter or margarine in a large saucepan, add the onion and carrots and fry, stirring frequently, for 4 minutes. Add the spinach, cream, salt, mace, paprika and chilli powder and stir well. Cook for 2–3 minutes, stirring constantly. Stir in the beaten eggs, mix thoroughly and remove from the heat.

3 Grease a 450 g (1 lb) loaf tin and line its base with foil. Spoon in the spinach mixture and even it over the top. Cover with another piece of foil.

4 Place this tin in a much larger one filled with enough water to come within 2.5 cm (1 inch) of the top of the loaf tin. Bake in a 180°C (350°) mark 4 oven for about 1¹/₂ hours. Remove from the oven, take out the loaf tin and leave to cool for 10 minutes. Place a large plate over the tin and carefully invert it. Leave to cool then refrigerate for at least 3–4 hours without removing the tin.

5 Loosen the sides of the pâté and carefully remove it from the tin. Peel off the foil, place on a serving dish and sprinkle with the herbs. Slice and serve.

espinafre saboroso

colombian spinach with cream

This makes a fine appetiser and you can if you wish bake the spinach in individual dishes.

700 g (1¹/₂ lb) fresh spinach, coarse and discoloured leaves and stems discarded
45 ml (3 tablespoons) lime or lemon juice
150 ml (¹/₄ pint) single cream
10 ml (2 teaspoons) salt
1.25 ml (¹/₄ teaspoon) black pepper
1.25 ml (¹/₄ teaspoon) nutmeg
75–90 ml (5–6 tablespoons) grated cheese (Parmesan or Cheddar)

Garnish
2 hard-boiled eggs, chopped

1 Wash the spinach very thoroughly under cold running water and then shake dry. Chop coarsely and place in a large bowl. Add all the remaining ingredients except the cheese and mix thoroughly.

2 Lightly grease a large ovenproof casserole and arrange the spinach mixture in it. Sprinkle the cheese evenly over the top. Bake in a 180°C (350°F) mark 4 oven for about 45–60 minutes or until the spinach is tender and the topping is golden.

3 Serve hot garnished with the chopped eggs.

gajar muli bharta
carrot and radish purée

'The poor seek food, the rich seek an appetite'
Hindi proverb

Bhartas are puréed vegetable dishes which are eaten as accompaniments to roasts or curries. They also make excellent appetisers when served as dips or spreads with bread.

There are many variations of this dish. Cauliflower, potato, spinach, turnips and tomatoes make excellent *bhartas*.

225g (8 oz) carrots, peeled and chopped
225 g (8 oz) white radish, peeled and chopped
You can also use red radishes, in which case there is no need to peel them
30 ml (2 tablespoons) ghee (see Glossary)
1 cm ($^1/_2$ inch) piece fresh ginger, peeled and finely chopped
1 onion, finely chopped
5 ml (1 teaspoon) salt
2.5 ml ($^1/_2$ teaspoon) garam masala (see Glossary)
2.5 ml ($^1/_2$ teaspoon) cayenne pepper
2 tomatoes, blanched, peeled and chopped

1 Place the chopped carrots and radishes in a saucepan with enough water to cover, bring to the boil, lower the heat, cover the pan and simmer for 15–20 minutes or until tender. Add a little more water if necessary. Drain and mash.

2 Melt the ghee in a frying pan, add the ginger and onion and fry gently until the onion is soft and turning golden. Add the mashed vegetables and remaining ingredients and cook, stirring frequently, until the mixture is a smooth purée and all the juices have evaporated. Serve hot.

hummus-bi-tahini

chickpeas with tahini

This magnificent Syrian dip has entered the world's repertoire of classics, and deservedly so. It, too, makes use of tahini. I remember spending hours in my mother's kitchen stirring the chickpeas with a long wooden spoon to first purée and then to mix them with the tahini. It was tiring work but well worth the effort. A piece of bread dipped into the hummus and all tiredness would disappear. However, when all is said and done, I still say 'Thank goodness for Mr Moulinex and his magnificent processing machine.'

450 g (1 lb) chickpeas, soaked overnight in cold water
3 garlic cloves, peeled
300 ml ($^1/_2$ pint) tahini paste (see Glossary)
5 ml (1 teaspoon) chilli powder
15 ml (3 teaspoons) salt
10 ml (2 teaspoons) ground cumin
juice of 2 lemons

Garnish
a little red pepper, cumin, olive oil, lemon juice and chopped parsley

1 Half fill a large pan with water and bring to the boil. Drain the chickpeas and add to the pan. Lower the heat, cover the pan and simmer for 1–1$^1/_2$ hours or until the chickpeas are tender. Remove any scum which appears on the surface and add more boiling water, if necessary.

2 When tender drain the chickpeas and rinse under cold running water. Retain a few to use as a garnish. Using a blender, reduce the rest to a thick paste or purée. You will need to add a little water to facilitate the blending, but take care not to add too much or the mixture will become too thin. While puréeing the chickpeas add the garlic — this will ensure that they are properly ground and distributed.

3 Empty the purée into a large bowl, add the tahini, chilli powder, salt, cumin and lemon juice and mix very thoroughly. Taste and adjust seasoning to your own liking.

4 To serve — use either individual bowls or one large dish. Smooth the hummus with the back of a soup spoon from the centre out so that there is a slight depression in the centre. Decorate in a star pattern with alternating dribbles of red pepper and cumin. Pour a little olive oil and lemon juice into the centre and then garnish with a little chopped parsley and the whole chickpeas.

tabouleh

burghul and vegetable salad

One other classic of the Syrian cuisine is this salad, prepared with cracked wheat (burghul) and vegetables, which is served as an appetiser with cos lettuce leaves. The ideal way to eat *tabouleh* is to make a parcel by folding a little of it up in a lettuce leaf or a pita bread.

75 g (3 oz) fine burghul (see Glossary)
1 cucumber, peeled and finely chopped
4 tomatoes, finely chopped
1 green pepper, seeded and finely chopped
$^1\!/_2$ onion, finely chopped
60 ml (4 tablespoons) finely chopped parsley
30 ml (2 tablespoons) dried mint or finely chopped fresh mint
5 ml (1 teaspoon) salt
juice of 2–3 lemons
60 ml (4 tablespoons) olive oil

To serve
1 lettuce, preferably cos, washed

1 Wash the burghul in a large bowl in several changes of water until the water you pour away is clean. Squeeze out any excess water. Put the chopped vegetables, parsley and mint into a bowl with the burghul and mix thoroughly. Stir in the salt, lemon juice and olive oil. Mix well together, leave for 15 minutes and then taste and adjust seasoning.

2 To serve, arrange the lettuce leaves around the edge of a serving plate and pile the salad into the centre.

babsalata

bean salad

In Hungary, this simple bean dish often appears on the buffet table.
Serve with lemon wedges and bread.

350 g (12 oz) dried beans (haricot, lima, cannellini or red kidney beans),
soaked overnight in cold water and drained
120 ml (4 fl oz) oil
2 onions, sliced into rings
2 large green or red peppers, seeded and sliced into rings
2 large tomatoes, blanched, peeled and chopped
juice of 1 lemon
10 ml (2 teaspoons) salt
10 ml (2 teaspoons) paprika

Garnish
45 ml (3 tablespoons) finely chopped parsley, coriander or dill

1 Half fill a large saucepan with water and bring to the boil. Add the beans and simmer, covered, for 45–60 minutes or until they are tender, adding more boiling water if necessary. Drain.

2 Meanwhile, heat the oil in a large saucepan, add the onion and fry, stirring frequently, until soft. Add the peppers and fry, still stirring, for a further 3 minutes. Now add the chopped tomatoes, cover the pan and cook over a low heat for 10 minutes.

3 Add the drained beans to the pan together with the lemon juice, salt and paprika and mix well. Remove from the heat, transfer to a serving dish and, when cool, refrigerate until needed. Serve garnished with the herb of your choice; use only one type.

yam fritters

Since yam is perhaps the most popular root vegetable in Africa I give one recipe which can go under the heading of appetiser. Serve warm with Harissa Sauce (see page 230) or Groundnut Sauce (see page 231).

700 g (1¹/₂ lb) yam
2 large green peppers, finely chopped
3 large tomatoes, finely chopped
3 eggs, beaten
1 onion, finely chopped
10 ml (2 teaspoons) salt
oil for frying

1 Peel and grate the yam. Place in a bowl with all the remaining ingredients and knead until well blended.

2 Heat a good depth of oil in a frying pan. Take a spoonful of the mixture, roll it between your palms and then flatten it gently and place in the oil. Fry gently for 4–5 minutes, turning once until cooked through and golden. Remove with a slotted spoon and keep warm while you cook the remaining mixture in the same way. You should be able to cook a few at a time depending on the size of your pan.

griyby ikraiy

mushroom caviar

Another Russian favourite which is always present on a *zakuski* table. You can use either pickled mushrooms (see page 243) or cooked dried mushrooms.

450 g (1 lb) pickled mushrooms
45–60 ml (3–4 tablespoons) oil
1 large onion, finely chopped
2.5 ml (¹/₂ teaspoon) white pepper
5 ml (1 level teaspoon) salt
15–30 ml (1–2 tablespoons) lemon juice

1 Wash and drain the mushrooms in a colander and then chop very finely.

2 Heat the oil in a frying pan, add the onion and fry until soft and just beginning to turn golden. Remove the onion with a slotted spoon, place in a bowl and leave to cool for a few minutes. Add the chopped mushrooms and remaining ingredients, mix well and serve.

salads

Salad, from the Latin 'sal' (salt), derives from the early Greek and Roman custom of dipping lettuce and endive leaves into salt — a custom which is still popular in the Middle East, where people sprinkle a few grains of salt over sliced cucumbers, tomatoes or radishes before eating them with relish. Iranians often dip lettuce leaves in a bowl of *sekanjabin*, a sweet and sour syrup prepared with mint, sugar and vinegar.

Apicius[1], in *The Roman Cookery Book*, noted several salads, vegetables and herbs which were popular in the Rome of his day. In the Middle Ages the European cuisines went into a decline, while those of the East, dominated by Islam, went from strength to strength. The Renaissance brought to light not only the great cultural works of the Ancients, but other aspects of their social life, including the art of cooking. Yet the concept of a bowl of salad as we know it did not really exist till the late nineteenth century. Markham's chatty work[2] included an entire chapter on salads 'Some sallets be simple, some compounded for use and adornation.' With these few words Markham succeeds in expressing everything one needs to know about salads; that they can be very simple fare or elaborate and, above all, attractive in colour, texture and taste.

Years later, in 1699, Evelyn[3] published what is perhaps the first book devoted to salads, where he named over 70 types of vegetables, herbs and salads, The cookery books of this period did occasionally note certain regional salads, but almost as an afterthought. Indeed, as late as the nineteenth century, when Brillat-Savarin remarked that a bowl of salad gave one a feeling of 'freshness without enfeebling and fortifies without irritating'[4], the art of salad-making was confined to a few places, notably the Middle East, North Africa and the newly emerging states of the Americas.

In our time it is to the credit of those American states with their abundant vegetables, fertile soil and ideas unhampered by European traditionalism that salads have reappeared and regained their deserving popularity.

Today, a bowl of salad on a dinner table is not only a must but also a sight full of beauty, aroma and inventiveness. For a good salad should not only taste good but look good as well.

Salads are very simple to prepare, but, I hasten to add, they do need care and attention. Throwing a few shredded leaves of lettuce, some chopped cucumber and tomatoes into a bowl does not make a salad — contrary to what most British restaurateurs think.

Use only the best vegetables and condiments and eat as soon after preparation as possible unless otherwise stated.

Toss or mix all salads at the last minute, again unless otherwise stated, and be careful with your garnishes.

All sauces, dressings and relishes used with these salads can be found in the appropriate chapters.

1   Apicius *'De re coquinaria/culinaria'*
2   Gervase Markham *The English Housewife*
3   John Evelyn Acetaria, *a Discourse of Sallets*
4   Brillat-Savarin *La Physiologie du Goût*

salads   67

tossed green salad

The first salad I have chosen is one that is regularly served in British restaurants. 'Green Salad' normally appears on the table as a small collection of tired lettuce leaves with a few onion rings and yellowing cucumber slices with or, as is often the case, without a dressing.

2 lettuce, cos or Webb's or 1 large Iceberg or 2 curly endive
1 bunch watercress, coarse and discoloured leaves discarded
30–45 ml (2–3 tablespoons) finely chopped chives or 3 spring onions, chopped
15 ml (1 tablespoon) finely chopped parsley
15 ml (1 tablespoon) finely chopped basil
1 garlic clove, finely chopped
150 ml ($^1/_2$ pint) vinaigrette (see page 228)

1 Wash the lettuces or endive and watercress thoroughly under cold water and shake off excess water. Leave to drain for 10–15 minutes. If you wish you can gently pat the leaves dry with a tea towel. Refrigerate leaves for 15 minutes then tear into smaller pieces.

2 Combine the lettuce or endive, watercress, chives or spring onions, parsley, basil and garlic in a large bowl. Spoon over the dressing, toss thoroughly and serve immediately.

VARIATION: Add other greens such as chicory, young spinach leaves, lamb's lettuce (mâche), diced celery or fennel or thinly sliced green pepper.

ensalada mejicana

mexican salad

Here is a brilliantly rich salad which would have pleased Markham. A 'compounded'
salad brimful of 'adornation'. This is also a filling salad, almost a meal in itself —
marvellous on a summer's day.

1 medium lettuce, cos or Iceberg, washed under cold water and drained
1 medium potato, cooked and diced
1 celery stick, thinly sliced
1 medium onion, thinly sliced crossways and separated into rings
1 green pepper, seeded and thinly sliced
75 ml (5 tablespoons) olive oil
45 ml (3 tablespoons) wine vinegar
5 ml (1 teaspoon) salt
2.5 ml ($^1/_2$ teaspoon) black pepper
1.25 ml ($^1/_4$ teaspoon) chilli powder
1.25 ml ($^1/_4$ teaspoon) dried oregano or basil
croutons

Garnish
1 avocado, peeled, stoned, thinly sliced and tossed
in a little lemon juice to prevent discolouring

1 Tear the lettuce into bite-sized pieces or shred finely and place in a large salad bowl.
Add the potato, celery, onion and green pepper and mix well.

2 When ready to serve add the olive oil, vinegar, salt, pepper, chilli powder and the
oregano or basil and toss thoroughly. Stir in the croutons, garnish with the avocado
slices and serve immediately.

fattoush

syrian bread salad

Bread, whether stale or fried, appears in salads all over the world. Sometimes bread is replaced by other ingredients such as cheese and olives. There are several such dishes well known in the Balkans, Greece and Turkey. Others, like Iranians, Afghanis and the Caucasians, prefer to eat their cheese separately, i.e., they cut a piece of cheese, eat it and then proceed with a lettuce leaf or a radish. Iranians never use a dressing on their greens, just a sprinkling of salt.

Simple, cheap yet deliciously textured, this salad is still eaten day in, day out by Syrian peasants — as it has been for generations.

Village women do not throw away their stale bread, they combine it with cucumbers, tomatoes, lettuce, herbs and spices to create this salad. Ideal on a buffet table or as an accompaniment to cold or roast meats.

You can prepare *fattoush* in advance and chill, but do not stir in the bread until just before serving or it will lose its crispness.

1 large cucumber, chopped
1 lettuce heart, shredded
5 tomatoes, chopped
10 spring onions, chopped
1 small green pepper, chopped
15 ml (1 tablespoon) chopped fresh coriander leaves
15 ml (1 tablespoon) chopped parsley
7.5 ml (1/2 tablespoon) finely chopped fresh mint
1 garlic clove, crushed
90 ml (6 tablespoons) olive oil
juice of 2 lemons
2.5 ml (1/2 teaspoon) salt
1.25 ml (1/4 teaspoon) black pepper
5 thin slices bread, lightly toasted and cut into small cubes

1 Place all the ingredients except the toasted bread in a large bowl. Toss the salad so that all the ingredients are well coated with the oil and lemon juice. Chill until ready to serve.

2 Stir in toasted bread cubes and serve immediately.

salade mimosa

A French classic that can be made with a wide variety of ingredients, but it should always incorporate a sprinkling of hard-boiled egg yolks — hence its name.

2 lettuce or endive, washed thoroughly under cold water and drained
2 hard-boiled egg yolks
45–60 ml (3–4 tablespoons) finely chopped parsley, basil or tarragon
5 ml (1 teaspoon) coarse salt
2.5 ml (1/2 teaspoon) black pepper
105–120 ml (7–8 tablespoons) vinaigrette dressing (see page 228)

1 Refrigerate drained leaves for 15 minutes as described in tossed green salad and then tear into bite-sized pieces and place in a salad bowl.

2 Pass the egg yolks through a fine wire sieve or strainer and mix in a small bowl with the chopped herb, salt and pepper.

3 Pour the dressing over the lettuce and toss thoroughly. Sprinkle with the egg yolk mixture and serve immediately.

salata horiatiki

village salad

This classic salad with cheese and olives is very popular throughout Greece.

If possible use cos lettuce since this was the original Greek lettuce native to the island of Kos in the Aegean Sea.

2 lettuce, cos or Iceberg, washed and drained
3 tomatoes, cut into wedges and seeded
1 onion, thinly sliced crossways and separated into rings
$^1/_2$ cucumber, peeled and thinly sliced
6–8 radishes, thinly sliced
1 green pepper, seeded and thinly sliced crossways
10–12 black olives
120 ml (8 tablespoons) olive oil
juice of 1 lemon
10 ml (2 teaspoons) coarse salt
2.5 ml ($^1/_2$ teaspoon) black pepper
2.5 ml ($^1/_2$ teaspoon) paprika
5 ml (1 teaspoon) dried mint or oregano
125 g (4 oz) feta cheese (see Glossary), crumbled

1 Shred the lettuce finely and refrigerate for 15 minutes.

2 Place the lettuce in a large salad bowl and add the tomatoes, onion, cucumber, radishes, green pepper and olives.

3 Mix the oil, lemon juice, salt, pepper, paprika and mint or oregano together in a small bowl and pour over the salad. Toss gently, sprinkle with the cheese and serve immediately.

VARIATION: The Caucasian *Shominiaghtsan* replaces the lettuce with fresh spinach. The leaves are washed under cold running water and any coarse stems and leaves discarded. Proceed as with the recipe above but add 3–4 tablespoons of roasted and chopped pine kernels or almonds or pistachios.

nigerian beetroot salad

Beetroot is consumed on a vast scale by the Slavic nations because it is one of the few fresh vegetables readily available and also because the Central Europeans have a love affair with the beetroot's deep red colour, its sweetness and the richness of its natural juices. Naturally, there are many 'classic' beetroot-based salads in Poland, Ukraine, Russia and the adjacent lands.

This recipe, however, comes from Nigeria, where the beetroots are smaller than their European counterparts.

1 small cos lettuce, washed, drained and shredded
3 large tomatoes, seeded and chopped
2 avocados, peeled, stoned, thinly sliced and tossed in a little lemon juice
450 g (1 lb) cooked beetroot, peeled and diced
1 green pepper, thinly sliced
3 hard-boiled eggs, quartered

Dressing
45 ml (3 tablespoons) vinegar
90 ml (6 tablespoons) oil
15 ml (1 tablespoon) finely chopped parsley
30 ml (2 tablespoons) finely chopped celery
5 ml (1 teaspoon) salt
2.5 ml ($^1/_2$ teaspoon) black pepper

1 Arrange the shredded lettuce in a salad bowl and top with the tomatoes, avocados, beetroot and green pepper.

2 Just before serving arrange the quartered eggs on the salad. Mix all the dressing ingredients together in a small bowl and pour evenly over the salad.

kalam sangi salatasi
kohlrabi salad

This is another member of the versatile cabbage family. The name kohlrabi has come to us from the German for cabbage-turnip. Indeed, it is to Central Europe and beyond that we must look for recipes for this little-used vegetable. We, potato eaters, used to feed our cattle with it.

Today kohlrabi is still relatively unused, but as this simple and delicious recipe illustrates it is highly popular in Kurdistan. The name in Persian and Kurdish means stone-cabbage, which well suggests the hardness of the bulb. Consequently it should be eaten when still relatively small — not larger than an apple or small orange. If left it will grow to a grapefruit size and become as hard as stone.

To prepare, cut off the leaves — which can also be used in salads and stews — and trim the roots.

4–5 small kohlrabi, peeled and coarsely grated
2 large onions, thinly sliced
3 medium carrots, peeled and grated
4 radishes, washed and thinly sliced
30 ml (2 tablespoons) sultanas
15 ml (1 tablespoon) slivered almonds, optional
juice of 1 large lime or lemon
30 ml (2 tablespoons) finely chopped tarragon
7.5 ml (1$^{1}/_{2}$ teaspoons) salt

Mix all the ingredients together in a large salad bowl and refrigerate for about 1 hour before serving.

jopan lousan

chinese asparagus salad

A delightful salad that can be eaten hot or cold. To prepare the ginger juice press a small piece of fresh ginger root through a garlic press. This salad serves four.

450 g (1 lb) fresh asparagus, tough ends removed
2 medium carrots, peeled and cut into thin rounds

30 ml (2 tablespoons) soy sauce
10 ml (2 teaspoons) sesame oil (see Glossary)
3.75 ml ($^3/_4$ teaspoon) sugar
2.5 ml ($^1/_2$ teaspoon) ginger juice

1 Scrape each asparagus stalk and then cut into 2.5 cm (1 inch) pieces.

2 Half fill a saucepan with water and bring to the boil. Add the carrot slices and simmer for 5–7 minutes or until just tender. Add the asparagus pieces and cook for a further 3–4 minutes. Drain in a colander and then transfer to a salad bowl.

3 In a small bowl, mix all the dressing ingredients together and pour over the vegetables. Toss gently but thoroughly and serve hot.

VARIATION: Add 50 g (2 oz) finely chopped walnuts to the dressing then refrigerate the salad for 1 hour before serving.

aubergine salads

Under this subheading I have included a few of the vast repertoire of aubergine-based recipes. The aubergine is not only a relatively new vegetable in Britain but also one of the most exciting and versatile. My acquaintance with this shiny purple-skinned vegetable started way back in my childhood. I can safely say I was brought up on my mother's milk, yogurt and aubergine in that order.

loligov sumpoog
aubergine and tomato salad

3 large aubergines
juice of 1 large lemon
4 medium tomatoes, finely chopped
2 spring onions, including the green parts, finely chopped
30 ml (2 tablespoons) finely chopped parsley
15 ml (1 tablespoon) chopped fresh dill or 5 ml (1 teaspoon) dried dillweed
45 ml (3 tablespoons) olive oil
5 ml (1 teaspoon) salt
2.5 ml ($^1/_2$ teaspoon) black pepper

Garnish
black olives
2–3 thinly sliced radishes
1 green pepper, thinly sliced

1 Make 2 or 3 slits in each aubergine and then cook over charcoal, under a hot grill or in a hot oven until the skins are black and the flesh feels soft when poked with a finger. Remove and when cool enough to handle peel off the skin, scraping off and reserving any flesh which comes away with it.

2 Place the flesh in a bowl, add the lemon juice and chop finely. Add all the remaining ingredients and mix well. Refrigerate until ready to serve. Serve with the garnishes.

brinjal salad

aubergine salad

This is a warm salad from Central Africa with Indian overtones. The vegetable was introduced to that continent by migrant Indian workers early in the twentieth century and the name 'Brinjal' derives from the Hindi 'Badingan'.

3 large aubergines, washed and dried
30 ml (2 tablespoons) oil
5 ml (I teaspoon) paprika
1 garlic clove, crushed
7.5 ml (1^1/$_2$ teaspoons) ground cumin
30 ml (2 tablespoons) malt vinegar
5 ml (1 teaspoon) salt

Garnish
lemon wedges

1 Cut the aubergines into 2.5 cm (1 inch) cubes and place in a large saucepan. Add enough water to cover by about 2.5 cm (1 inch), then add all the remaining ingredients and bring to the boil.

2 Lower the heat, cover the pan and simmer, stirring occasionally, for about 30 minutes or until the aubergines are tender and most of the water has evaporated.

caponata

sicilian aubergine salad

A rich colourful salad from the homeland of the Mafiosi.

4 celery sticks, cut into 1 cm ($^1/_2$ inch) pieces
90 ml (3 fl oz) olive oil
3 large aubergines, washed, dried and cut into 2 cm ($^3/_4$ inch) cubes
1 large onion, coarsely chopped
3 large tomatoes, coarsely chopped
1 green pepper, seeded and thinly sliced
15 ml (1 tablespoon) tomato purée
45 ml (3 tablespoons) capers, rinsed
50 g (2 oz) green olives, stoned
45 ml (3 tablespoons) wine vinegar
30 ml (2 tablespoons) finely chopped parsley
5 ml (1 teaspoon) salt
5 ml (1 teaspoon) paprika
2.5 ml ($^1/_2$ teaspoon) dried dillweed

1 Bring 600 ml (1 pint) lightly salted water to the boil in a saucepan, add the celery pieces and cook for 6–8 minutes. Drain.

2 Meanwhile, heat two-thirds of the oil in a large saucepan, add the aubergine cubes and fry for 3–4 minutes, stirring frequently. Remove the aubergines with a slotted spoon and drain on kitchen paper.

3 Add the remaining oil to the pan, add the onion and celery and fry for about 5 minutes or until soft. Remove with a slotted spoon and reserve.

4 Add the tomatoes, green pepper and tomato purée to the pan and cook over a low heat for 4–5 minutes. Return all the fried vegetables to the pan and add all the remaining ingredients. Cook over gentle heat, stirring frequently, for 10–15 minutes or until the aubergines are just tender. Transfer to a serving dish and, when cold, refrigerate until ready to serve.

haiver ot patladzani i sirene

aubergine and cheese salad

This recipe is from Bulgaria, which is famed for its cheeses, one of which is *sirene*, a cottage cheese usually made with sheep's milk and which is much firmer than our own versions. I suggest you substitute feta cheese, which is more readily available.

The dish is also called 'aubergine caviar', a title that appears throughout Central Europe as well.

3 large aubergines
75 g (3 oz) feta cheese, crumbled (see Glossary)
45 ml (3 tablespoons) oil
2 garlic cloves, crushed
30 ml (2 tablespoons) vinegar
5 ml (1 teaspoon) salt
30 ml (2 tablespoons) finely chopped parsley

Garnish
30 ml (2 tablespoons) finely chopped fresh tarragon or mint
3 hard-boiled eggs, quartered
6 green olives
6 black olives

1 Prepare the aubergines as described in *Loligov Sumpoog* (Aubergine and Tomato Salad) on page 76.

2 Chop the aubergine flesh and place in a salad bowl with all the remaining ingredients and mix well. Garnish and serve.

takenoko sarada

japanese bamboo shoot salad

The Far East and India do not possess as rich a salad repertoire as the Mediterranean and Middle East. However, this is a tasty and popular salad from Japan. Similar salads also appear in Korea and China.

Fresh bamboo shoots are still difficult to find, but canned ones are readily available from Chinese stores and some large supermarkets (see Glossary).

1 fresh bamboo shoot or 1 can bamboo shoots
60 ml (4 tablespoons) vinegar
30 ml (2 tablespoons) mirin (see Glossary)
3.75 ml ($^3/_4$ teaspoon) salt
30 ml (2 level tablespoons) brown sugar
1.25 ml ($^1/_4$ teaspoon) monosodium glutamate, optional
2 small red peppers, seeded and cut into thin rings

1 If using a fresh bamboo shoot, scrape off the skin and boil it in water for 5–8 minutes or until tender. If using canned ones then drain, rinse and drain again. Cut into thin strips and arrange in a salad bowl.

2 In a small saucepan mix the vinegar, mirin, salt, sugar and monosodium glutamate, if using, together and cook over a low heat, stirring constantly, until the sugar has dissolved. Add the red pepper rings and cook for 2–3 minutes. Remove from the heat and pour over the bamboo shoot strips. When cold refrigerate for 20–30 minutes and then serve.

breadfruit salad

Breadfruit (*Artocarpus communis*) thrives in the hot, humid tropics and is one of the staple foods of Pacific and Caribbean islands. A versatile vegetable fruit, breadfruit can be roasted, boiled, baked and fried. It has a nutty flavour, its seeds are edible and its blossom (with its slight banana flavour) is also eaten. It is sold in most Indo-Pakistani and West Indian shops and weighs somewhere between 1–1.5 kg (2–3 lb). This popular Caribbean salad makes an excellent addition to a buffet or an accompaniment to cold meats.

1 well-ripened breadfruit, washed
3 hard-boiled eggs, whites and yolks separated
1 medium onion, grated
15 ml (3 teaspoons) English or American mustard
25 g (1 oz) butter, melted
75 ml (5 tablespoons) single cream
dash of Worcestershire sauce
7.5 ml (1¹/₂ teaspoons) salt
2.5 ml (¹/₂ teaspoon) black pepper
45 ml (3 tablespoons) wine vinegar or 30 ml (2 tablespoons) lemon juice

1 Place the breadfruit in a large ovenproof dish. Add enough water to cover the base of the dish by about 1 cm (¹/₂ inch). Put in a 180°C (350°F) mark 4 oven and bake for about 1 hour. Remove and set aside until cool enough to handle.

2 Peel and core the breadfruit and slice thinly. Arrange the slices on a large salad plate.

3 Chop the egg whites and sprinkle over the slices together with the grated onion.

4 Place the egg yolks in a bowl, add all the remaining ingredients and mash with a fork until smooth. Taste and adjust seasoning, if necessary. Pour the dressing over the salad and serve.

coleslaw

A delightful salad popularised in North America.

There are many variations, but the main ingredient is always white cabbage coated with mayonnaise.

450 g (1 lb) white cabbage, finely shredded
3 medium carrots, peeled and grated
1 medium onion, thinly sliced
90 ml (6 tablespoons) mayonnaise
15 ml (1 tablespoon) lemon juice
10 ml (2 teaspoons) caraway seeds
5–7.5 ml (1–1$^1/_2$ teaspoons) salt
2.5 ml ($^1/_2$ teaspoon) black pepper

Place all the vegetables in a large salad bowl and add the mayonnaise, lemon juice and caraway seeds. Stir with a wooden spoon until evenly mixed. Add salt and pepper to taste. Cover and refrigerate until ready to serve.

VARIATIONS: Add sliced apples and pears or other fruit, chopped dates, roasted peanuts, chopped walnuts or toasted almonds. If you are extravagant you can even add cashew nuts or pistachios. Other vegetables could include peppers, cress, sliced radishes and any sprouted beans. You can also combine red cabbage with the white and yogurt with the mayonnaise. There are no set rules.

mdzavay komposto

pickled cabbage salad

In the Caucasian mountains, where folk live to a very ripe old age (one of my great aunts made 109), this popular Georgian salad is prepared and served in large quantities. The idea is to pickle a white cabbage for several days until it turns red. No, you cannot use red cabbage. First, because it is not traditional and, second, the flavour is not the same.

The pickled cabbage is often served as a salad by itself simply cut into pickling quarters.

For the pickled white cabbage

900 g (2 lb) white cabbage, washed, trimmed and with
coarse outer leaves discarded
900 g (2 lb) beetroot, peeled and cut into 2.5 cm (1 inch) pieces
10 parsley sprigs
leaves of 6 celery sticks
450 ml (³/₄ pint) red wine vinegar
10 ml (2 teaspoons) paprika

1 First pickle the cabbage: put it in a large saucepan, cover with water, bring to the boil and simmer for about 30 minutes. Remove the cabbage from the water, set aside to drain and leave until cool enough to handle. Pull back the outer leaves gently and carefully open and separate the inner ones, but without detaching them from their base. Put the cabbage into a large casserole.

2 Add the remaining ingredients and sufficient water to cover the cabbage by about 7.5 cm (3 inches). Cover and leave for approximately 1 week.

3 At the end of the week remove the cabbage, which should now be deep red in colour and have a marvellously piquant flavour. Now make the salad.

For the salad

450 g (1 lb) pickled white cabbage (see above)
50 g (2 oz) finely chopped walnuts
2 spring onions, including green parts, finely chopped
15 ml (1 tablespoon) sesame seeds
1 garlic clove, crushed
5 ml (1 teaspoon) salt
2.5 ml (¹/₂ teaspoon) paprika
2.5 ml (¹/₂ teaspoon) basil
5 ml (1 teaspoon) sumac powder (see Glossary)

Garnish
**15 ml (1 tablespoon) finely
chopped parsley or tarragon**

Shred the cabbage and place in a salad bowl. Add the remaining ingredients and mix thoroughly. Refrigerate for about 2 hours before serving.

surówskaz kisonej kapusty

sauerkraut and apple salad

'Fair words butter no cabbage'
Serbo-Croatian saying

For a Pole, and indeed for a Russian, there is the Father, Son and Holy Ghost to feed his soul and beetroot, cabbage and potato to feed his stomach. This recipe is part of the vast cabbage repertoire of Central Europe.

**75 ml (5 tablespoons) oil
10 ml (2 teaspoons) caraway seeds
10 ml (2 teaspoons) sugar
5 ml (1 teaspoon) salt
700 g (1¹/₂ lb) sauerkraut (see page 244), drained
2 large tart cooking apples, peeled, cored,
diced and tossed in a little lemon juice**

1 Place the oil, caraway seeds, sugar and salt in a salad bowl and whisk well.

2 Wash the sauerkraut under cold running water, place in a bowl of water and leave to soak for 15 minutes. Squeeze the sauerkraut until dry and chop it finely. Place it in the salad bowl and add the chopped apples. Toss thoroughly to coat with the dressing and refrigerate until ready to serve.

VARIATIONS: You can add other fruits, vegetables and herbs to the basic recipe: grated carrots, chopped celery, bilberries or pickled mushrooms (see page 243). Cinnamon goes particularly well with cabbage-fruit combinations.

yung chung – chang kar

mongolian cucumber and onion salad

There isn't much in Mongolia (Inner or Outer) except vast, desolate spaces, a large number of horses and a few million people. The food varies from region to region. In the south it is the Chinese school that dominates, in the north it is the Russian and in the east the Korean-Japanese. Overall, simple kebab-type dishes and pastas are eaten. There are, however, a few very interesting vegetable dishes such as this tasty salad. This recipe is from Tolun in the east of the country near Korea.

1 cucumber, washed and very thinly sliced
1 large onion, very thinly sliced
225 g (8 oz) white radishes, peeled and thinly sliced
10 ml (2 teaspoons) salt
10–15 ml (2–3 teaspoons) rice vinegar or wine vinegar
2.5 ml ($1/2$ teaspoon) cayenne pepper
30 ml (2 tablespoons) toasted sesame seeds, crushed (see Glossary)
30 ml (2 tablespoons) sesame oil (see Glossary)

Mix all the ingredients together in a bowl and refrigerate until ready to serve.

flower drum salad

hawaiian tangerine and chinese leaf salad

This fascinating salad from the Pacific islands has a great deal in common with similar recipes from mainland China.

A multicoloured, richly textured recipe which is well worth the effort. Chinese leaves can nowadays be bought from most greengrocers.

2 tangerines, peeled and segmented
6 Chinese leaves, washed and coarsely shredded, discarding
the coarse base of each leaf
125 g (4 oz) slivered bamboo shoots (see Glossary)
50 g (2 oz) sliced water chestnuts (see Glossary)
3 spring onions, thinly sliced
45 ml (3 tablespoons) watercress, washed and chopped

Dressing
60 ml (4 tablespoons) oil
45 ml (3 tablespoons) vinegar or juice of 1 large lemon
10 ml (2 teaspoons) soy sauce
10 ml (2 teaspoons) sugar
1.25 ml ($^1/_4$ teaspoon) dry mustard
2.5 ml ($^1/_2$ teaspoon) salt
1.25 ml ($^1/_4$ teaspoon) black pepper
15 ml (1 tablespoon) toasted sesame seeds (see Glossary)

1 Refrigerate tangerine segments and shredded leaves.

2 Place bamboo shoots, water chestnuts, spring onions and watercress in a large salad bowl.

3 Place all the dressing ingredients in a small bowl and beat thoroughly. Pour over the salad in the bowl, toss well and refrigerate for about 1 hour.

4 When ready to serve add the tangerine pieces and shredded leaves to the salad and toss well.

arnabit antakiyeh

antioch-style salad

*'Cauliflower is nothing but a cabbage
with a college education'*
Mark Twain

This is a family recipe handed down from my maternal grandparent who hailed
from the biblical city of Antioch (modern Antakya) in Turkey.

The cauliflower florets are lightly boiled and then coated with a creamy mixture of
tahini paste seasoned with herbs and spices. Makes a beautiful salad.

1 large cauliflower, broken into florets and washed
150 ml (¼ pint) tahini paste (see Glossary)
2 garlic cloves, crushed
juice of 1 large lemon
5 ml (1 teaspoon) salt
30 ml (2 tablespoons) finely chopped parsley
150 ml (½ pint) cold water

Garnish
2.5 ml (½ teaspoon) paprika
2.5 ml (½ teaspoon) ground cumin

1 Half fill a large saucepan with lightly salted water and bring to the boil. Add the
cauliflower florets, lower the heat, cover the pan and simmer for 5–7 minutes or until
just tender.

2 Meanwhile, mix the tahini in a bowl with the garlic, lemon juice, salt and half the
parsley and water. Beat thoroughly with a fork and then gradually add enough of the
remaining water to produce a creamy dressing about the consistency of mayonnaise.

3 Drain the cauliflower and break into smaller florets, if necessary. Transfer to a salad
bowl, pour the tahini dressing over the top and mix well. Sprinkle with the paprika and
cumin and garnish with the remaining parsley. Serve warm or cold.

VARIATIONS: The Balkans substitute a lemon and olive oil dressing, Lemonolatho, for
the tahini mixture above. To prepare the dressing mix together 45 ml (3 tablespoons)
olive oil, juice of 1 lemon, 2.5 ml (½ teaspoon) dried mint (or dill or thyme), 30 ml (2
tablespoons) finely chopped spring onions, 1 crushed garlic clove, 5 ml (1 teaspoon)
salt and 2.5 ml (½ teaspoon) paprika. The North Africans love to add ½ teaspoon
Harissa (see page 230) and ½ teaspoon caraway.

chayote en salade

chayote salad

A Caribbean speciality. Chayote is better known as Christophene in the West Indies. Although relatively bland in flavour, when cooked with other vegetables and spices it acquires a uniquely 'tropical' taste.

It is well worth experimenting with this 'new' vegetable to our shores. You should be able to find it in most West Indian and many Indo-Pakistani shops. It looks something like a very large, unripe green quince or pear.

2 large chayotes, peeled and quartered lengthways
4 spring onions, including green parts, chopped

Dressing
90 ml (6 tablespoons) olive oil
45 ml (3 tablespoons) lemon juice
1 garlic clove, crushed
5 ml (1 teaspoon) salt
1.25 ml (¼ teaspoon) black pepper
15 ml (1 tablespoon) finely chopped parsley
2.5 ml (½ teaspoon) dillweed
2.5 ml (½ teaspoon) paprika
2.5 ml (½ teaspoon) ginger
2.5 ml (½ teaspoon) chilli powder, optional

1 Half fill a large saucepan with lightly salted water and bring to the boil. Add the quartered chayotes and simmer for about 20 minutes or until tender. Drain and leave until cool enough to handle.

2 Meanwhile, place the spring onions and dressing ingredients in a salad bowl and mix well.

3 When cool enough to handle cut the chayote quarters into 1 cm (½ inch) slices. Although the seeds are edible you can discard them if they are a little tough. Add to the salad bowl and toss well. Serve cold.

cacik

cucumber and yogurt salad

Cucumber and yogurt have a great affinity and these two ingredients appear in numerous salad variations. I have never liked the cucumbers sold in plastic skins. They may be large, but that is about all that can be said for them. The cucumbers I prefer are much smaller, usually about 15 cm (6 inches) long, and can often be found in ethnic Middle Eastern grocery stores. My absolute favourite is twisted and deformed (called *adjour* in Arabic) but alas I have never seen that kind in Britain. However, I have been able to find it pickled — marvellous! No wonder Middle Eastern donkeys and mules crunch them happily as they cart the world's weight on their backs. *Cacik* is the classic salad of Anatolia.

600 ml (1 pint) yogurt
2.5 ml (¹/₂ teaspoon) salt
1 garlic clove, crushed
1 cucumber, peeled and diced
15 ml (1 tablespoon) finely chopped fresh mint or
5 ml (1 teaspoon) dried mint

Garnish
pinch chilli powder

1 Place the yogurt in a large bowl and stir in the salt, garlic, cucumber and mint. Refrigerate until ready to serve.

2 Pour into individual side dishes and sprinkle with the chilli powder.

VARIATION: MIZERIA This is the Polish name for a cucumber and soured cream salad which is popular throughout Central Europe.

Into 600 ml (1 pint) soured cream stir 30 ml (2 tablespoons) finely chopped fresh dill leaves, 2.5 ml (¹/₂ teaspoon) sugar and 30 ml (2 tablespoons) vinegar. Pour this mixture over one peeled and chopped cucumber, mix well and chill until ready to serve.

insalata di arancia

orange and cucumber salad

I was served this salad in a Tangiers hotel a few years ago. The menu called it 'Chalatit Bartogal wa Khiar'. A very similar recipe appears in Marcella Hazan's *Classic Italian Cookbook*, where it is claimed to be of Sicilian origin. Sicilian, Moroccan or, for all I know, Algerian, this is a very tasty and refreshing salad. I particularly like the use of fresh mint.

3 oranges, peeled and with as much
white pith removed as possible
1 cucumber, thinly sliced
6–8 radishes, washed and thinly sliced
4–5 fresh mint leaves, chopped
5 ml (1 teaspoon) salt
juice of 1 small lemon or lime
30 ml (2 tablespoons) olive oil

Garnish
About 15 green or black olives, stoned
2 hard-boiled eggs, quartered

1 Cut the oranges into thin rounds and remove all pips. Place in a large salad bowl with all the remaining ingredients and toss gently but well.

2 Garnish with the olives and quartered eggs.

VARIATION: A Tunisian-Algerian version will also include 1/2 a finely shredded Iceberg lettuce, 15–30 ml (1–2 tablespoons) orange flower water and 2.5 ml (1/2 teaspoon) chilli powder.

t'ang ts'u ou p'ien

fresh lotus root salad

The lotus arrived in China and Japan from the Caucasus and Caspian Sea region. While hardly used in its original homeland all parts of the lotus — the leaves, flower petals, seeds and especially the roots — are much used in Far Eastern cookery.

This recipe is from the Shantung region of mainland China.

Fresh or canned lotus roots can be bought from Chinese grocery stores, but the latter are more readily available.

450 g (1 lb) fresh lotus roots or 2 canned lotus roots (see Glossary)

Dressing
15 ml (1 tablespoon) sesame oil (see Glossary)
15 ml (1 tablespoon) vinegar
25 ml (1½ tablespoons) soy sauce
15 ml (1 tablespoon) brown sugar
2.5 ml (½ teaspoon) salt

1 If using fresh roots wash them thoroughly under cold running water, peel and trim and discard the end of each root. Cut them into 3 mm (⅛ inch) slices. Drop immediately into a bowl of acidulated water to prevent discoloration. Drain, place in a bowl and cover with boiling water. Leave for 5 minutes and then drain again. Rinse under cold running water and pat dry. Transfer to a salad bowl.

2 Mix the dressing ingredients together in a small bowl and pour over the slices. Toss thoroughly and refrigerate before serving.

3 If using canned lotus roots, drain them, slice thinly and marinate in the dressing overnight. Drain, refrigerate for about 1 hour and serve.

VARIATION: Japanese cooks make a dressing with 120 ml (4 fl oz) sake, 45–60 ml (3-4 tablespoons) sugar, 50 ml (2 fl oz) water, 2.5 ml (½ teaspoon) salt and 1.25 ml (¼ teaspoon) monosodium glutamate, which they bring slowly to the boil in a small pan. It is then poured over the thinly sliced lotus roots and set aside for 30 minutes. The slices are then drained, refrigerated for about 1 hour and served.

prikalida me rapania

dandelion and radish salad

Some people find dandelion leaves rather bitter, but the variety that grows in abundance in Greece has a mild flavour. It is the young leaves that go to make this colourful salad.

Once very popular in England, the name comes from the French *dent de lion* (lion's tooth), well describing the jagged edges of the leaves. Dandelion is still very popular in Greece and the neighbouring Balkan lands, where it often replaces spinach, lamb's lettuce, endive or fennel.

30 young dandelion leaves, washed and chopped
$\frac{1}{2}$ large cos lettuce, finely shredded
12 red radishes, thinly sliced
4–5 spring onions, thinly sliced
3 large tomatoes, halved and thinly sliced
10–12 black olives
small bunch watercress, chopped
90 ml (6 tablespoons) olive oil
juice of 1 lemon
10 ml (2 teaspoons) salt
2.5 ml ($\frac{1}{2}$ teaspoon) paprika
15 ml (1 tablespoon) finely chopped fresh dill or
5 ml (1 teaspoon) dried dillweed

Place all the ingredients in a large salad bowl and toss well. Refrigerate until ready to serve.

bekoula

berber-style mallow salad

Our everyday common mallow (*malva sylvestris*) is completely ignored by our cooks. Fortunately it survives in the Mediterranean cuisines. This North African recipe, a speciality of the Holy City of Meknez in Morocco, cleverly mixes the mallow with coriander, celery, olives and pickled lemons.

The mallow has large green leaves rather like spinach and is found in abundance in waste places, rubbish dumps, fields and on roadsides. If not readily available you can use fresh spinach instead and produce an equally delicious salad.

125 g (4 oz) mallow or spinach, chopped
50 g (2 oz) parsley, finely chopped
25 g (1 oz) fresh coriander or tarragon, finely chopped
2 celery sticks, including leaves, finely chopped
3 garlic cloves
zest of 1/2 pickled lemon, optional (see Glossary)
10 ml (2 teaspoons) paprika
2.5 ml (1/2 teaspoon) chilli powder
7.5 ml (1 1/2 teaspoons) salt
60 ml (4 tablespoons) oil
10–12 black olives, stoned
juice of 1 large lemon

1 Place the chopped vegetables in a colander and wash thoroughly under cold water. Shake off excess moisture and place in a large saucepan with the whole cloves of garlic. Cook over a medium heat for about 10 minutes, stirring frequently. Do not add any water as that retained by the vegetables will be sufficient.

2 Remove the garlic cloves, peel, crush and return to the pan. Add the lemon zest, if using, paprika, chilli powder, salt and oil, lower the heat and simmer, stirring occasionally, until all the water has evaporated. Stir in the lemon juice and olives and cook for a further 2 minutes.

3 Transfer to a salad bowl and leave to cool. Taste, adjust seasoning, if necessary, and serve.

salada a lisbonense

lisbon salad

Endive (*Cichorium endivia*) is a variety of chicory with a curly crisp head. It has a slightly bitter flavour which, in this well-known salad from Portugal, is contrasted with the sweet touch of beetroot.

There are two basic varieties of endive available in Britain, Batavian Green and Green Curled. The best, Red Verona, is not easily found here, but is much appreciated in Europe.

Some people like to cook the endive lightly before preparing this dish, but I prefer it raw. If you wish to cook it, then trim, wash, drop into lightly salted boiling water and cook for 1 minute. Drain and shred.

3 endives, trimmed, washed and shredded
4–5 tomatoes, thinly sliced
4 medium carrots, grated
3 medium beetroot, cooked and cut into julienne strips
2 hard-boiled eggs
150 ml (¹/₄ pint) vinaigrette (see page 228)

1 Put the shredded endives in a large salad bowl and arrange the tomato slices overlapping around the edge. Heap the carrots and beetroot in the centre.

2 Chop the egg yolks and whites separately and use to garnish the top of the salad attractively. Pour the vinaigrette over the salad and serve.

kachumbar

parsee onion salad

The onion, which originated in the homelands of the Indo-Iranian races — modern Turkey, Caucasus, Iran and northern India — still dominates the cuisines of these peoples. Here, in this Parsee salad, the two sister cultures of Persia and India combine to perfection.

2 large onions, thinly sliced
10 ml (2 teaspoons) salt
15 ml (1 tablespoon) tamarind juice (see Glossary)
30 ml (2 tablespoons) brown sugar
3 medium tomatoes, chopped
10 ml (2 teaspoons) finely chopped fresh ginger
1–2 chillies, seeded and sliced
5 ml (1 teaspoon) salt
45 ml (3 tablespoons) chopped fresh coriander

1 Place the onion slices in a large dish, sprinkle with the salt and set aside for 1 hour. Transfer to a colander and squeeze out as much liquid as possible. Rinse in cold running water and leave to drain.

2 Meanwhile, place the tamarind juice in a small bowl and stir in 3 tablespoons of water. Add all the remaining ingredients except the onion slices and mix well.

3 Arrange the onion slices in a salad bowl, pour over the tamarind mixture, cover and refrigerate until ready.

VARIATION: In the Balkans tamarind is replaced by a mixture of olive oil and vinegar as with this Albanian salad called *SALAT QEPE TIRANË* — Tirana-style onion salad. Prepare, salt and drain the onions as above. Prepare a dressing with 30 ml (2 tablespoons) olive oil, 30 ml (2 tablespoons) vinegar, 2.5 ml (¹/₂ teaspoon) black pepper and 2 finely chopped garlic cloves. Pour over the onion slices, toss well, refrigerate and serve.

peyvez

onion salad

Ancient Egyptians loved it, the Chinese worshipped it, the Israelites in the Sinai Desert lamented on it, our medieval ancestors ate it as a fruit. Indeed, modern Iranians and Afghanis eat it raw like an apple, but a fifth-century French bishop had an intense dislike for *Allium cepa* — to give it its official name — and this is how he expressed his feelings:

Wouldst know what terrifies my muse,
What is it she complains on?
How can she write a six foot line
With seven feet of patron?
O happy eyes! O happy ears!
Too happy, happy nose
That smells not onions all day long,
For whom no garlic grows.
Poetry in the Dark Ages — Sidonius Apollinaris

Had he tasted this simple salad, which usually accompanies all kinds of kebabs, he may have dampened his muse a trifle.

Serve it with all kinds of stews, cooked vegetables and pickles.

2 large onions, thinly sliced
1 bunch fresh parsley or tarragon, finely chopped
30–45 ml (2–3 tablespoons) sumac powder (see Glossary)

Mix all the ingredients together in a salad bowl and serve.

el ajo de la mano

spanish potato salad

The literal translation of this dish is 'garlic of the hand'. Why? I have not been able to find out. There is a Cervantesian clove of an idea somewhere hidden in the potato slices which escapes me, but the taste cannot.

This is one of the numerous potato-based dishes from the people who first introduced it to Europe.

Farther north on the western coast of the Black Sea chopped spring onions, onions or shallots are added to the potatoes together with shredded lettuce. Greeks like to garnish their potato salads with olives, while the Romanians add hard-boiled eggs.

You can add any favourite herb or spice. The Russians like to garnish their potato salads with dill and parsley, while the Caucasians prefer chopped fresh tarragon or basil or a sprinkling of sumac powder (see Glossary).

900 g (2 lb) potatoes
3 dried or fresh red or green chillies
4–6 garlic cloves, crushed
10 ml (2 teaspoons) salt
5 ml (1 teaspoon) paprika
15 ml (1 tablespoon) lemon juice
30 ml (2 tablespoons) olive oil

1 Hall fill a large saucepan with water and bring to the boil. Add the potatoes and chillies and cook until just tender. Drain and leave until cool enough to handle.

2 Meanwhile, in a small bowl mix together all the remaining ingredients.

3 When the potatoes are cool enough to handle, peel and cut into 2.5 cm (1 inch) cubes. Slice the chillies. Place potatoes and chillies in a salad bowl, add the garlic dressing and mix well. Serve warm or cold.

karjalan perunat

karelian potato salad

Here is a fine potato recipe from Karelia in Finland. It is a part of the world I have not visited but feel I know well through the music of one of my favourite composers, Sibelius, whose suite of the same name I adore as much as I do this simple dish with its egg dressing.

900 g (2 lb) new potatoes, preferably small

Munavoi — Butter and egg dressing
125 g (4 oz) butter
5 ml (1 teaspoon) salt
1.25 ml ($^1/_2$ teaspoon) black pepper
3 hard-boiled eggs, chopped

Garnish
15 ml (1 tablespoon) chopped fresh dill or
5 ml (1 teaspoon) dried dillweed

1 Drop the potatoes into a pan of boiling water. Simmer for 20 minutes or until just tender. Drain and when cool enough to handle, peel and, if necessary, halve.

2 Melt the butter in a saucepan, add the potatoes, salt and pepper and stir until the potatoes are well coated with butter. Stir in the chopped eggs. Spoon into a salad bowl and sprinkle with the dill. Serve warm or cold.

kaiso sarada

seaweed salad

125 g (4 oz) kelp or wakame seaweed (see Glossary)
$^1/_2$ cucumber, thinly sliced
1 medium white radish, peeled and grated
60 ml (4 tablespoons) wine vinegar
60 ml (4 tablespoons) soy sauce
30 ml (2 tablespoons) sugar
5 ml (1 teaspoon) salt
$^1/_8$ teaspoon monosodium glutamate, optional

1 Soak the seaweed in water until tender. The time will vary depending on the freshness of the vegetable, but it usually takes 15–20 minutes.

2 Place the cucumber slices in a colander, lightly salt and leave for 20–30 minutes to drain.

3 Drain away as much of the radish juice as possible by squeezing it out with your hands.

4 When the seaweed is ready, cut into 5 cm (2 inch) lengths. Place in a salad bowl and add the vinegar, soy sauce, sugar, salt and monosodium glutamate, if used. Mix well.

5 Drain the cucumber slices, add to the bowl and mix thoroughly. Make a well in the centre, pile in the grated radish and serve.

salata ot surov spanak

spinach salad, balkan style

The word spinach derives from the Persian *espanakh* and was first cultivated on the slopes of Mount Ararat and the Elburz mountain ranges some 2,000 years ago. Today, as in the past, the most exciting spinach-based dishes come from that geographical area. Only fresh spinach should be used here.

450 g (1 lb) fresh spinach
6 spring onions, sliced

Dressing
150 ml ($^1/_4$ pint) yogurt
60 ml (4 tablespoons) oil
3 hard-boiled eggs, chopped
10 ml (2 teaspoons) salt
2.5 ml ($^1/_2$ teaspoon) black pepper

1 Discard the coarse leaves and thick stems of the spinach. Wash the leaves thoroughly under cold running water and then pat dry. Tear into smaller pieces and place in a large salad bowl with the onions.

2 Mix all the dressing ingredients together in a small bowl and pour over the spinach. Toss well and refrigerate for 30 minutes before serving.

gado-gado

indonesian mixed salad

I have chosen two only from scores of well-known mixed vegetable salads. This one is from South East Asia and the other from the West Indies and both illustrate the rich, colourful and imaginative way salads can be prepared.

125 g (4 oz) fresh bean sprouts
125 g (4 oz) cabbage, shredded
125 g (4 oz) green beans, trimmed and cut into 2.5 cm (1 inch) lengths
3 carrots, peeled and thinly sliced
2 potatoes, peeled
1 bunch watercress, washed

Garnish
1/2 cucumber, peeled and thinly sliced
2 large tomatoes, thinly sliced
3 hard-boiled eggs, cut into wedges

Saus kacang
Peanut Sauce (see page 228)

1 Wash the bean sprouts in a colander under cold running water, then pour boiling water over them and finally rinse with cold water again. Drain.

2 Cook separately in lightly salted boiling water the green beans, cabbage, carrots and potatoes until just tender and then drain.

3 Spread the watercress on a serving plate and arrange the various vegetables in separate sections on top.

4 Garnish the edges of the plate with the cucumber and tomato slices and put the eggs in the centre. Cover and chill for 30 minutes.

5 Meanwhile, prepare the peanut sauce.

6 Serve the salad with the peanut sauce in a separate bowl.

port au prince salad

west indian mixed salad

1 crisp lettuce, finely shredded
1 large green pepper, seeded and cut into rings
4 celery sticks, chopped
8 small shallots or spring onions, quartered lengthways
3 medium carrots, peeled and diced
$1/_2$ cooked breadfruit (see Joy's Creamed Breadfruit, page 113),
peeled and diced
50 g (2 oz) butter
1 garlic clove, crushed
4 thick slices bread, cut into 1 cm ($1/_2$ inch) cubes
1 large or 2 small avocado pears
juice of 1 large lime or lemon
150 ml ($1/_4$ pint) vinaigrette (see page 228)

Garnish
5 ml (1 teaspoon) paprika

1 Arrange the shredded lettuce on a large serving plate.

2 Halve each pepper ring and place in a bowl with the celery, shallots or spring onions, carrots and breadfruit.

3 Melt the butter in a frying pan, add the garlic and fry for 1 minute. Add the bread cubes and fry until golden and crisp. Remove with a slotted spoon, add to the bowl of vegetables and mix well.

4 Peel, stone and slice the avocado. Place the slices in a small bowl, add the lime or lemon juice and toss thoroughly to prevent discoloration.

5 Pile the vegetable and bread mixture on top of the lettuce. Arrange the avocado slices over the vegetables and pour the vinaigrette dressing evenly over them. Sprinkle with the paprika and serve.

cooked vegetables

'One of the greatest luxuries in dining is to be able to command plenty of good vegetables well served up. But this is a luxury vainly hoped for at set parties. The vegetables are made to figure in a very secondary way.'
The Art of Dining
Thomas Walker, London 1835

This is as true today as of Victorian Britain. We really ought to do something about the way we cook and serve vegetables. The generations-old method of boiling good, wholesome potatoes, carrots, peas, beans and sprouts in water and then serving them, still floating in water, should be banned — if need be by royal decree.

Vegetables are too important to be treated in such a 'mean' manner and, as the recipes in this chapter will verify, should never be made 'to figure in a very secondary way'.

The first recipe, from the Balkans, illustrates how other people have devised methods to enhance both the taste and flavour of such normally bland vegetables as artichokes and broad beans.

agginares me koukia

artichokes and broad beans

A typical Greek dish. The fresh broad beans can be substituted by others such as runner beans, chickpeas, lentils, black-eyed beans and *ful* beans — as indeed they often are in the Balkans, Turkey and Armenia. If using black-eyed beans, chickpeas or *ful* beans remember to soak them overnight in cold water and then drain and parboil (see Glossary) before proceeding with the recipe below. Serve with bread or a pilav or a salad.

6 artichoke hearts (see Glossary)
900 g (2 lb) fresh broad beans
3 large potatoes, peeled and cut into 5 cm (2 inch) pieces
1 large onion, thinly sliced
2–3 garlic cloves, crushed
15 ml (1 tablespoon) finely chopped parsley
15 ml (1 tablespoon) finely chopped fresh tarragon
2.5 ml ($^1/_2$ teaspoon) dried dillweed
10 ml (2 teaspoons) salt
2.5 ml ($^1/_2$ teaspoon) black pepper
5 ml (1 teaspoon) paprika
2.5 ml ($^1/_2$ teaspoon) ground cumin

1 Quarter the hearts and keep in acidulated water (see Glossary) until ready to cook.

2 If using very young broad beans, just string and halve the pods, otherwise shell them.

3 Place all the ingredients in a large saucepan and mix thoroughly. Add enough water to cover by 0.5 cm ($^1/_4$ inch) and bring to the boil. Lower the heat, cover the pan and simmer until the vegetables are tender and the water has evaporated.

4 Turn into a large bowl and serve.

broccoli all'aglio

broccoli with garlic

Try this tasty southern Italian dish. I like to serve it with a tomato and cashew nut sauce (see page 234) and with rice or pasta — lovely!

900 g (2 lb) fresh broccoli heads, washed and trimmed
75 ml (5 tablespoons) oil
3–4 garlic cloves, crushed
45 ml (3 tablespoons) finely chopped parsley or coriander
5 ml (1 teaspoon) salt
2.5 ml (1/2 teaspoon) black pepper
2.5 ml (1/2 teaspoon) chilli powder
2.5 ml (1/2 teaspoon) basil

Garnish
30 ml (2 tablespoons) toasted sesame seeds (see Glossary)

1 Divide the broccoli heads into small spears and cook in lightly salted water for 5–7 minutes. Drain and reserve.

2 Heat the oil in a large frying pan, add the garlic and fry for 2 minutes, stirring frequently. Mix in the parsley or coriander, salt, pepper, chilli powder and basil. Add the broccoli and turn to coat with the oil. Cook over a low heat for about 5 minutes, carefully turning the broccoli a few times. Turn into a large shallow serving dish and sprinkle with the sesame seeds.

ghalieh-ye kadoo

lentils with courgettes

A delicious recipe from Shiraz (Iran). You can substitute small vegetable marrow or pumpkin for the courgettes.

Serve with a rice or burghul pilav and with either yogurt or, as is often the custom in the land of Saidi and Khayyam, with a yogurt and garlic sauce (see page 234).

25 g (1 oz) butter
2 onions, thinly sliced
350 g (12 oz) whole lentils, washed thoroughly
3–4 courgettes, cut crossways into 1 cm ($^1/_2$ inch) slices
15 ml (1 tablespoon) lemon juice
7.5 ml (1$^1/_2$ teaspoons) salt
2.5 ml ($^1/_2$ teaspoon) black pepper
5 ml (1 teaspoon) ground cumin

Garnish
15 ml (1 tablespoon) butter
1 small onion, finely chopped
30 ml (2 tablespoons) finely chopped parsley

1 Melt the butter in a large saucepan. Add the onions and fry until golden. Add the lentils and enough water to cover by about 2.5 cm (1 inch) and bring to the boil. Lower the heat, cover the pan and simmer for 15 minutes.

2 Stir the courgettes into the lentils, cover and simmer for a further 15–20 minutes or until the courgettes and lentils are tender. Add the lemon juice, salt, pepper and cumin and stir thoroughly.

3 Make the garnish: melt the butter in a small pan, add the onion and fry until lightly browned.

4 To serve, transfer the lentil-courgette mixture to a large dish and sprinkle with the fried onion and parsley.

sparga siitve

asparagus hungarian style

Hungarian asparagus is long, thick and white, but the green British variety will do just as well. You can also use yogurt instead of soured cream. A very tasty dish which can be served with other vegetables or salads and with bread or a pilav.

Serves four as a main dish or six as a starter or side dish.

900 g (2 lb) asparagus, trimmed and scraped
2.5 ml ($\frac{1}{2}$ teaspoon) sugar
300 ml ($\frac{1}{2}$ pint) soured cream or yogurt
5 ml (1 teaspoon) plain flour
1 large egg yolk
5 ml (1 teaspoon) salt
5 ml (1 teaspoon) paprika
2.5 ml ($\frac{1}{2}$ teaspoon) sugar
25 g (1 oz) fresh breadcrumbs
25 g (1 oz) unsalted butter

1 Wash and drain the asparagus thoroughly. Simmer for 5 minutes in boiling water and drain. Pat dry with kitchen paper and arrange in a large greased ovenproof dish.

2 In a small bowl, mix together thoroughly the soured cream or yogurt, flour, egg yolk, salt, paprika and sugar. Pour this evenly over the asparagus. Sprinkle the breadcrumbs over the top and then dot with small knobs of the butter. Bake in a 200°C (400°F) mark 6 oven for about 15 minutes or until the top is golden.

ching chiao shao chie tzu

aubergines with capsicums

This dish is best made in a wok, but if you do not have one use a large shallow saucepan or frying pan.

This is one of the numerous stir-fry dishes of China. It is a method of cooking which retains the crispness and freshness of the vegetables as well as saving cooking time and fuel. Other vegetables can also be prepared in this way.

Serve with boiled rice if you wish to be authentic. Personally, I prefer a good rice or burghul pilav. The Chinese may claim, as indeed they do, that 'In China we have only three religions, but we have a hundred dishes we can make from rice' — but all they offer you, over and over again, is boiled rice and, if they really have taken a liking to you, fried rice. In short, they may have first cultivated the grain and it may be their natural cereal, but they have a great deal to learn from the Iranians and Turks and even the Italians when it comes to making dishes from rice.

Tou shih — salted black beans — are sold in cans or plastic bags at all Chinese groceries and are used mainly to flavour vegetables and curds.

150 ml (¹/₄ pint) corn or groundnut oil
2 large aubergines, halved lengthways and then cut across into 0.5 cm (¹/₄ inch) slices
1–2 garlic cloves, thinly sliced
4 capsicums (green peppers), seeded and cut into 2.5 cm (1 inch) squares
30 ml (2 tablespoons) salted black beans (*tou shih*)
60 ml (4 tablespoons) soy sauce
15 ml (1 tablespoon) brown sugar
300 ml (¹/₂ pint) water

1 Heat the oil in a wok, add the aubergine slices a few at a time and fry until both sides are lightly golden. Remove with a slotted spoon, drain on kitchen paper and reserve. Add a little more oil if necessary.

2 When all the slices are fried add the garlic and peppers to the pan and stir-fry for 2 minutes or until just tender. Push the garlic and peppers to one side, add the salted black beans and stir-fry for 1 minute. Return the fried aubergines to the pan and add the soy sauce, sugar and water. Stir well, cover the pan and simmer for 5–7 minutes.

3 Remove the cover, stir thoroughly and cook for a further 2 minutes before serving.

wake-ewa

black-eyed beans in pepper sauce

A very tasty and simple dish from West Africa. You can also use other dried beans such as chickpeas, pinto or haricot beans.

These bean dishes are served with a hot pepper sauce (see *Egbo*, page 222) and *garri* (see Glossary), but you can also serve them with any *fufu* dishes (see page 206) as well as *Eba* (see page 206) or Breadfruit or Plantain chips (see page 207).

350 g (12 oz) black-eyed beans, washed,
soaked overnight in cold water and drained
15 ml (1 tablespoon) sugar
5 ml (1 teaspoon) salt

Pepper Sauce
See page 222

1 Half fill a large saucepan with water and bring to the boil. Add the beans, sugar and salt. Lower the heat, cover the pan and simmer for 30–40 minutes or until tender — time will depend on age and type of beans used.

2 Meanwhile, prepare the pepper sauce and keep warm.

3 When tender drain the beans and serve with the pepper sauce. You can either serve them separately or stir the beans into the sauce.

aubergines in coconut milk

This Caribbean dish is similar to the many Indo-Pakistani coconut with vegetable dishes. Serve with rice, baked potatoes, sweet potatoes or yams.

2 large aubergines, cut crossways into 1 cm ($^1/_2$ inch) slices
3 large onions, thinly sliced
10 ml (2 teaspoons) salt
2 small green chillies, seeded and thinly sliced
2.5 ml ($^1/_2$ teaspoon) black pepper
5 ml (1 teaspoon) paprika
450 ml ($^3/_4$ pint) coconut milk (see Glossary)

1 Lightly grease a large ovenproof casserole and arrange the aubergine slices in layers in it. Spread the onions over the top. Sprinkle with the sliced chillies, salt, black pepper and paprika.

2 Pour in the coconut milk, cover the dish and bake in a l80°C (350°F) mark 4 oven for about 50 minutes or until the aubergines are tender. Remove the lid and cook uncovered for a further 10 minutes. Serve immediately.

patrizani borani
aubergines with walnut sauce

This is how the twelfth-century Moorish poet Ibn Sara described the aubergine:

Fire to the taste they are,
Smoothly globular,
Fed by the sweet brook
In their shady nook.

Fronds at the top and toe
Clutch them round as though
they are hearts of sheep
In the eagle's grip.
Anthology of Moorish Poetry

Curiously enough it has fallen to the non-Arab people of Iran, Turkey and the Caucasus to expand the many-faceted qualities of this vegetable. This popular dish from Armenia makes use of an equally famed sauce of walnuts and coriander from the neighbouring land of Georgia, renowned for her dancers, beautiful women and two notorious sons — Stalin and Beria.

This method of cooking vegetables is equally popular in Iran, where it is reputed to have originated. *Borani* is named after the Iranian Queen Borantoukht, who, it appears, was fond of yogurt. Hence all *borani* dishes (traditionally at least) incorporate yogurt either as part of the dish or as a sauce. In similar vein you can prepare spinach, courgettes, green beans and many other vegetables.

90 ml (6 tablespoons) oil
3 medium onions, thinly sliced
6 medium aubergines, cut crossways into 0.5 cm (¼ inch) slices
3 large tomatoes, blanched, peeled and coarsely chopped
15 ml (1 tablespoon) finely chopped fresh basil or 5 ml (1 teaspoon) dried basil
15 ml (1 tablespoon) finely chopped fresh mint or 5 ml (1 teaspoon) dried mint
30 ml (2 tablespoons) finely chopped parsley
5 ml (1 level teaspoon) cinnamon
7.5 ml (1½ teaspoons) salt
2.5 ml (½ teaspoon) black pepper
2.5 ml (½ teaspoon) sumac powder (see Glossary)

Walnut and Coriander Sauce
See page 235

Heal the oil in a large saucepan, add the onions and fry until soft, stirring frequently. Add all the remaining ingredients and mix well. Cook over a moderate heat, stirring occasionally, for about 20 minutes or until the aubergines are tender. Add a little more oil if necessary as aubergines 'drink' oil. Serve with walnut and coriander sauce.

tavce

beans with onions and chillies

From Macedonia, the homeland of Philip and Alexander the Great and now divided between Yugoslavia, Greece and Bulgaria, comes this dish which also has divided origins and loyalties. It has a Turkish-based name *tavce* meaning small *tava* (frying pan) from the Arabic *tawa*. The style of cooking is typically Ottoman, the only Macedonian part is the use of hot chillies.

Serve with breads, pickles and fresh salads.

150 ml (¹/₄ pint) oil
3 large onions, thinly sliced
2 garlic cloves, crushed
10 ml (2 teaspoons) paprika
2.5 ml (¹/₂ teaspoon) black pepper
2 bay leaves
3 chillies, seeded and thinly sliced
350 g (12 oz) dried beans (cannellini, flageolet, or *ful*),
soaked overnight in cold water and drained
600 ml (1 pint) boiling water
7.5 ml (1¹/₂ teaspoons) salt

1 Heat half the oil in a saucepan, add the onions and fry until soft. Add the garlic, paprika, black pepper, bay leaves and chillies and fry for 2 minutes, stirring frequently. Remove from the heat.

2 Lightly grease a large ovenproof dish and spread half the beans over the bottom. Arrange half the onion mixture over them. Spread remaining beans over the onions and then top with the remaining onion mixture. Pour remaining oil and the water into the dish and bake in a 180°C (350°F) mark 4 oven for 60–90 minutes or until the beans are tender. Season with the salt.

joy's creamed breadfruit

On some of the West Indian islands breadfruit is cooked with okra to make the famed *Coo-coo*, which is undoubtedly related to the African *fufu*. Cooked breadfruit tastes very much like potatoes. If fresh breadfruit is not available you can use canned breadfruit which can be found in Indo-Pakistani as well as West Indian shops. Serve with salad and pickles or as an accompaniment to a vegetable stew.

1–1.5 kg (2–3 lb) fresh or 2 x 450 g (1 lb) canned breadfruit
25 g (1 oz) butter
10 ml (2 teaspoons) salt
2.5 ml ($1/2$ teaspoon) black pepper
2.5 ml ($1/2$ teaspoon) chilli powder
1.25 ml ($1/4$ teaspoon) nutmeg
200 ml ($1/3$ pint) milk

1 Cook the fresh breadfruit in a large saucepan of boiling salted water for about 40 minutes or until tender. Drain, peel and core. Then chop the flesh roughly. If using canned breadfruit, drain and chop coarsely.

2 Place the chopped flesh in a large bowl, add the butter, salt, pepper, chilli powder and nutmeg. Mash the mixture with a fork, gradually stirring in enough of the milk to make a creamy but still stiff mixture.

3 Grease an ovenproof dish, put in the mashed breadfruit and smooth over the surface with the back of a spoon. Bake in a 200°C (400°F) mark 6 oven for 15–20 minutes or until the top is golden. Serve hot.

VARIATION: You can, of course, serve the mashed breadfruit without baking it just as you would mashed potatoes.

costanos y champinones
chestnuts with mushrooms

'Unless you learn' said the father to the son,
'How to tell a horse chestnut from a chestnut
horse you may have to live on soup made
from the shadow of a starving pigeon.'
Carl Sandburg

Fresh chestnuts are not always readily available and I therefore suggest that you use either canned or dried ones. The latter should be soaked for 6–8 hours in water before using.

Serve with vegetables of your choice or a plain pasta dish and a fresh salad.

700 g (1¹/₂ lb) chestnuts, shelled
90 ml (6 tablespoons) oil
450 g (1 lb) button mushrooms, wiped clean
45 ml (3 tablespoons) flour
600 ml (1 pint) soured cream or yogurt
5 ml (1 teaspoon) salt
2.5 ml (¹/₂ teaspoon) paprika
2.5 ml (¹/₂ teaspoon) grated lemon rind
15 ml (1 tablespoon) finely chopped parsley

Garnish
black and green olives and sliced radishes

1 Put the fresh or drained dried chestnuts in a large saucepan, add enough water to cover and bring to the boil. Lower the heat, cover the pan and simmer for about 20 minutes. Drain and leave until cool enough to handle and then quarter them with a sharp knife and reserve.

2 Heat the oil in a large saucepan, add the mushrooms and fry, stirring frequently, for 2–3 minutes. Add the chestnuts and fry for a further 3–4 minutes.

3 Sprinkle in the flour and stir to thicken the mixture. Reduce the heat to very low and gradually stir in the soured cream or yogurt. Add the salt, paprika and lemon rind, mix well and simmer for 8–10 minutes.

4 Transfer to a serving dish and sprinkle with the parsley. Garnish and serve.

kraut mit paprika und paradeisern

cabbage with tomatoes and peppers

This recipe from the German-Austrian cuisine is also popular in the adjacent lands, particularly in Romania and Hungary, hence the appearance of paprika, the Hungarian national vegetable.

50 g (2 oz) butter or margarine
1 medium onion, finely chopped
3 large tomatoes, blanched, peeled and coarsely chopped
2 green peppers, thinly sliced
900 g (2 lb) white cabbage, finely shredded
15 ml (1 level tablespoon) caraway seeds
10 ml (2 teaspoons) salt
1.25 ml ($^1/_4$ teaspoon) black pepper
5 ml (1 teaspoon) paprika
30 ml (2 tablespoons) malt vinegar
30 ml (2 tablespoons) flour mixed to a smooth paste
with 90 ml (6 tablespoons) water

Garnish
Soured cream or yogurt

1 Melt the butter or margarine in a large saucepan, add the onions and fry, stirring frequently, for 3 minutes. Add the tomatoes and green peppers and cook, stirring occasionally, for 3 more minutes. Now add the shredded cabbage, caraway seeds, salt, pepper, paprika and vinegar and mix well. Cover the pan and cook over a low heat, stirring occasionally, for 20–30 minutes or until the cabbage is tender.

2 Stir in the flour mixture and cook for a further 2–3 minutes. Remove from the heat and serve immediately. Either pour the soured cream or yogurt over the cabbage mixture in its serving dish or serve it in a separate bowl.

tungku chuan hsin tsay
cabbage with mushrooms and bamboo shoots

From the native homeland of cabbage comes this simple but typical and very popular recipe. You can use any Chinese cabbage that is available locally — *Choy Sum* (flowering cabbage) or pak choi (white cabbage) or *Wong nga Baak* (Peking cabbage).

Serve with Chinese-style boiled or fried rice.

900 g (2 lb) cabbage, trimmed, quartered and cored
10–12 dried winter mushrooms (enoki), soaked in water for 1 hour
45 ml (3 tablespoons) oil
75–90 ml (5–6 tablespoons) water
75 g (3 oz) bamboo shoots, thinly sliced (see Glossary)
10 ml (2 teaspoons) salt
5 ml (1 teaspoon) sugar

1 Cut the cabbage quarters into 2.5 cm (1 inch) slices.

2 Drain the mushrooms and reserve the soaking liquid. Discard the stems and thinly slice the caps.

3 Heat a wok or large frying pan on a high heat and add the oil. Add the cabbage and sprinkle with the water to prevent the cabbage from burning. Stir-fry for 2 minutes. Add the bamboo shoots and stir-fry for a further 2 minutes. Now add the mushrooms and fry for 2 more minutes. Season with the salt and sugar and add 150 ml (1/4 pint) of the soaking liquid — making it up to that amount with water, if necessary. Mix well, cover the pan and cook for 2–3 minutes.

4 To serve, mix thoroughly, turn into a large dish and serve.

voroskaposzta almaval

red cabbage with apples and raisins

In the same vein, again from Central Europe, here is a recipe where red cabbage is mixed with a fruit — in this case apples. This is a standard method prevalent throughout Europe and the Balkans. This recipe is from Budapest in Hungary. Use firm under-ripe eating apples or cooking apples. If the latter, add a little sugar.

Serve with vegetables, bread and pickles.

900 g (2 lb) red cabbage, finely shredded
15 ml (1 tablespoon) salt
25 g (1 oz) butter or margarine
450 g (1 lb) apples, peeled and thinly sliced
75 g (3 oz) raisins
2.5 ml ($1/2$ teaspoon) black pepper
5 ml (1 teaspoon) thyme

Garnish
150 ml ($1/4$ pint) soured cream or yogurt

1 Place the shredded cabbage in a colander, sprinkle with 5 ml (1 teaspoon) salt and set aside for 30 minutes. Squeeze as much of the liquid out as possible.

2 Melt the butter or margarine in a large pan, add the cabbage and fry, stirring frequently, for 5 minutes. Add the apple slices and fry gently for a further 5 minutes. Stir in the remaining ingredients, lower the heat and cook for 20–30 minutes, stirring carefully occasionally.

3 Transfer to a large serving dish, pour over the soured cream or yogurt and serve.

couve-flor da meia noite

midnight cauliflower

Try as I did I was unable to find out why this South American recipe is so named. There is a similar Portuguese dish with the same name, so perhaps it is Portuguese in origin. As for the name, I drew a blank.

Traditionally the vegetable is baked whole and you can do so if you wish, but I prefer it broken into florets. This is a fine dish.

Serve it with roast potatoes or yams.

1 large cauliflower (about 700 g/1^1/$_2$ lb),
trimmed, washed and drained
300 ml (^{1}/$_2$ pint) boiling water
15 ml (1 tablespoon) butter or margarine
1 onion, finely chopped
2 garlic cloves, crushed
120 ml (4 fl oz) oil
6–8 black olives, stoned and thinly sliced
300 ml (^{1}/$_2$ pint) single cream or yogurt blended with
15 ml (1 tablespoon) flour
10 ml (2 teaspoons) salt
2.5 ml (^{1}/$_2$ teaspoon) black pepper
2.5–5 ml (^{1}/$_2$–1 teaspoon) chilli powder, according to taste

Garnish
30–45 ml (2–3 tablespoons) finely chopped parsley

1 Either place the whole cauliflower head down in a large saucepan or break into florets before placing in the pan. Add the boiling water, cover the pan and simmer for 5–10 minutes. Drain in a colander.

2 Lightly grease a large ovenproof casserole and place the cauliflower in it. If using a whole cauliflower place it head upwards.

3 Melt the butter or margarine in a small saucepan, add the onion and garlic and fry until soft and turning golden.

4 Place the contents of the pan with all the remaining ingredients in a bowl and mix thoroughly. Pour the mixture over the cauliflower and bake in the centre of a 180°C (350°F) mark 4 oven for about 30 minutes, basting regularly with the pan juices.

5 Remove from the oven, garnish with the parsley and serve.

ful bit tewm

broad beans with garlic

If you like garlic this is the dish for you — of course it will help if you also have a penchant for broad beans. The beans should be fresh and shelled, but you can use dried ones, which should first be soaked for about 6–8 hours in cold water and then drained. Add salt only when they are cooked.

I have deliberately kept the quantity of garlic low so that you can then increase it according to your taste.

Serve with rice or couscous (see page 208) or with vegetables of your choice.

900 g (2 lb) fresh broad beans
4 garlic cloves (or more), crushed
30 ml (2 tablespoons) finely chopped coriander or parsley
25 ml (1^1/$_2$ tablespoons) vinegar or lemon juice
30 ml (2 tablespoons) olive oil
10 ml (2 teaspoons) salt
2.5 ml (^{1}/$_2$ teaspoon) black pepper
1.25 ml (^{1}/$_4$ teaspoon) cayenne pepper
300 ml (^{1}/$_2$ pint) water

Place all the ingredients in a large saucepan, mix thoroughly and bring to the boil. Lower the heat, cover the pan and simmer until the beans are tender. If using dried beans they will take about 1 hour and may need a little extra water.

spicy carrots

This dish appears on many restaurant and hotel menus. About its nationality I do not know, but of its taste I do — it is excellent.

Serve with other vegetables and salads.

900 g (2 lb) carrots, peeled and cut crossways
into 0.5 cm ($^1/_4$ inch) slices
75 g (3 oz) raisins or sultanas
50 g (2 oz) butter
1 small onion, finely chopped
7.5 ml (1$^1/_2$ teaspoons) salt
5 ml (1 teaspoon) chilli powder
1.25 ml ($^1/_4$ teaspoon) nutmeg
150 ml ($^1/_4$ pint) water
25 g (1 oz) soft brown sugar

Garnish
30 ml (2 tablespoons) slivered almonds, toasted

1 Place the carrots in a large saucepan with all the remaining ingredients except the sugar. Cook over a low heat, stirring occasionally, for about 15 minutes or until the carrots are just tender.

2 Add the sugar, mix well and continue to cook until the sugar has dissolved. Turn into a large dish, sprinkle with the toasted almonds and serve.

selery z serem

celeriac au gratin

Celeriac, or celery roots, is a relative of celery, which is particularly popular in Central European cuisines.

This Polish-inspired recipe is one of those nineteenth-century creations that enriched both the French and the Polish-Russian cuisines.

Gratin simply means that the top is browned either under the grill or in the oven.

Serve with a bowl of fresh salad, bread and pickles.

900 g (2 lb) celeriac, peeled
15 ml (1 tablespoon) wine vinegar
350 g (12 oz) cheese, Gruyère or Cheddar, grated
50 g (2 oz) butter or margarine
5 ml (1 teaspoon) sugar
10 ml (2 teaspoons) salt
1.25 ml ($^{1}/_{4}$ teaspoon) black pepper
150 ml ($^{1}/_{4}$ pint) soured cream or yogurt
15 ml (1 tablespoon) flour mixed to smooth paste with 45 ml (3 tablespoons) water
60 ml (4 tablespoons) lightly toasted fresh breadcrumbs

1 Half fill a large pan with lightly salted water and bring to the boil. Add the celeriac and vinegar, cover the pan and simmer for 20 minutes. Drain and, when cool enough to handle, cut into 3 mm ($^{1}/_{8}$ inch) slices.

2 Lightly grease a large casserole and fill with alternate layers of celeriac slices and grated cheese, each layer dotted with butter and sprinkled with salt, black pepper and sugar. Finish with a layer of cheese.

3 In a small bowl, mix together the soured cream or yogurt and the dissolved flour. Pour evenly over the top. Sprinkle over the toasted breadcrumbs and bake in the centre of a 180°C (350°F) mark 4 oven for 20–25 minutes. At this point you can, if necessary, remove the casserole from the oven and complete the browning under a hot grill.

VARIATION: While celeriac, like celery, has a natural affinity with cheese, there is no real reason why you should not make this dish with other root vegetables such as parsnips, turnips or swedes, or a mixture of all three.

aaloo aur seengh ki sabzi

drumsticks with potatoes

Drumsticks are found now almost all year round in Indo-Pakistani groceries. Long, thin and with ridged skins they make an excellent chutney (see page 256) and are used in stews and soups.

You must never eat the skins, just suck their tender insides.

Serve with a rice pilav of your choice.

About 10 drumsticks, washed and cut into 5 cm (2 inch) pieces
45 ml (3 tablespoons) oil
15 ml (1 tablespoon) mustard seeds
5 ml (1 level teaspoon) chilli powder
2.5 ml ($^1/_2$ teaspoon) turmeric
5 ml (1 teaspoon) salt
1 onion, finely chopped
450 g (1 lb) tomatoes, blanched, peeled and coarsely chopped
60 ml (4 tablespoons) water
450 g (1 lb) potatoes or sweet potatoes, peeled and
cut into 5 cm (2 inch) cubes
450 ml ($^3/_4$ pint) water or vegetable stock (see Glossary)

Garnish
30 ml (2 tablespoons) finely chopped parsley or coriander

1 Half fill a large pan with lightly salted water and bring to the boil. Add the drumsticks, lower the heat, cover the pan and simmer for 20 minutes. Drain and set aside.

2 Heat the oil in a large pan, add the mustard seeds and fry for about 1 minute or until they begin to pop. Add the chilli powder, turmeric, salt and onion and mix well. Fry, stirring frequently, for 2–3 minutes before adding the chopped tomatoes and the water. Lower the heat and simmer, stirring occasionally, for about 10 minutes or until the tomatoes are reduced to a pulp.

3 Add the potatoes and water or vegetable stock and mix thoroughly. Cover the pan and simmer for about 20 minutes or until tender. Add the drumsticks, stir and simmer for a further 5 minutes. Turn into a large serving dish and garnish with the parsley.

finocchi al latte

fennel with milk

Fennel is now readily available in our shops and there are many fine ways of preparing this aromatic flowering plant, but none I believe is as good, or as simple, as the recipe below from the homeland of the vegetable — Italy.

If you find the Parmesan cheese too strong either use Cheddar or Gruyère or combine them with the Parmesan.

900 g (2 lb) fennel bulbs, trimmed, tough outer stalks removed
50 g (2 oz) butter
200 ml (¹/₃ pint) milk
60–75 ml (4–5 tablespoons) freshly grated Parmesan
2.5 ml (¹/₂ teaspoon) paprika

Garnish
15 ml (1 tablespoon) finely chopped coriander or parsley

1 Slice the fennel bulbs horizontally and wash thoroughly.

2 Half fill a large saucepan with lightly salted water and bring to the boil. Add the fennel slices and simmer for 7–8 minutes or until just tender. Drain.

3 Melt the butter in a large pan, add the fennel slices and fry for 2–3 minutes, turning carefully. Add the milk, cover the pan and simmer, turning the slices occasionally, for 5–7 minutes or until most of the milk has evaporated.

4 Transfer the fennel to a shallow heatproof dish and sprinkle with the cheese and paprika. Cook under a hot grill for 2–3 minutes or until the top is golden. Garnish and serve.

calam ghomri khoresh
afghan-style kohlrabi

This Afghan dish is typical of the *khoresh*-named dishes of Iran and neighbouring Soviet Tadzhikistan and Turkmenistan.

It is traditionally served with one of the many exquisite rice pilavs for which the Iranian cuisine is particularly famed.

30 ml (2 tablespoons) ghee (see Glossary) or butter
1 large onion, finely chopped
2 garlic cloves, crushed
700 g (1¹/₂ lb) kohlrabi, peeled and cut into 5 cm (2 inch) slices
225 g (8 oz) carrots, peeled and cut into 1 cm (¹/₂ inch) rounds
2 medium turnips, peeled and cut into 5 cm (2 inch) slices
50 g (2 oz) chickpeas, soaked overnight in cold water and drained
1 large potato, peeled and cut into 5 cm (2 inch) pieces
60 ml (4 tablespoons) finely chopped parsley or coriander
600 ml (1 pint) water
2.5 ml (¹/₂ teaspoon) marjoram
10 ml (2 teaspoons) salt
1.25 ml (¹/₄ teaspoon) black pepper
1.25 ml (¹/₄ teaspoon) cayenne pepper
25 ml (1¹/₂ tablespoons) tomato purée

1 Melt the ghee or butter in a large saucepan, add the onion and garlic and fry, stirring constantly, for 3 minutes.

2 Add all the remaining ingredients, mix thoroughly, and bring to the boil. Lower the heat, cover the pan and simmer for 60–75 minutes or until the chickpeas are tender. Add a little more water, if necessary. Serve hot.

tomates con lentejas asados

tomatoes with lentils

This is a tasty and filling dish typical of South American cooking. It is popular throughout Mexico, Cuba and the other Spanish-speaking countries of that vast continent.

Serve with pickles, bread and fresh vegetables of your choice including avocados, pawpaws and hot chillies.

700 g (1$^{1}/_{2}$ lb) whole lentils, washed, cooked until just tender and drained
125 g (4 oz) mushrooms, wiped clean and thinly sliced
1 small onion, finely chopped
6–8 black olives, stoned and thinly sliced
50 g (2 oz) fresh breadcrumbs, lightly toasted
25 g (1 oz) slivered almonds, lightly toasted
5 ml (1 teaspoon) salt
1.25 ml ($^{1}/_{2}$ teaspoon) black pepper
2.5 ml ($^{1}/_{2}$ teaspoon) cumin
5 ml (1 level teaspoon) chilli powder
6 tomatoes, sliced into thick rounds
350 g (12 oz) cheese, Cheddar, Gruyère or mozzarella, grated

Garnish
lemon wedges

1 Grease a large ovenproof casserole and spread the lentils over the base.

2 In a bowl, mix all the remaining ingredients together except the tomatoes and cheese, and spread evenly over the lentils. Arrange the tomato slices over the top and then cover with the cheese.

3 Bake in a 180°C (350°F) mark 4 oven for 20–30 minutes or until the top is golden and the cheese is bubbling. Garnish with the lemon wedges and serve.

ku kua tou shih

bitter melon with salted black beans

Bitter melon or gourd, the *karela* of India, is equally popular in China. To reduce its bitterness parboil for 3–4 minutes before proceeding with the recipe, which is simple, cheap and tasty.

Tou shih (salted black beans) are beans preserved in salt and can be bought from Chinese stores. Bitter gourds can be found in most Indian or Pakistani greengrocers.

4 bitter melons or gourds, washed, halved lengthways,
blanched in boiling water for 3–4 minutes and drained
75–90 ml (5–6 tablespoons) oil
50 g (2 oz) salted black beans
7.5 ml (1¹/₂ teaspoons) brown sugar
10 ml (2 teaspoons) salt
60 ml (4 tablespoons) water
15 ml (1 tablespoon) soy sauce

1 Remove and discard the seeds and soft central part of each *karela* and then cut each one crossways into 0.5 cm (¹/₄ inch) slices.

2 Heat a wok until very hot. Add half the oil and stir-fry the *karela* for 3–4 minutes or until it acquires a dark green sheen. Remove with a slotted spoon and set aside on a plate.

3 Add the remaining oil to the wok and stir-fry the black beans for 3 minutes. Add the sugar, salt, water, soy sauce and *karela* and mix well. Stir-fry for 3–4 minutes and serve immediately.

The love of mushrooms is legendary among the people of Central Europe, particularly of Poland and Russia, where, without a doubt, the most varied, rich and exciting mushroom-based dishes are found. By far the most popular type of mushroom is called 'Polish mushroom'. This variety has a refined aroma, exquisite flavour and retains its colour during cooking. In short, not only do they taste good, they look good too.

The first recipe is therefore understandably from Poland. It is as tasty as it is simple to prepare.

pieczarki po polsku

polish-style mushrooms

When the mushroom-picking season is on people from the towns and villages pour into the forests and woods to gather the many types of edible fungi. Baskets full of mushrooms are taken home, and since their life expectancy is short various methods are used to extend their edible life by salting and pickling. Serve with roast or boiled potatoes or a *kasha* (buckwheat) pilav.

1.4 kg (3 lb) mushrooms, wiped clean and thinly sliced
125 g (4 oz) butter
1 large onion, finely chopped
30 ml (2 tablespoons) flour, sifted
450 ml (³/₄ pint) soured cream
10 ml (2 teaspoons) salt
1.25 ml (¹/₄ teaspoon) white pepper

Garnish
60 ml (4 tablespoons) finely chopped parsley
5 ml (1 teaspoon) paprika

1 Half fill a large pan with lightly salted water and bring to the boil. Add the mushroom slices and cook for 3–4 minutes. Drain.

2 Melt the butter in a large frying pan, add the onion and fry, stirring occasionally, for 3 minutes. Add the mushroom slices, lower the heat and fry, stirring, for 15 minutes.

3 Sprinkle in the flour and stir well. Blend in the soured cream and continue to cook gently, stirring, until the mixture thickens. Stir in the salt and pepper and transfer to a serving dish. Garnish with the parsley and paprika.

VARIATION: In the Ukraine they add 3 egg yolks to the soured cream.

zarkoye

mushrooms with vegetables

A rich dish from Russia which is best served with a rice or *kasha* (buckwheat) pilav, bread and pickles.

75 g (3 oz) butter or margarine
900 g (2 lb) mushrooms, wiped clean and thinly sliced
450 g (1 lb) potatoes, peeled and cut into 2 cm (³/₄ inch) cubes
1 medium carrot, peeled and cut crossways into thin rounds
1 parsley root or celeriac, washed, peeled and thinly sliced
1 large onion, finely chopped
300 ml (¹/₂ pint) soured cream blended with 15 ml (1 tablespoon) flour
30 ml (2 tablespoons) tomato purée
10 ml (2 teaspoons) salt
1.25 ml (¹/₄ teaspoon) white pepper
2 bay leaves
225 g (8 oz) peas

Garnish
30 ml (2 tablespoons) finely chopped parsley

1 In a large saucepan, heat one-third of the butter or margarine. Add the mushroom slices and fry, stirring frequently, for 4–5 minutes. Remove from the heat.

2 Melt another third of the fat in a small saucepan and add the potatoes, carrots and parsley root. Fry, stirring, for 4–5 minutes and add to the mushrooms.

3 Melt the remaining fat in the pan, add the onion and fry, stirring, for 3 minutes. Spoon into the mushroom pan.

4 Mix all the vegetables in the large pan together thoroughly and stir in the soured cream, tomato purée, salt, pepper and bay leaves. Cover the pan and cook over a low heat for 10 minutes. Add the peas and cook, stirring occasionally, for a further 8–10 minutes or until the potatoes and peas are tender.

5 Serve garnished with the parsley.

dunn's river okra

west indian-style okra

Whether it was the Indian traders or the African slaves who first transported the okra to the West Indies is uncertain, but that okra is very popular and much used we know for sure. Most West Indians fry or stew okra and eat it as a meal with a bowl of rice. The recipes are simple. For fried okra, dip each one in beaten egg, roll in fresh breadcrumbs seasoned with salt and pepper and then fry in oil. A slightly more elaborate dish is this recipe from Jamaica.

Serve with a rice pilav.

50 g (2 oz) butter
1 large onion, cut into thin rings
1 garlic clove, crushed
4 large tomatoes blanched, peeled and coarsely chopped
10 ml (2 teaspoons) salt
2.5 ml ($1/_2$ teaspoon) black pepper
2.5–5 ml ($1/_2$–1 teaspoon) chilli powder, depending on taste
2.5 ml ($1/_2$ teaspoon) cumin
700 g ($1^1/_2$ lb) small, firm okra, stalks trimmed

Melt the butter in a large pan, add the onion and garlic and fry, stirring, for 3 minutes. Add the tomatoes, salt, pepper, chilli powder and cumin and fry for a further 3 minutes. Stir in the okra, lower the heat, cover the pan and cook gently, stirring occasionally, for 20–30 minutes.

*Eat leeks in March, garlic in May; all the
rest of the year, the doctors may play*
English expression (Sussex)

The medicinal qualities of leeks and garlic have been known for thousands of years. Ancient Egyptians and Romans held this cylindrical-shaped *Allium* in great esteem. Indeed it is reported that no lesser person than Nero loved leek soup, for he was anxious to retain a clear and sonorous voice for his oratory and musical renderings.

The Welsh, who have a legendary connection with leeks, dating back to King Cadwallader (AD 640), have no doubt been aware of the vegetable's 'nasal goodness' for how else can they go on and on producing such beautiful voices? Yet when it comes to cooking the leek they have a great deal to learn from the people of the Balkans, North Africa and Iran.

prasiluk
leek casserole

This recipe is from Serbia

700 g (1¹/₂ lb) leeks, trimmed, cut into 5 cm (2 inch) pieces
and thoroughly washed
90 ml (6 tablespoons) oil
60 ml (4 tablespoons) long grain rice, washed thoroughly
under cold running water and drained
450 g (1 lb) tomatoes, blanched, peeled and coarsely chopped
3 green peppers, thinly sliced
10 ml (2 teaspoons) salt
1.25 ml (¹/₄ teaspoon) black pepper
2.5 ml (¹/₂ teaspoon) cayenne pepper
2.5 ml (¹/₂ teaspoon) basil
2.5 ml (¹/₂ teaspoon) sage
150 ml (¹/₄ pint) water

Garnish
juice of 2 medium lemons
5 ml (1 teaspoon) paprika

1 Half fill a large saucepan with lightly salted water and bring to the boil. Add the leeks and simmer, covered, for 8 minutes. Drain and set aside.

2 Heat the oil in a large pan, add the leeks and green peppers and fry, stirring, for about 10 minutes. Remove from the heat and spread the leeks evenly over the bottom of a large, greased ovenproof casserole. Sprinkle the rice over the leeks and peppers and then layer with the tomatoes. Mix the seasoning, herbs and spices together in a small bowl and sprinkle evenly over the vegetables. Pour in the water, cover the dish and cook in a 180°C (350°F) mark 4 oven for about 45 minutes.

3 Just before serving sprinkle with the lemon juice and the paprika.

Sublime potatoes! that, from Antrim's shore
To famous Kerry, form the poor man's store;
Agreeing well with every place and state —
the peasant's noggin, or the rich man's plate,
Much prized when smoking from the teeming pot,
Or in turf-embers roasted crisp and hot.
Welcome, although you be our only dish;
Welcome, companion to flesh, fowl or fish;
But to the real gourmands, the learned few,
Most welcome, steaming in an Irish stew
An Anthology of the Potato
Thomas Groffon Groker

I would have liked to have given you the recipe for the famed Irish stew, but I cannot — the meat content being the prime culprit. There again, I wished to include a potato recipe from Ireland, but I cannot since, in the words of the poet *although you be our only dish*, the Irish, who are excellent at mashing, frying, roasting and baking the potato, do very little that is unusual with their only vegetable — except perhaps for that very Irish dish called colcannon, which is a mash of potatoes, leeks and kale mixed with milk, seasoned with salt, pepper and ground mace and served with melted butter on Hallowe'en.

So, we go to Italy for a delectable recipe using the humble potato.

gnocchi di patate
potato gnocchi

Gnocchi can be made from flour, semolina or potato. This very popular recipe is of Austro-Hungarian origin.

Serve with a tomato sauce: *sugo di pomodoro* (see page 232) or with a liberal garnishing of Parmesan cheese, and a fresh salad.

1.4 kg (3 lb) potatoes, scrubbed
3 eggs
50 g (2 oz) butter
2.5 ml (¹/₂ teaspoon) nutmeg
salt
2.5 ml (¹/₂ teaspoon) black pepper
350 g (12 oz) plain flour, preferably wholemeal
grated Parmesan cheese

1 Half fill a large pan with lightly salted water, add the potatoes and simmer until tender. Drain and, when cool enough to handle, peel. While still warm either pass through a sieve or mash until smooth. Add the eggs, butter, nutmeg, 10 ml (2 teaspoons) salt and the pepper and continue to mash until well blended. Gradually

add the flour and knead until smooth.

2 Keeping your hands lightly floured take walnut-sized pieces of the dough and roll into balls. Gently flatten each ball by pressing on it with the back of a fork to give the traditional gnocchi marks.

3 Half fill a large saucepan with water, add 15 ml (1 tablespoon) salt and bring to the boil. Add the gnocchi, a few at a time, and cook for 4 minutes. Remove with a slotted spoon and transfer to a large ovenproof dish. Keep warm while you cook the remaining gnocchi. Arrange them in layers and sprinkle each layer generously with Parmesan cheese.

papas arequipena

peruvian-style potatoes

From the original homeland of the potato this simple offering is from Arequipa, in the shade of the mighty Andes range.

900 g (2 lb) medium-sized potatoes, peeled and halved

Sauce
50 g (2 oz) unsalted peanuts
150 ml (¹/₄ pint) milk
60 ml (2 fl oz) oil
1 green chilli, seeded
1 small onion, coarsely chopped
50 g (2 oz) cheese, Gouda, Cheddar or feta (see Glossary), grated
5 ml (1 teaspoon) salt, or more depending on taste
1.25 ml (¹/₄ teaspoon) black pepper

Garnish
6 hard-boiled eggs, quartered
olives, radishes, sliced cucumber and tomatoes

1 Half fill a large saucepan with lightly salted water and bring to the boil. Add the potatoes, lower the heat, cover the pan and simmer for 12–15 minutes or until the potatoes are tender. Do not overcook.

2 Meanwhile, place all the sauce ingredients in a blender and process until smooth.

3 When the potatoes are done, drain and arrange, cut side down, in a large serving dish. Pour the peanut sauce over them and garnish with the eggs, olives and vegetables.

muglai aloo
mogul-style potatoes

The Indian cuisine, although not famed for its potato dishes, still has a few worthy of wider recognition. Here is one from Rajasthan fit for kings, hence its title — although I'm not sure whether the Moguls had anything to do with its conception. I suspect they had long disappeared by the time the potato arrived in their territories.

Cream was once used with all Muglai dishes, but I suggest you use yogurt, not only because it is cheaper, but also tastier and healthier.

45 ml (3 tablespoons) ghee (see Glossary) or butter
1.4 kg (3 lb) small, new potatoes, scrubbed and scraped
3 cloves
seeds from 2 cardamom pods
2 green chillies, seeded
5 ml (1 teaspoon) finely chopped fresh ginger
3 cloves garlic
150 ml (1/4 pint) yogurt
7.5 ml (1 1/2 teaspoons) salt
1 large onion, finely chopped
5 ml (1 teaspoon) ground cumin
5 ml (1 teaspoon) ground coriander
2.5 ml (1/2 teaspoon) turmeric
300 ml (1/2 pint) water

Garnish
5 ml (1 teaspoon) paprika
30 ml (2 tablespoons) finely chopped fresh parsley or coriander

1 Melt 30 ml (2 tablespoons) of the ghee or butter in a large saucepan, add the potatoes and fry, stirring regularly until nicely coated with butter and evenly golden.

2 Meanwhile, either in a blender or mortar, grind the cloves, cardamom seeds, chillies, ginger and garlic until it forms a paste. Add 15 ml (1 tablespoon) water if necessary.

3 With a slotted spoon remove the potatoes and transfer to another large pan and add the spice paste, yogurt and salt to them. Mix thoroughly and set aside.

4 Add the remaining ghee or butter to any that remains in the first pan and melt. Add the onion and fry, stirring frequently, for 3 minutes. Stir in the cumin, coriander and turmeric and fry for a further 3 minutes. Add the potato mixture and water and mix thoroughly. Bring to the boil, lower the heat, cover the pan and simmer for 15–20 minutes or until the potatoes are tender and most of the liquid has evaporated. Turn into a large dish, sprinkle with the paprika and parsley or coriander and serve immediately.

hawaiian sweet potatoes
with pineapple

In the Hawaiian, Melanesian and Micronesian islands, as well as in the Caribbean, the sweet potato is much in demand. It is sometimes substituted with other tubers such as eddos, dasheen (a hairy root about the size of a large potato and similar in taste), tannia or taro. Since only the sweet potato is easily available in our shops I suggest you prepare this simple dish with this particular vegetable.

A little on the sweet side, this casserole is best served with pickles (as a contrast to the sugary flavour), pastas and fresh salads.

Use fresh pineapple and orange juice if possible. If you use canned pineapple rings use those that are unsweetened.

salt
1.4 kg (3 lb) sweet potatoes, peeled and cut into
2.5 cm (1 inch) pieces
75 g (3 oz) butter, softened
juice of 1 small orange
50 g (2 oz) brown sugar
$^1/_2$ average fresh pineapple, peeled, cored and cut into rings

1 Half fill a large pan with water, add 10 ml (2 teaspoons) salt and bring to the boil. Add the sweet potatoes and simmer for about 15 minutes or until tender. Drain and place the potato pieces in a large bowl. Add the butter, orange juice, sugar and salt to taste and mash until smooth.

2 Chop the pineapple rings and then add half to the potato mixture and stir well. Spoon into a large, greased ovenproof dish and smooth over the top with the back of a spoon. Sprinkle the remaining pineapple pieces evenly over the top. Bake in a 180°C (350°F) mark 4 oven for about 30 minutes. Remove and serve immediately.

plaintains in coconut milk

This is a very attractive and popular dish from the West Indies. It also appears throughout Africa (where instead of rice cassava is eaten as an accompaniment) and in South East Asia.

Plantains are also fried like potato chips and mashed with lime juice, butter, cinnamon, chilli powder and nutmeg.

Serve on a bed of rice pilav of your choice and, to give it extra piquancy, some pickles and a little Harissa Sauce (see page 230). Plantains can vary considerably in size. Use either 6 long ones or 8 medium ones.

6-8 plantains
50 g (2 oz) butter or margarine
7.5 ml (1¹/₂ teaspoons) garam masala (see Glossary)
7.5 ml (1¹/₂ teaspoons) salt
2.5 ml (¹/₂ teaspoon) black pepper
1 small onion, finely chopped
600 ml (1 pint) thick coconut milk (see Glossary)
2 eggs, beaten

Garnish
5 ml (1 teaspoon) paprika

1 Peel the plantains and slice lengthways. If they are long cut each slice in half.

2 Melt the fat in a large frying pan, add the garam masala, salt, pepper and onion and fry, stirring frequently, for 4-5 minutes or until the onion is soft. Add the plantain slices and fry, turning carefully, for 2 minutes, until golden.

3 Gradually pour in the coconut milk and stir carefully. Lower the heat and simmer for 20-30 minutes. Remove pan from the heat and stir in the beaten eggs. Serve when the eggs have set. Turn out into a serving dish, sprinkle the paprika on top and serve.

mamao a espirito santo

brazilian-style pawpaw

I think pawpaws (papayas) are at their very best when eaten as they are — just cut the ripe fruit in half, remove the seeds and scoop out the flesh with a spoon. However, while still green they can be cooked in many interesting ways. The best pawpaws available in this country are from Brazil, whence, too, comes this recipe.

Serve with rice or a pasta dish of your choice.

3 very green, medium-sized pawpaws
45 ml (3 tablespoons) butter or margarine
2 large onions, coarsely chopped
3 large tomatoes, blanched, peeled and chopped
15 ml (1 tablespoon) finely chopped chives
10 ml (2 teaspoons) salt
1.25 ml ($^1/_4$ teaspoon) black pepper
2.5 ml ($^1/_2$ teaspoon) dried mint
75 g (3 oz) fresh breadcrumbs

1 Half fill a large saucepan with water, add the pawpaws and simmer for 30–40 minutes. Drain and, when cool enough to handle, cut each in half lengthways and remove and discard the seeds. Scoop out the pulp with a spoon, chop and place in a bowl. Reserve the skins.

2 Heat 30 ml (2 tablespoons) of the butter or margarine in a large frying pan, add the onions and fry until soft. Add the tomatoes and chives and fry, stirring frequently, for a further 3–4 minutes. Remove from the heat, add to the pawpaw flesh and season with the salt, pepper and mint. Mix thoroughly. Carefully spoon the onion and pawpaw mixture back into the pawpaw shells and arrange them side by side in an ovenproof dish. Sprinkle the breadcrumbs over each and dot with the remaining butter. Bake in a 180°C (350°F) mark 4 oven for about 20 minutes or until the crumbs are golden. Serve immediately, piping hot.

sughtoradz tetum
pumpkin with yogurt and garlic sauce

Throughout Africa, America and the Indian subcontinent pumpkins, marrows and gourds (they are often interchanged in recipes) are very popular and cooked in a variety of ways. The simplest, and one of the most popular, is to divide the vegetable into wedges or quarters, peel, remove the seeds, place in an ovenproof dish, dot with ghee or butter, season with salt and pepper and bake. The pumpkin is then served as an accompaniment.

This is a slightly more elaborate recipe from the slopes of Mount Ararat in Armenia. The pumpkin is fried and served with a yogurt–garlic sauce.

900 g (2 lb) pumpkin
15 ml (1 tablespoon) salt
125 g (4 oz) ghee (see Glossary) or butter
75–90 ml (5–6 tablespoons) flour, sifted
Yogurt and Garlic Sauce (see page 234)
2.5 ml ($^1/_2$ teaspoon) cayenne pepper
5 ml (1 teaspoon) sumac powder (see Glossary)

1 Cut the pumpkin in half and peel it. Discard the seeds and cut the flesh into 2.5–3. 5 cm (1–1$^1/_2$ inch) cubes. Place in a colander, sprinkle with the salt and set aside for 5–7 minutes. Drain.

2 Melt the ghee or butter in a large saucepan. Toss the pumpkin cubes in the flour until well coated. Add to the pan and fry until tender, turning carefully from time to time and adding a little more butter, if necessary.

3 Pile the cubes into a serving dish and sprinkle with the cayenne pepper and sumac. Serve the sauce in a separate bowl.

sansafil maghli

libyan fried salsify

You can use either salsify or scorzonera (see Glossary) for this delicious North African recipe, which can be eaten as an appetiser or, with a fresh salad, bread and pickles, as a meal.

700 g (1¹/₂ lb) salsify, topped and tailed

Batter
125 g (4 oz) plain flour, sifted
5 ml (1 teaspoon) baking powder
1 egg
15 ml (1 tablespoon) olive oil
150 ml (¹/₄ pint) water
1.25 ml (¹/₄ teaspoon) Harissa Sauce (see page 230)
2.5 ml (¹/₂ teaspoon) cumin
1.25 ml (¹/₄ teaspoon) dried thyme
5 ml (1 teaspoon) salt
oil, for frying

To serve
lemon wedges

1 Wash the salsify under cold running water using a scrubbing brush if necessary to remove all the sand. Cut each root in half.

2 Half fill a large pan with lightly salted water and bring to the boil. Add the salsify and simmer, covered, for 30 minutes. Drain and rinse under cold running water. When cool enough to handle peel the salsify and cut the roots into 7.5 cm (3 inch) pieces.

3 To prepare the batter mix all the ingredients together in a shallow bowl.

4 Heat sufficient oil to cover the base of a large frying pan by 5 cm (2 inches). Dip several pieces of the salsify into the batter and fry in the oil until crisp and golden. Remove with a slotted spoon and keep warm while you cook the remaining salsify in the same way. Serve hot with the lemon wedges.

les navets au sucre

turnips with sugar

'There is no getting blood out of a turnip'
Tunisian proverb

A classic recipe from Maine (France). It is simple and to the point. Serve it with roast vegetables, fresh salad and pickles.

If you like to be experimental, substitute the turnips with cologassi (see Glossary), which have a slightly turnipy flavour.

50 g (2 oz) butter
50 g (2 oz) sugar
1.4 kg (3 lb) turnips, peeled. If young and small leave whole, otherwise cut into
5 cm (2 inch) pieces
300 ml ($^1/_2$ pint) water
10 ml (2 teaspoons) salt
2.5 ml ($^1/_4$ teaspoon) black pepper

Garnish
30–45 ml (2–3 tablespoons) finely chopped parsley

1 Melt the butter in a large saucepan, add the sugar and mix well. Add the turnips and fry for 5–7 minutes, turning regularly. Add the water, salt and pepper, stir well, cover the pan and simmer for 15–20 minutes or until the turnips are tender.

2 Transfer to a large dish, sprinkle with the parsley and serve.

jimikand

yam in hot sauce

The African yam is also popular in India, where it goes under the name of *suren* (elephant's food). The recipe chosen, from south India, is also worthy of the elephant's owner. And I am not being facetious. Here I quote Laurens van der Post's impressions:

'All along the west coast of Africa, the yam is not just an ingredient for food but part of the emotions of people. These emotions are even stronger than the Irish feel for the potato. The truth is that for all its deficiencies the yam enables the West African to survive. Yam feast days are still common in West Africa. They are seen at their best in Ghana, where yam dishes are brought in to the ceremonies that accompany birth, marriage, recovery from accident or ill-health and the overcoming of sorrow after death.'
First Catch Your Eland

What then is good enough for one's best friend (the elephant) is good enough for you.

700 g (1¹/₂ lb) yam, peeled and cut into 2.5 cm (1 inch) cubes
15 ml (1 tablespoon) plus 10 ml (2 teaspoons) salt
135 ml (9 tablespoons) oil
5 ml (1 teaspoon) whole cumin seeds
1 large onion, finely chopped
2 garlic cloves, crushed
15 ml (1 tablespoon) grated fresh ginger
30–45 ml (2–3 tablespoons) water
2.5 ml (¹/₂ teaspoon) cayenne pepper
2.5 ml (¹/₂ teaspoon) turmeric
3 large tomatoes, blanched, peeled and chopped
60 ml (4 tablespoons) yogurt mixed with 1 tablespoon flour
600 ml (1 pint) water

Garnish
5 ml (1 teaspoon) garam masala (see Glossary)
30 ml (2 tablespoons) finely chopped parsley

1 Place the yam cubes in a colander, sprinkle with 15 ml (1 tablespoon) salt and set

aside for 20 minutes.

2 Heat 75 ml (5 tablespoons) oil in a large pan, add the cumin seeds and fry gently for 3 minutes. Add the onion and garlic and fry for 3 minutes, stirring frequently. Add the ginger and water and fry for a further 2 minutes before stirring in the cayenne pepper, turmeric, 10 ml (2 teaspoons) salt and the tomatoes. Cook over a low heat, stirring frequently, for about 10 minutes or until the tomatoes are reduced to a pulp. Gradually stir in the yogurt and water, lower the heat and simmer, stirring occasionally, for about 10 minutes.

3 Rinse the yam and dry with kitchen paper. Heat the remaining oil in a large frying pan, add the yam cubes and fry, turning regularly, for a few minutes, until nicely browned. Remove with a slotted spoon and drain on kitchen paper. Add to the simmering sauce, mix thoroughly, cover the pan and continue to simmer for 12–15 minutes. Transfer to a large dish and mix in the garam masala. Sprinkle with the parsley and serve with rice or bread.

lanttulaatikko

swede casserole

The cuisines of Scandinavia are relatively poor in vegetable dishes of any distinction. In the past, apart from a few hardy vegetables such as cabbage, potato, cauliflower, turnip, swede and mushroom, there was little else available. During Christmas Swedish and Finnish housewives prepare special vegetable dishes, two of which are worthy of note. Perunelaatikko (potato bake) and this recipe for swedes. Traditionally these dishes were baked alongside the meat in a wood-burning stove for several hours while the family did their farm work, cleaned the house, went to church and then returned home to their Christmas feast. This family recipe was given to me by a Finnish relation.

1.4 kg (3 lb) swedes, peeled and cut into 5 cm (2 inch) pieces
600 ml (1 pint) water
10 ml (2 teaspoons) salt
50 g (2 oz) fresh breadcrumbs
150 ml ($^1/_4$ pint) single cream
25 g (1 oz) butter
30 ml (2 tablespoons) golden syrup
2.5 ml (4 teaspoon) grated fresh ginger
1.25 ml ($^1/_4$ teaspoon) nutmeg
1.25 ml ($^1/_4$ teaspoon) white pepper
2 eggs, beaten

Garnish
30–45 ml (2–3 tablespoons) fresh breadcrumbs
15 ml (1 tablespoon) butter

1 Put the swedes into a large pan, add the water and salt and bring to the boil. Lower the heat, cover the pan and simmer for 15–20 minutes or until the swedes are tender.

2 Meanwhile, put the breadcrumbs in a small bowl and cover with the cream.

3 Drain the swedes and reserve the cooking liquid. Place the swedes in a large bowl and mash until smooth. Add the cream mixture and all the remaining ingredients and continue to mash until well blended and really smooth. Spoon the mixture into a large, greased ovenproof dish and smooth over the top with the back of a spoon. Pour 50–90 ml (2–3 fl oz) of the reserved liquid over the top and set aside for 5 minutes. Sprinkle the breadcrumbs evenly over the top and dot with the butter. Bake in a 180°C (350°F) mark 4 oven for about 1 hour or until the top is golden.

ghalieh esfanaj

spinach in pomegranate juice

Pomegranate juice gives an extra piquancy to this tasty dish from the Caspian region of Iran. It is also popular in the Caucasus and southern Russia.

175 g (6 oz) whole lentils, rinsed
30 ml (2 tablespoons) butter
1 onion, thinly sliced
700 g (1¹/₂ lb) fresh spinach, coarse leaves and
tough stems discarded, washed thoroughly
5 ml (1 teaspoon) salt
45 ml (3 tablespoons) pomegranate juice (see page 238)

1 Half fill a large saucepan with lightly salted water and bring to the boil. Add the lentils, lower the heat and simmer for 30–40 minutes or until tender. Drain and set aside.

2 Melt the butter in a large saucepan, add the onion and fry, stirring frequently, until golden. Chop the spinach and add to the pan. Stir well, cover the pan, lower the heat and simmer for 10 minutes. Stir in the lentils, salt and pomegranate juice, cover and simmer for a further 20 minutes. Transfer to a large dish and serve immediately.

stuffed vegetables

In the heyday of Kings Darius and Xerxes of Achaemenian Persia the court chefs of their capital city, Istakhar (Persepolis to the Greeks), busied themselves using vine leaves to enfold all kinds of meats, nuts, fruits and vegetables — including the newly introduced grains of the plant *Oryza sativa* (rice) from faraway India and China. With these ingredients they incorporated locally found herbs and spices such as dillweed, marjoram, basil, fenugreek and sumac as well as such expensive imports as pepper.

The Greeks, on the other side of the Bosphorus, were equally diligent in wrapping small fish, pieces of meat or wheat or barley in vine leaves, fig leaves, silver beet leaves and even apricot leaves.

The art of stuffing vegetables is of ancient vintage and not necessarily confined solely to the Middle Eastern cuisines, for the people of China and those in the Indian subcontinent were also well versed in this form of cooking. However, it is to the Middle Eastern people that one must give the credit for mastering this ingenious method of vegetable cookery. The adjacent North Africans, Italians, French and those living in the Balkans adopted this technique and today stuffed vegetables appear in most of the world's cuisines.

Aubergines, courgettes, onions, marrows, peppers, cucumbers, artichokes and even whole pumpkins and melons are treated in this way; as well as the lesser-known bean curds, lotus roots, chayote and karela.

In the first part of this chapter I have given a variety of fillings. The quantities given are approximately sufficient to stuff 6 medium aubergines, 8 medium-large tomatoes, 8 medium peppers or courgettes, 6–8 pickling-size cucumbers or 10–12 artichoke hearts.

Unless the recipe states otherwise, prepare each vegetable for stuffing by slicing off the stalk end and then, using an apple corer, remove as much flesh as possible, leaving a shell about 0.5 cm (¼ inch) thick. Take care not to split or make a hole in the shell.

rice-based filling

Any vegetables with a rice filling should be placed in a saucepan, openings uppermost, and held in place with an inverted plate and a weight. Cover with a sauce, stock or water and cook over a medium heat or in the oven for about 60 minutes or until tender. For typical sauces see pages 228-237

FILLING 1:
This is a Turkish favourite which is also used to fill apples and quinces.

225 g (8 oz) long grain rice, washed thoroughly
under cold running water and drained
1 large onion, finely chopped
45 ml (3 tablespoons) parsley, finely chopped
30 ml (2 tablespoons) raisins
10 ml (2 teaspoons) salt
2.5 ml ($^1/_2$ teaspoon) black pepper

FILLING 2:
A classic Middle Eastern stuffing. In Armenian and Turkish cooking rice is often replaced by burghul (cracked wheat) and this makes an equally delicious filling.

175 g (6 oz) long grain rice, washed thoroughly
under cold running water and drained
3 tomatoes, blanched, peeled and chopped
1 large onion, finely chopped
45 ml (3 tablespoons) finely chopped parsley
30 ml (2 tablespoons) pine kernels
15 ml (1 tablespoon) raisins
7.5 ml (1$^1/_2$ teaspoons) salt
5 ml (1 teaspoon) dillweed
2.5 ml ($^1/_2$ teaspoon) black pepper
2.5 ml ($^1/_2$ teaspoon) ground cinnamon

To prepare both fillings, place all the ingredients in a large bowl and mix until well blended. Stuff the vegetables, remembering not to overfill as the rice will swell while cooking.

This is an Italian favourite called *peperoni ripieni*. It is a filling for peppers but can be used with other vegetables.

60 ml (4 tablespoons) oil
2 medium onions, finely chopped
225 g (8 oz) long grain rice, washed thoroughly
under cold running water and drained
50 g (2 oz) sultanas
15 ml (1 tablespoon) tomato purée
600 ml (1 pint) boiling water
10 ml (2 teaspoons) salt
2.5 ml ($1/2$ teaspoon) black pepper
5 ml (1 teaspoon) paprika
5 ml (1 teaspoon) basil

Sauce
30 ml (2 tablespoons) oil
15 ml (1 tablespoon) tomato purée
300 ml ($1/2$ pint) water
5 ml (1 teaspoon) sugar
2.5 ml ($1/2$ teaspoon) oregano

1 Heat the oil in a saucepan, add the onions and fry, stirring frequently, until soft. Stir in the rice and fry for 1–2 minutes and then add all the remaining ingredients and mix well. Bring to the boil, lower the heat, cover the pan and simmer until all the water has evaporated. Remove from the heat, stir gently and set aside for 10 minutes.

2 Spoon the stuffing into the vegetables and replace their tops. Stand upright in a casserole dish.

3 Mix the sauce ingredients together and pour into the dish. Cover and bake in a 180°C (350°F) mark 4 oven for 30–40 minutes or until the vegetables are tender.

4 Remove from the oven and serve hot or, as is often the custom, cold.

50 g (2 oz) chickpeas, soaked overnight in cold water,
then drained and cooked in simmering water for
1^1/$_2$ hours or until tender
125 g (4 oz) long grain rice, washed thoroughly
under cold running water and drained
3 tomatoes, blanched, peeled and chopped
1 large onion, finely chopped
5 ml (1 teaspoon) dried mint
5 ml (1 teaspoon) dried tarragon
5 ml (1 teaspoon) dillweed
5 ml (1 teaspoon) salt
2.5 ml (^{1}/$_2$ teaspoon) black pepper
2.5 ml (^{1}/$_2$ teaspoon) cinnamon

Place all the ingredients in a large bowl and mix until well blended.

vegetable-based fillings

Vegetables are often filled with their own pulp previously sautéed in oil with herbs
and spices, as well as with such other vegetables as onions, garlic, carrots,
potatoes and celery.

The recipe below from Bulgaria is typical of this kind of filling and it has a tasty
yogurt-based sauce.

You can use any vegetables, but I suggest large tomatoes, green peppers or
courgettes.

150 ml (¹/₄ pint) oil
1 large onion, finely chopped
3 medium carrots, peeled and chopped into
0.5 cm (¹/₄ inch) pieces
3 celery sticks, chopped into 0.5 cm (¹/₄ inch) pieces
1 large potato, peeled and cut into 0.5 cm (¹/₄ inch) pieces
2 garlic cloves, crushed
3 tomatoes, blanched, peeled and coarsely chopped
5 ml (1 teaspoon) salt
2.5 ml (¹/₂ teaspoon) black pepper
30 ml (2 tablespoons) finely chopped parsley
125 g (4 oz) feta, haloumi (see Glossary) or Cheddar cheese, grated
150 ml (¹/₂ pint) water

Sauce
150 ml (¹/₄ pint) yogurt
2 eggs
15 ml (1 tablespoon) flour
1.25 ml (¹/₄ teaspoon) black pepper
2.5 ml (¹/₂ teaspoon) paprika

1 Heat the oil in a large saucepan, add the onion, carrots, celery, potato and garlic and fry, stirring frequently, for 10 minutes. Add the tomatoes, salt and pepper and cook, stirring occasionally, for a further 10 minutes. Stir in the parsley and cheese, cook for 5 minutes and then remove from the heat and set aside for 10 minutes.

2 Spoon the filling into the vegetables of your choice and replace the tops. Stand them upright in a casserole dish and pour in the water. Cover the dish and bake in a 180°C (350°F) mark 4 oven for 30 minutes.

3 Meanwhile, mix the sauce ingredients together in a bowl and, after the 30 minutes, pour over the vegetables. When the sauce has thickened and is golden remove from the oven and serve immediately.

450 g (1 lb) small yams
60 ml (4 tablespoons) oil
1 onion, finely chopped
50 g (2 oz) slivered almonds
50 g (2 oz) sultanas
10 ml (2 teaspoons) salt
1.25 ml ($^1/_4$ teaspoon) black pepper
2.5 ml ($^1/_2$ teaspoon) chilli powder
1.25 ml ($^1/_4$ teaspoon) nutmeg
2.5 ml ($^1/_2$ teaspoon) ground ginger
30 ml (2 tablespoons) finely chopped parsley

Sauce
25 ml (1$^1/_2$ tablespoons) tomato purée
900 ml (1$^1/_2$ pints) boiling water
1 garlic clove, crushed
5 ml (1 teaspoon) salt
2.5 ml ($^1/_2$ teaspoon) black pepper
5 ml (1 teaspoon) thyme

1 Place the yams in a pan of lightly salted boiling water and cook for about 20 minutes or until tender. Drain and, when cool enough to handle, peel off the skin. Mash the vegetables until smooth.

2 Meanwhile, heat the oil in a frying pan, add the onion and fry until soft and golden. Add the almonds and sultanas and fry, stirring constantly, until the nuts are lightly golden. Remove from the heat and add the mixture to the yams together with the remaining ingredients and mix well.

3 Stuff the vegetables of your choice and arrange upright in a casserole. Mix the sauce ingredients together in a bowl and pour into the casserole. Cover and place in a l80°C (350°F) mark 4 oven and bake for 45–60 minutes or until the vegetables are tender — the length of time will depend on the vegetables used.

pulse-based fillings

Chickpeas, lentils, dried peas and beans are often used as fillings.

This recipe uses chickpeas, but you can use any bean you like. Remember that lentils do not need soaking overnight. This mixture is usually used to fill courgettes, but other vegetables can be used. The filling is sufficient for 12 courgettes.

125 g (4 oz) chickpeas, soaked overnight in cold water
90 ml (6 tablespoons) oil
1 onion, finely chopped
3 tomatoes, blanched, peeled and chopped
125 g (4 oz) rice or burghul (cracked wheat), washed
under cold running water and drained
15 ml (1 tablespoon) finely chopped parsley
5 ml (1 teaspoon) tarragon
5 ml (1 teaspoon) dillweed
10 ml (2 teaspoons) salt
2.5 ml ($^1/_2$ teaspoon) black pepper
2.5 ml ($^1/_2$ teaspoon) chilli powder

1 Drain the chickpeas, place in a pan of boiling water and simmer for 1$^1/_2$ hours or until tender. Add more boiling water if necessary. Drain.

2 Heat the oil in a saucepan, add the onion and fry until golden. Add the chickpeas and all the remaining ingredients and mix thoroughly. Three-quarters fill each courgette (or other vegetables). Place side by side in a saucepan, cover completely with lightly salted water and bring to the boil. Lower the heat, cover the pan and simmer for about 1–1$^1/_2$ hours or until cooked. Keep the water level topped up so that the courgettes are cooked through.

VARIATION: Omit the rice and substitute lentils or any other beans.

patlindan punsene sa sirom

aubergines stuffed with cheese

This recipe is from Croatia. It is simple and tasty with the pulp of the aubergines being mixed with other ingredients and used as the stuffing. Courgettes can be prepared in the same way.

Serve with rice or roast potatoes and a bowl of fresh salad.

6 medium aubergines, wiped clean and with stalks cut off
25 g (1 oz) melted butter
1 large onion, finely chopped
225 g (8 oz) feta (see Glossary), Cheddar or Edam cheese, grated
2 eggs
30 ml (2 tablespoons) finely chopped parsley or coriander
5 ml (1 teaspoon) paprika
2.5 ml (1/2 teaspoon) black pepper
salt to taste

1 Half fill a large saucepan with water, add 10 ml (2 teaspoons) salt and bring to the boil. Drop in the aubergines and cook for 5–7 minutes or until just tender — check by piercing the skins with the point of a sharp knife. Drain.

2 When cool enough to handle cut each aubergine in half lengthways and scoop out most of the flesh, taking care not to damage the skins. Chop the flesh, place in a bowl and add the remaining ingredients. Taste before adding salt because the amount needed will depend on the type of cheese you use — feta, for example, is saltier than others. Mix together thoroughly.

3 Arrange the aubergine shells side by side in a shallow, greased ovenproof dish. Spoon the mixture into the shells. Do not overfill. If there is any mixture left arrange it between the shells — it will still taste good.

4 Bake in a 180°C (350°F) mark 4 oven for 40–45 minutes or until golden. Serve warm or cold.

k'uia hua t'ang ou

stuffed lotus roots

A fascinating recipe from China.

The lotus plant's roots grow in the mud under water, while its leaves, blossoms and seed pods are attached to long stems and are above water. *Ou* is the rhizome of the lotus and looks like short links of salami. Lotus is rather expensive and very difficult to find fresh, although there are tinned versions available.

Sweet rice is ground from glutinous rice and is used just like rice flour. It is sold in all Chinese grocery stores.

Although traditionally this dish is served as a dessert, I think it is equally good as a starter, although in that case I suggest you halve the sugar content.

**2 fresh lotus roots (the centre sections) with knots
still intact on both sides
125 g (4 oz) sweet rice, washed under cold running water,
drained and then spread out on a kitchen towel to dry thoroughly
30 ml (2 tablespoons) brown sugar
2.5 ml (¹/₂ teaspoon) cinnamon**

1 Wash the lotus roots in cold water, drain and dry. With a sharp knife cut 1 cm (¹/₂ inch) off one root end of each lotus root and reserve. Stuff the rice into the lotus root cavities, pushing it all the way through with a skewer or chopstick. Replace the cut end of the lotus root and hold it in place with a few toothpicks.

2 Arrange the roots in a long baking tin and add enough water to cover by 5 cm (2 inches). Place a long plate over the roots and hold in place with a weight to prevent them moving and the rice coming out while cooking. Now cook over a very low heat for about 4 hours or until the roots are very tender.

3 Carefully transfer the roots to a large dish and, equally carefully, peel off the skins and allow to cool for 30 minutes. Cut crossways into ¹/₂–1 cm (¹/₄–¹/₂ inch) pieces and sprinkle with the sugar and cinnamon. Cover with a cloth.

4 Place in a larger dish or pan containing water and bring to the boil. Lower the heat and steam the roots for 20–25 minutes.

5 Serve immediately as a starter or to finish a meal.

qar mahch bi lubiya
courgettes stuffed with beans

In North Africa this stuffing is used in gourds or locally grown marrows called 'Qar Maghrabi'. You can of course use a vegetable marrow if you wish, but I prefer courgettes for their crispness and adaptability.

As for the beans, virtually any kind will do, but the people of Fez (Morocco) prefer red kidney beans while those on the Mediterranean coast go for white or *ful* beans.

This is an Andalusian style of cooking which the Spanish Muslims brought back with them when they were expelled in the fourteenth to sixteenth centuries from Muslim Spain.

225 g (8 oz) red or white kidney beans, soaked overnight in cold water
6 large courgettes, wiped clean and with stems cut off
75 ml (5 tablespoons) oil
1 large onion, finely chopped
2 garlic cloves, crushed
4 medium tomatoes, blanched, peeled and coarsely chopped
25 ml (1¹/₂ tablespoons) tomato purée
2.5 ml (¹/₂ teaspoon) harissa (see page 230)
5 ml (1 teaspoon) salt
2.5 ml (¹/₂ teaspoon) ground or pulverised caraway
5 ml (1 teaspoon) cinnamon
50 g (2 oz) fresh breadcrumbs
75 g (3 oz) cheese, feta (see Glossary), Cheddar or Edam, grated

Garnish
30 ml (2 tablespoons) finely chopped parsley, coriander or mint

1 Half fill a large saucepan with water and bring to the boil. Drain the beans, add to the pan and simmer for about 60–90 minutes or until just tender. Drain.

2 Meanwhile, cut the courgettes in half lengthways and scoop out and discard the pulp, taking care not to damage the shells. Arrange them side by side in a shallow, lightly greased ovenproof dish.

3 Heat the oil in a saucepan, add the onion and garlic and fry gently until the onion is golden. Add the tomatoes, tomato purée and harissa, stir well and cook for 3 more minutes. Add the beans, salt, caraway and cinnamon and simmer over a low heat for a few more minutes.

4 Remove from the heat and spoon the mixture into the courgette halves. Sprinkle each first with breadcrumbs and then with grated cheese.

5 Bake in a 180°C (350°F) mark 4 oven for about 45 minutes or until the courgettes are tender and the filling golden. Serve warm with one of the garnishes sprinkled over the top.

stuffed pawpaw

pawpaw stuffed with vegetables and rice

This recipe comes from that easy-going island in the sun, Jamaica, where the humble pawpaw feeds rich and poor alike. Pawpaw is often found in West Indian shops and in some large supermarkets and greengrocers. Serve with fresh salads and a chutney or pickle of your choice.

For this recipe you need unripe, green pawpaws.

3 large green pawpaws, about 450 g (1 lb) each
30 ml (2 tablespoons) oil
1 small onion, finely chopped
2 garlic cloves, finely chopped
2 large tomatoes, blanched, peeled and coarsely chopped
50 g (2 oz) long grain rice, washed thoroughly
under cold running water and drained
25 g (1 oz) raisins
25 g (1 oz) slivered, blanched almonds
1 small red pepper, seeded and finely chopped
1 fresh green chilli, thinly sliced
5 ml (1 teaspoon) salt
1.25 ml ($^1/_4$ teaspoon) black pepper
2.5 ml ($^1/_2$ teaspoon) garam masala (see Glossary)
30 ml (2 tablespoons) port or sherry
120 ml (4 fl oz) water
50 g (2 oz) Cheddar cheese, grated
45 ml (3 tablespoons) oil

1 Peel the pawpaws, halve and discard the seeds. Drop the halves into a large pan of lightly salted boiling water and simmer for 10 minutes. Drain and set aside.

2 Meanwhile, heat the oil in a saucepan, add the onion and garlic and fry, stirring frequently, for 3 minutes. Add the tomatoes, rice, raisins, almonds, red pepper, chilli, salt, pepper and garam masala and fry, stirring, for a further 2–3 minutes. Stir in the port or sherry and the water and bring to the boil. Lower the heat, cover the pan and simmer until the water has been absorbed.

3 Arrange the pawpaw halves side by side in a lightly greased, shallow ovenproof dish. Spoon some of the rice mixture into each and sprinkle with the cheese. Pour 7.5 ml (1$^1/_2$ teaspoons) of oil over each half and bake in a 180°C (350°F) mark 4 oven for about 30 minutes.

christophene au gratin
chayote stuffed with onions and cheese

Chayote is also known as christophene in the West Indies, where this recipe comes from, but the roots of the recipe lie in Europe in the Franco-Italian cuisine, where the pulp of the vegetable is mixed with other ingredients and then used as the filling.

The only West Indian things about this dish are the use of chayotes and sultanas. Serve with a salad and pickles.

3 large chayotes or 6 small ones
75 g (3 oz) margarine or butter
1 large onion, finely chopped
1 garlic clove, crushed
50 g (2 oz) sultanas
2.5 ml ($\frac{1}{2}$ teaspoon) nutmeg
10 ml (2 teaspoons) salt
2.5 ml ($\frac{1}{2}$ teaspoon) black pepper
2.5 ml ($\frac{1}{2}$ teaspoon) ginger
175 g (6 oz) Cheddar or Edam cheese, grated

Garnish
5 ml (1 teaspoon) paprika

1 Bring a large saucepan half filled with lightly salted water to the boil. Add the chayotes and simmer for about 30 minutes or until tender. Drain and leave to cool for 10 minutes.

2 Cut each vegetable in half lengthways and carefully scoop out the pulp and seeds. Reserve the shells and place the pulp in a bowl. Mash until smooth.

3 Heat two-thirds of the margarine or butter in a frying pan, add the onion and garlic and fry gently until golden. Add the chayote pulp, sultanas, nutmeg, salt, pepper and ginger and cook for 3–4 minutes, stirring frequently. Stir in 125 g (4 oz) of the grated cheese and cook for a further 3 minutes. Remove from the heat.

4 Arrange the chayote shells in a shallow, lightly greased ovenproof dish. Fill with the cheese mixture and sprinkle with the remaining cheese. Dot with the remaining margarine or butter and bake in a 180°C (350°F) mark 4 oven for about 20 minutes or until the filling is lightly golden. Garnish with the paprika.

carciofi imbottiti alla siciliana

sicilian-style stuffed artichokes

6 globe artichokes, prepared (see Glossary)
125 g (4 oz) fresh breadcrumbs
175 g (6 oz) pecorino or Parmesan cheese or a
mixture of the two or Cheddar, grated
1 onion, finely chopped
2 garlic cloves, crushed
75 ml (5 tablespoons) finely chopped parsley
15 ml (1 tablespoon) finely chopped fresh tarragon,
mint or coriander
10 ml (2 teaspoons) salt
2.5 ml ($\frac{1}{2}$ teaspoon) black pepper
3–4 pieces lemon rind
90 ml (6 tablespoons) olive oil

Garnish
lemon wedges

1 Mix the breadcrumbs, cheese, onion, garlic, parsley, tarragon, mint or coriander, salt and pepper together well. Take one artichoke at a time out of the acidulated water and spread out its leaves. Spoon a little of the breadcrumb mixture into the centre and press down with the back of a spoon. Repeat with the remaining artichokes.

2 Arrange the stuffed artichokes upright in a large saucepan. Add sufficient water to come halfway up the artichokes, season with 5 ml (1 teaspoon) salt and the pieces of lemon rind and the oil and bring to the boil. Lower the heat, cover the pan and simmer for 30–40 minutes.

3 Remove the artichokes from the pan, arrange on a serving dish and serve immediately with the lemon wedges.

derevi blor

stuffed vine leaves

A Middle Eastern classic. Vine leaves are either filled with meat, nuts and spices and served hot or filled with meatless mixtures and served cold. There are several regional fillings: the most popular ones are the first two given at the beginning of this chapter. A recipe from the Caucasus has a filling of lentils, burghul (cracked wheat) and prunes and is traditionally served during the 40 days of Lent. A Turkish version makes use of coarsely ground pearl barley, while the Iranians prefer a combination of split lentils and rice.

**350 g (12 oz) fresh or preserved vine leaves, washed,
cooked and drained (see Glossary)**

Filling
Prepare either filling 1 or 2 on page 145.

Sauce
**15 ml (1 tablespoon) tomato purée
1.1–1.7 litres (2–3 pints) water
4 garlic cloves, crushed
5 ml (1 teaspoon) salt
2.5 ml ($\frac{1}{2}$ teaspoon) chilli powder
45 ml (3 tablespoons) lemon juice**

1 Prepare the filling of your choice.

2 To make each blor spread a leaf out flat, smooth side down and veins uppermost. Arrange a small ridge of filling across the centre. Remove the stalk and fold the bottom of the leaf over the filling. Now fold each side of the leaf over the middle and roll up like a small cigar (see opposite).

3 When you have used up all the filling and leaves, use any remaining broken leaves to cover the bottom of a medium-sized saucepan — this helps to prevent burning. Pack the blor carefully and closely into the saucepan in layers, then put a plate on top to cover as many of the blor as possible. Hold it down with a small weight — this will prevent the blor from moving around while cooking and so coming undone.

4 Mix the ingredients for the sauce together in a bowl and pour into the saucepan. The sauce should cover the blor completely. If it doesn't, then add a little more water. Bring to the boil, lower the heat, cover the pan and simmer for $1\frac{1}{2}$–2 hours. Top up with a little water if necessary. Remove the pan from the heat, take off the weight and plate and remove one blor to test if the leaf is tender. If it is, remove all from the saucepan when cool enough to handle and arrange on a plate.

stuffing vine leaves

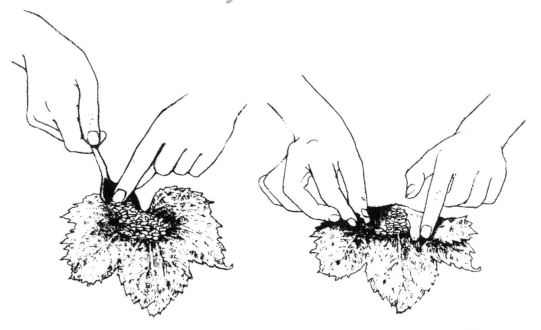

1 Place a teaspoon of filling in centre of leaf, vein-side uppermost.

2 Fold bottom of leaf over filling.

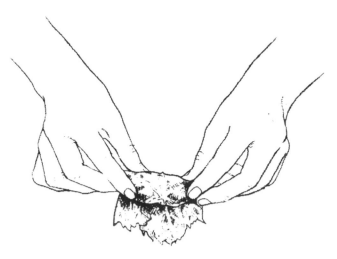

3 Fold sides over and roll up leaf into a firm cigar shape.

dolmé bargé mo

iranian stuffed vine leaves

350 g (12 oz) fresh or preserved vine leaves, washed,
cooked and drained (see Glossary)

Filling

60 ml (4 tablespoons) oil
1 large onion, finely chopped
75 g (3 oz) split red lentils, washed
75 g (3 oz) long grain rice, washed thoroughly
under cold running water and drained
30 ml (2 tablespoons) sultanas
5 ml (1 teaspoon) salt
2.5 ml ($1/_2$ teaspoon) black pepper
15 ml (1 tablespoon) finely chopped parsley
5 ml (1 teaspoon) dillweed
5 ml (1 teaspoon) sugar
30 ml (2 tablespoons) lemon juice
300 ml ($1/_2$ pint) water

Sauce

300 ml ($1/_2$ pint water)
15 ml (1 tablespoon) oil
5 ml (1 teaspoon) salt
3 halved bay leaves

1 To prepare the filling, heat the oil in a saucepan, add the onion and fry until soft. Add the lentils and rice and fry, stirring frequently, for 2–3 minutes. Add all the remaining ingredients, stir well and bring to the boil. Lower the heat, cover the pan and simmer until all the water has been absorbed. Leave to cool.

2 To fill the leaves and prepare for cooking follow the instructions above.

3 Mix the sauce ingredients together and pour over the vine leaves. If they are not completely covered then add a little more water. Bring to the boil, lower the heat, cover the pan and simmer for $1^1/_2$–2 hours. Add a little more water if necessary. Take out one vine leaf and test to see if tender. If it is, remove the pan from the heat, take off the weight and plate and, when cool enough to handle, arrange the stuffed vine leaves on a dish. Serve warm or cold.

golubtsy
stuffed cabbage leaves

A very versatile vegetable for stuffing is the cabbage. In some recipes the leaves are separated and wrapped around a filling, while in others the whole cabbage is hollowed out and then stuffed.

Loved by the ancient Greeks, Romans and Chinese, the cabbage was unknown in the Middle East until about a thousand years ago.

It arrived in Europe from China before the Aryan races had been formulated and tribalised and it is still the favourite vegetable of northern and Central Europe. Naturally, therefore, the finest stuffed cabbage recipes are of Central European origin, although many of them contain meat.

I have chosen the Slavonic name for stuffed cabbage leaves — *golubtsy* — as a general heading since they are the true masters of this much used yet underrated vegetable with which Europeans have developed a love-hate relationship.

The three fillings given below, from Russia, France and Turkey, reflect the differing approaches.

Each of the following 3 fillings is sufficient for stuffing 1–1.4 kg (2–3 lb) white cabbage.

FILLING 1:
This is a favourite Russian recipe.

45 ml (3 tablespoons) butter or margarine
1 large onion, finely chopped
350 g (12 oz) mushrooms, wiped clean and coarsely chopped
125 g (4 oz) long grain rice, washed thoroughly
under cold running water and drained
10 ml (2 teaspoons) salt
2.5 ml ($^1/_2$ teaspoon) black pepper
5 ml (1 teaspoon) paprika
150 ml ($^1/_4$ pint) water
2 hard-boiled eggs, chopped

1 To prepare the cabbage leaves, fill a large saucepan two-thirds full with lightly salted water and bring to the boil. With the point of a sharp knife remove as much of the hard core of the cabbage as possible. Place the cabbage in the water and boil for 7–8 minutes. Remove the cabbage to a large plate and, when cool enough to handle, carefully peel away the outer leaves taking care not to tear them. When it becomes difficult to remove the leaves return the cabbage to the water and boil for a few more minutes. Continue removing leaves until you have all that you need. Put the leaves in

a colander to cool. Reserve the small inner leaves.

2 To prepare the filling, melt the butter or margarine in a saucepan, add the onion and fry until soft. Add the mushrooms and fry, stirring occasionally, for a few minutes. Stir in the rice, salt, pepper, paprika and the water and bring to the boil. Lower the heat, cover the pan and simmer until the water has been absorbed. Remove from the heat and stir in the hard-boiled eggs.

3 To fill a leaf, place one on a board, veins uppermost, and cut out the hard stem. With the cut end towards you place 15 ml (1 tablespoon) filling — exact amount depends on the size of the leaf in a ridge across the leaf near the cut end. Fold the cut end over the filling and then fold the sides over the filling towards the centre. Roll the leaf up towards the tip and the result will be a cigar-shaped parcel. Continue in this way until you have used up all the leaves and filling. Use any remaining leaves to cover the base of a medium-sized saucepan. Pack the parcels carefully and closely into the saucepan in layers. Place a plate over the leaves to cover as many as possible and hold down with a small weight — this prevents the leaves unwrapping during cooking.

4 To cook, pour in enough water to cover and bring to the boil. Lower the heat and simmer for about 1 hour or until the leaves are tender. Add a little more water, if necessary. Remove from the heat, take off the weight and plate and serve warm or cold.

FILLING 2:
This is a popular filling from northern France and the Low Countries.

30 ml (2 tablespoons) butter or margarine
1 large onion, finely chopped
900 g (2 lb) curd cheese, cottage cheese, panir or feta (see Glossary)
5 ml (1 teaspoon) oregano
30–45 ml (2–3 tablespoons) caraway seeds
5 ml (1 teaspoon) paprika
2.5 ml ($1/2$ teaspoon) chilli powder (optional)
10 ml (2 teaspoons) salt
2.5 ml ($1/2$ teaspoon) black pepper
1 large egg, beaten
oil, for frying
Tomato Sauce (see page 232)
30 ml (2 tablespoons) finely chopped parsley

1 Prepare the cabbage leaves as described in the instructions for Filling 1. When you have separated as many leaves as you can, return them to the pan of boiling water for a few minutes until just tender. Drain.

2 To make the filling, heat the fat in a small pan, add the onion and fry until soft and just turning golden. Transfer the onion and fat to a bowl and add the cheese, oregano, caraway seeds, paprika, chilli powder, if you are using it, salt, black pepper and egg. Knead until the mixture is well blended.

3 Fill the leaves as described in the instructions for Filling 1.

4 To cook, heat a little oil in a frying pan, add a few of the stuffed cabbage leaves and fry for 15–20 minutes, turning occasionally until both cabbage and filling are cooked. Remove and keep warm while you fry the remaining stuffed leaves in the same way. Add a little more oil if necessary.

5 Arrange the stuffed cabbage leaves in a large shallow serving dish, pour the hot tomato sauce over them and sprinkle with the parsley. Serve hot.

FILLING 3:
A delicious Turkish recipe where the leaves are filled with rice, nuts and spices. You can either serve them with lemon wedges in the Greek style or yogurt as is the Turkish way.

45 ml (3 tablespoons) oil
2 onions, finely chopped
125 g (4 oz) long grain rice, washed under
cold running water and drained
15 ml (1 tablespoon) pine kernels
15 ml (1 tablespoon) blanched almonds, coarsely chopped
15 ml (1 tablespoon) raisins
2.5 ml (1/2 teaspoon) allspice
2.5 ml (1/2 teaspoon) paprika
7.5 ml (11/2 teaspoons) salt
2.5 ml (1/2 teaspoon) black pepper
240 ml (8 fl oz) water
juice of 1 lemon

1 Prepare the cabbage leaves as described in the instructions for Filling 1.

2 To prepare the filling, heat the oil in a saucepan, add the onions and fry until soft. Add the rice, pine kernels and almonds and fry, stirring frequently, until the nuts begin to turn golden. Add the raisins, spices, seasoning and water and bring to the boil. Lower the heat, cover the pan and simmer until the water has been absorbed. Remove from the heat, stir in half the lemon juice and set aside.

3 Fill the leaves and prepare for cooking as described in the instructions for Filling 1.

4 Sprinkle the remaining lemon juice over the stuffed cabbage leaves in the saucepan and then place a plate over the leaves to cover as many as possible and hold down with a small weight to prevent the leaves unwrapping while cooking. Pour in enough water to cover and bring to the boil. Lower the heat, cover the pan and simmer for about 1 hour or until the leaves are tender. Add a little more water if necessary. Remove from the heat and take off the plate and weight. Arrange the cabbage rolls on a serving plate and serve warm or cold.

sabzi bharay kali ton

stuffed vegetable marrows

This lovely North Indian dish has a filling of beans and cheese. The vegetables are cooked in a sauce spiced with turmeric and garam masala.

Very tasty and filling.

Avoid large marrows as they tend to be too watery. I suggest you use 2 small ones about 1.1 kg (2¹/₂ lb) each. Serve with rice pilav and a pickle or chutney of your choice.

2 small marrows, washed and stems trimmed
30 ml (2 tablespoons) ghee (see Glossary)
1 large onion, finely chopped
1 garlic clove, crushed
1 large tomato, blanched, peeled and chopped
1–2 hot chillies — depending on taste — thinly sliced
15 ml (1 tablespoon) finely chopped coriander
125 g (4 oz) butter beans, soaked overnight in cold water, drained, cooked in boiling water for 1¹/₂ hours or until tender and then drained
125 g (4 oz) peas, cooked in boiling water until just tender
75 g (3 oz) panir (see Glossary) or drained cottage cheese
7.5 ml (1¹/₂ teaspoons) salt
2.5 ml (¹/₂ teaspoon) black pepper

Sauce
30 ml (2 tablespoons) ghee (see Glossary)
2 small onions, finely chopped
5 ml (1 teaspoon) salt
15 ml (1 tablespoon) finely chopped fresh ginger
2.5 ml (¹/₂ teaspoon) turmeric
5 ml (1 teaspoon) garam masala (see Glossary)
2.5 ml (¹/₂ teaspoon) chilli powder
300 ml (¹/₂ pint) water

1 Lay the marrows on their sides. Cut a 1 cm (¹/₂ inch) slice from along the top of each and reserve. With a spoon scoop out the seeds and a little of the flesh to prepare space for the filling. Discard the seeds and reserve the pulp.

2 Half fill a large saucepan with lightly salted water and bring to the boil, add the marrows and simmer for 12–15 minutes. Remove and drain.

3 Meanwhile, prepare the filling by melting the ghee in a saucepan and frying the onion and garlic until soft. Add the remaining ingredients including the reserved chopped flesh and fry, stirring frequently, for a further 2–3 minutes. Spoon this mixture into the marrows and replace the lids, securing them in place with wooden cocktail sticks.

4 Make the sauce in a saucepan or casserole large enough to hold the marrows side by side. Melt the ghee, add the onions and fry until soft and then stir in all the remaining sauce ingredients. Arrange the marrows in the sauce and bring gently to the boil. Lower the heat, cover the pan and simmer for about 45 minutes, basting the marrows occasionally with the sauce.

VARIATION: You can, of course, use courgettes instead of marrows for this dish. Prepare them for stuffing as indicated on page 153 in Courgettes Stuffed with Beans. Do not overcook the courgettes.

casseroles and stews

In the world of cookery the greatest innovation may have been the discovery of fire, but it was with the introduction of the cauldron that real culinary progress was made. Nomads roaming the desert lands or the steppes of Asia carried with them large earthenware or metal cauldrons in which they cooked their food, which, understandably, consisted of soups, thicker soups, stews and more stews. In this way the great dishes of the world were evolved.

Basically a stew is a stew. The difference between one stew and the next lies in the variety of meat cuts and, of course, the vegetables used.

A casserole dish technically means a meal made with rice, but in recent years it has come to mean any vegetable dish cooked in the oven, the basis of which can be rice or pasta or meat or a variety of vegetables in a sauce.

Different cuisines have come to evolve their own methods of preparing stews and casseroles. One of the most exciting is the vast repertoire of curry dishes of South East Asia. Curry (*kari*) is, in essence, a combination of ground spices cooked in ghee (clarified butter) or oil with vegetables and meat. The finest exponents of this stew are of course the people of the Indian subcontinent. The second recipe, given to me by Mr Kantilal Vara, is for chickpeas, haricot beans and tindora — which is sold in most Indian shops. It is a small vegetable about 5 cm (2 inches) long which is sliced thinly and cooked in curry dishes. It adds a delicious 'cucumberish' flavour to the stew.

vatakka kari

pumpkin curry

'Long, long are the pumpkins!
They are milky and long.
He sleeps all night with me,
But in the day he calls me sister,
Often, often he plays with my firm breasts.
They are his playthings.'
Folk Song from Central India
The Unwritten Song

Pumpkins have never been as popular in Britain as they are in America or, for that matter, in France. However, it is in the Middle East and the Indian subcontinent that this large, delicately flavoured vegetable comes into its own. A versatile vegetable, it can be used in soups, salads, stews and even desserts. The recipe below is from Sri Lanka.

Dried curry leaves and fenugreek seeds can easily be bought from Indian or Pakistani grocers.

Serve with a rice pilav of your choice, bread and pickles.

450g (1 lb) pumpkin flesh
1 small onion, finely chopped
2 garlic cloves, finely chopped
3 green chillies, seeded and finely chopped
8 curry leaves
2.5 ml (¹/₂ teaspoon) fenugreek seeds
2.5 ml (¹/₂ teaspoon) turmeric
350 ml (12 fl oz) thin coconut milk (see Glossary)
5 ml (1 teaspoon) salt
120 ml (4 fl oz) thick coconut milk (see Glossary)
5 ml (1 teaspoon) black mustard seeds

1 Cut the pumpkin flesh into 2.5 cm (1 inch) cubes and place in a large saucepan with all the remaining ingredients except the thick coconut milk and the mustard seeds. Bring slowly to the boil and then simmer gently for about 15 minutes, stirring occasionally, until the pumpkin is almost tender.

2 Crush the mustard seeds in a mortar and mix them into the thick coconut milk. Add to the pan, simmer for a further 5 minutes and then serve.

sukh falli kari

curried dried beans with tindora

125 g (4 oz) chickpeas, soaked overnight in cold water
125 g (4 oz) haricot beans, soaked overnight in cold water
30 ml (2 tablespoons) ghee (see Glossary) or margarine
1 large onion, finely chopped
2–3 spring onions, finely chopped
2–3 garlic cloves, crushed
10 ml (2 teaspoons) salt
15 ml (1 tablespoon) finely chopped fresh ginger
15 ml (1 level tablespoon) turmeric
7.5 ml (1$\frac{1}{2}$ teaspoons) garam masala (see Glossary)
4 medium tomatoes, blanched, peeled and chopped
2 green chillies, seeded and thinly sliced
225 g (8 oz) tindora, cut crossways into 1 cm ($\frac{1}{2}$ inch) slices
45 ml (3 tablespoons) chopped fresh mint or
15 ml (1 tablespoon) dried mint
juice of 1 lemon

1 Drain the beans and rinse under cold water. Place in a large saucepan, add sufficient boiling water to cover by at least 5 cm (2 inches) and simmer for about 60–90 minutes or until tender. Add more boiling water if necessary. Drain and reserve the cooking liquid.

2 In another saucepan heat the ghee, add the onions and garlic and fry, stirring constantly, for 3 minutes. Add the beans and all the remaining ingredients and mix well.

3 Add 300 ml ($\frac{1}{2}$ pint) of the reserved bean liquid, making it up to the required amount with water if necessary. Bring to the boil, lower the heat, cover the pan and simmer, stirring occasionally, for 15–20 minutes or until the curry has a thick consistency.

bhendi kari

okra curry

Okra (or lady's finger), although of African origin, is today much more used in the Indo-Pakistani cuisines than in its original homeland. It is chutnied, pickled, fried in spices and used in sauces and curries. This South Indian recipe is very typical of many such vegetable curries cooked in coconut milk.

Any vegetables of your choice can be used, for example pumpkin, bitter gourds, gourds, courgettes and aubergines.

Buy small, fresh, tender okra and most certainly avoid large ones as their seeds are too large for comfort and they tend to be tough and stringy. Serve with rice, bread and pickles.

30 ml (2 tablespoons) ghee (see Glossary) or oil
2 large onions, thinly sliced
1.25 ml ($^1/_4$ teaspoon) black mustard seeds
1.25 ml ($^1/_4$ teaspoon) cumin seeds
1.25 ml ($^1/_4$ teaspoon) fennel seeds
1 small green chilli, seeded and thinly sliced
1 garlic clove, crushed
2.5 ml ($^1/_2$ teaspoon) finely chopped fresh ginger
1.25 ml ($^1/_4$ teaspoon) ground fenugreek
2.5 ml ($^1/_2$ teaspoon) turmeric
450 g (1 lb) okra, washed and stalks trimmed
2 medium courgettes, cut crossways into 1 cm ($^1/_2$ inch) slices
7.5 ml ($1^1/_2$ teaspoons) salt
450 ml ($^3/_4$ pint) coconut milk (see Glossary)

1 Heat the ghee or oil in a large saucepan, add the onions and mustard, cumin and fennel seeds and fry for 3 minutes, stirring constantly. Now add the chilli, garlic, ginger, fenugreek and turmeric and fry, stirring, for a further 3 minutes. Add the okra and courgettes and fry for 4 minutes, stirring frequently.

2 Stir in the salt and coconut milk and bring to the boil. Lower the heat and simmer for 12–15 minutes or until the vegetables are just tender.

plantain curry

The recipe below is from the West Indies, but of Eastern origin, and was no doubt carried across the seas by Indian immigrants. Similar recipes can be found throughout India, Sri Lanka and Indonesia. Serve with rice.

For this recipe make sure that you select really unripe plantains, which are sold in all Indian and West Indian shops.

6 very unripe plantains, peeled
5 ml (1 teaspoon) salt
5 ml (1 teaspoon) turmeric
150 ml ($^1/_4$ pint) oil
1 onion, thinly sliced
600 ml (1 pint) coconut milk (see Glossary)
3 small green chillies, seeded and thinly sliced
2.5 ml ($^1/_2$ teaspoon) cinnamon
2.5 ml ($^1/_2$ teaspoon) fenugreek seeds
5–6 curry leaves

1 Halve the plantains crossways and then quarter lengthways. Arrange on a plate and sprinkle with the salt and turmeric. Rub in gently and set aside.

2 Heat all but 30–45 ml (2–3 tablespoons) of the oil in a frying pan and then carefully add a few of the plantain slices. Fry, turning occasionally, until golden. Remove with a slotted spoon, drain on kitchen paper and set aside on a plate. Cook the remaining plantain pieces in the same way.

3 Meanwhile, heat the remaining oil in a large saucepan, add the onion and fry until soft. Add the remaining ingredients and simmer, covered, for 15 minutes. Carefully add the fried plantains and simmer for a further 15–20 minutes or until the sauce has thickened. Serve immediately.

tazi khumben kari

new potatoes and mushroom curry

You can prepare this dish with ordinary potatoes or sweet potatoes, but the standard way is with small new potatoes, mushrooms and peas.

This is a typical 'curried' dish from North India.

Serve with rice, fresh salad, bread and chutney.

450 g (1 lb) small new potatoes
30 ml (2 tablespoons) ghee (see Glossary) or margarine
1 onion, finely chopped
2 garlic cloves, crushed
5 ml (1 teaspoon) finely chopped fresh ginger
5 ml (1 teaspoon) turmeric
5 ml (1 level teaspoon) cayenne pepper
450 g (1 lb) button mushrooms, wiped clean
175 g (6 oz) peas
10 ml (2 teaspoons) salt
2.5 ml ($^1/_2$ teaspoon) black pepper
150 ml ($^1/_4$ pint) water
5 ml (1 teaspoon) garam masala (see Glossary)
30 ml (2 tablespoons) finely chopped coriander
30 ml (2 tablespoons) finely chopped parsley
10–12 small radishes, wiped clean

1 Wash and scrub the new potatoes. If using old or sweet potatoes peel and wash them and cut into 3 cm ($1^1/_2$ inch) cubes.

2 Melt the fat in a large saucepan, add the onion and fry, stirring frequently, for 3 minutes. Add garlic and ginger and fry, stirring, for a further 3 minutes.

3 Stir in the turmeric, cayenne pepper, mushrooms, potatoes, peas, salt, pepper and water and mix well. Bring to the boil, lower the heat, cover the pan and cook for 12–15 minutes.

4 Add the garam masala, coriander, parsley and radishes, mix well, cover the pan and cook for a further 10 minutes or until the potatoes are tender and the radishes still firm.

sayur marak lemak
malaysian vegetable stew

'The man who is not hungry says the coconut has a hard shell'
Arab saying

This and Vegetables in Coconut Gravy (see page 177) have been reproduced —
with slight modifications — from Charmaine Solomon's excellent book *The
Complete Asian Cookbook.*

1 large onion, finely chopped
2 garlic cloves, crushed
2 green chillies, seeded and thinly sliced
2.5 ml ($^1/_2$ teaspoon) turmeric
2.5 ml ($^1/_2$ teaspoon) garam masala (see Glossary)
300 ml ($^1/_2$ pint) thin coconut milk (see Glossary) or
150 ml ($^1/_4$ pint) canned coconut milk mixed
with 150 ml ($^1/_4$ pint) water
450 g (1 lb) potatoes, peeled and cut into 1 cm ($^1/_2$ inch) cubes
1 medium courgette, cut crossways into 0.5 cm ($^1/_4$ inch) slices
350 g (12 oz) cabbage, shredded
7.5 ml ($1^1/_2$ teaspoons) salt
300 ml ($^1/_2$ pint) thick coconut milk (see Glossary)
juice of 1 lemon

1 Put the onion, garlic, chillies, turmeric, garam masala and thin coconut milk into a
large saucepan and bring to the boil. Lower the heat, cover the pan and simmer for 10
minutes.

2 Add the potatoes and courgette slices, stir well and cook for 10 minutes. Add the
cabbage, salt and thick coconut milk, mix well and cook for 5–7 minutes or until the
cabbage is just tender. Remove from the heat, stir in the lemon juice and serve
immediately.

par say saw

mixed braised vegetables

In the past most Chinese restaurants (today only a few) would include a few curry dishes on their menus simply because they wished to satisfy the Englishman's penchant for the hot and spicy curry-based dishes of India.

Yet curry dishes do not exist in all the diversely rich Chinese regional cuisines and never have. It was all a matter of expediency.

What the Chinese have always had are wonderfully rich pork-based dishes and a vast array of vegetable dishes. A good example of the latter is this recipe from Canton, proverbial for its fine food. 'One should be able to eat in Canton, to live in Soochow and to die in Hangchow' — which suggests that in the whole of China Canton has the best food, Soochow the best women and Hangchow the finest coffins.

Serve with boiled rice.

30 ml (2 tablespoons) oil
1 garlic clove, crushed
2.5 cm (1 inch) piece fresh ginger, peeled and grated
350 g (12 oz) Chinese cabbage, trimmed and sliced
350 g (12 oz) vegetables — leeks, cauliflower, spring onions, green beans —
trimmed and sliced
120 ml (4 fl oz) hot water
15 ml (1 tablespoon) soy sauce
2.5 ml ($^{1}/_{2}$ teaspoon) salt
2.5 ml ($^{1}/_{2}$ teaspoon) monosodium glutamate (optional)
7.5 ml (1$^{1}/_{2}$ teaspoons) cornflour mixed to a smooth paste
with 30–45 ml (1–2 tablespoons) water

1 Heat the oil in a wok or large frying pan, add the garlic and ginger and fry for 1 minute.

2 Add all the prepared vegetables and fry, stirring constantly, for 2 minutes.

3 In a small bowl mix together the hot water, soy sauce, salt and monosodium glutamate, if you are using it. Stir the mixture into the vegetables, cover the pan and simmer for 4 minutes. Push the vegetables to one side, add the cornflour mixture to the middle of the pan and stir until it has thickened. Toss the vegetables in the sauce and serve immediately.

soop houa phak sao souan

laotian vegetable stew

If pork is the mainstay of Chinese cookery, then fish is its equivalent in Thailand, Cambodia, Kampuchia and Laos, where it has a close rival in rice, which appears on Laotian tables from breakfast through to supper and beyond.

There are few vegetable dishes of note in this part of the world. One way or another meat (i.e. pork, or fish or poultry in that order) nearly always appears in the pot. That said I found a magnificent vegetable recipe in a unique cookery book, *Traditional Recipes of Laos*, that I had to include, with minor adaptations. This is a rich stew which I have enjoyed preparing over and over again to the delight of family and friends. Traditionally, the shallots and garlic used in this recipe were cooked in the embers of a charcoal fire, but they can be cooked in a hot oven or under the grill. Serve it with a rice pilav — if you want to be really authentic then it should be sweet rice or sticky rice.

45 ml (3 tablespoons) unsalted peanuts
30 ml (2 tablespoons) sesame seeds
6 shallots, peeled
2 garlic heads, cloves separated and peeled
7.5 ml (1^1/$_2$ teaspoons) chilli powder
90 ml (6 tablespoons) finely chopped coriander or parsley
2 spring onions, green parts only, finely chopped
10 ml (2 teaspoons) salt
2.5 ml (^{1}/$_2$ teaspoon) black pepper
150 ml (^{1}/$_4$ pint) boiling water
4 hard-boiled eggs, separated
3 medium carrots, scraped and thinly sliced
350 g (12 oz) white radish, scraped and cut into 1 cm (^{1}/$_2$ inch) cubes
350 g (12 oz) potatoes, peeled and cut into 1 cm (^{1}/$_2$ inch) cubes
350 g (12 oz) cauliflower florets broken into small sprigs
125 g (4 oz) mangetout, stringed and halved

1 Place the peanuts in a small pan and toast over a medium heat for 3–4 minutes, shaking the pan occasionally. Remove and when cool enough to handle rub off the skins and set aside. Next toast the sesame seeds in the same way. Put these, with the peanuts, either in a mortar or in a blender and reduce to a powder. Place in a large mixing bowl.

2 Put the shallots and garlic in a hot oven or under the grill and cook for 8–10 minutes, turning once or twice. Blend or pound the onions and garlic to a paste with the chilli powder. Add to the peanut mixture together with the coriander or parsley, spring onions, salt, black pepper and hot water. Mash the egg yolks, add to the bowl and thoroughly mix all the ingredients.

3 Half fill a large saucepan with lightly salted water and bring to the boil. Add the vegetables and simmer for 4–5 minutes. Drain and place the vegetables in the mixing bowl. Chop the egg whites and add to the bowl. Toss gently until the vegetables are coated with the sauce. Turn the mixture into a serving dish and serve immediately.

Apropos the African cuisine, in general certain characteristic traits are evident which reflect not only the nature of the continent, but her immediate colonial past. I once asked a Ghanaian student working part-time in one of my restaurants, 'What are the basic characteristics of African food.' He burst out laughing (they tend to be happy almost all the time), flashed his snow-white teeth and exclaimed for all the world to hear, 'Anything we can lay hands on from the trees or the ground.' A good answer, but not an entirely satisfactory one.

African food is primitive and basic, depending on the yam, cassava and other root vegetables as well as fruits. There is little meat, fish or poultry available and what there is, is simply prepared. Much is made of groundnuts, maize, plantain (*matoke*) and coconut.

In the southern part of the continent the white man brought with him his ancestral European food. In the east it is the Arab and Javanese kitchens which have influenced the local cuisines. In the west one sees the influence of Portugal and Spain, but in the interior of that vast continent the nomadic and pastoral people have maintained their special foods based on the milk and blood of their animals and on insects such as locusts and grasshoppers, which are boiled in salty water, dried in the sun and then cooked with plantain or a porridge made of maize.

In parts of Africa, where people of Indian descent were brought over to work on the railways and the farms, a strangely interesting cuisine evolved which was a mixture of the local and the Indian.

ponkie

ghanaian vegetable stew

The word *'ponkie'* means pumpkin and so this is a dish of pumpkin with aubergines, onion and tomatoes. A vegetarian version of an equally popular meat ponkie.

Serve with boiled yam, cassava, any of the *fufu* dishes (see page 206) or rice.

75 ml (5 tablespoons) groundnut oil
1 large onion, coarsely chopped
3 large tomatoes, blanched, peeled and coarsely chopped
1–1.4 kg (2–3 lb) pumpkin, skinned, seeded and cut into 5 cm (2 inch) cubes
2 green peppers, thinly sliced
2 medium aubergines, cut crossways into 2.5 cm (1 inch) slices
5 ml (1 teaspoon) chilli powder
5 ml (1 teaspoon) freshly chopped coriander
10 ml (2 teaspoons) salt
5 ml (1 teaspoon) finely chopped fresh ginger

1 Heat the oil in a large saucepan, add the onion and fry until soft, stirring frequently. Add the tomatoes, pumpkin, green peppers and aubergines and mix thoroughly. Fry for 5 minutes, stirring occasionally.

2 Stir in the remaining ingredients, cover the pan and simmer for about 20–30 minutes or until the vegetables are tender, stirring occasionally. Serve immediately.

atieke

west african vegetable stew

'If I beat up cassava leaf
And mix it with green-green
And eat my fill of it,
And then take my drum
And beat it with a will,
Ah! then my mind goes back
And I remember your caresses
Ah! how sweet it was —
In that little room —
Where we first told our love!
Breathe it to no-one!'
The Unwritten Song — 'Love Song' Temne People SW Africa

A rich stew of vegetables from the Ivory Coast, but also popular in Nigeria, Senegal and Sierra Leone.

Cassava grains (*garri*) can be bought in most West Indian and Indian shops, but if you wish you can substitute this with couscous (see page 208) or with a rice pilav.

150 ml (¹/₄ pint) oil
2 large onions, sliced
2 garlic cloves, chopped
450 g (1 lb) ripe tomatoes, blanched, peeled and chopped
30 ml (2 tablespoons) tomato purée diluted in 600 ml (1 pint) water
7.5 ml (1¹/₂ teaspoons) salt
5 ml (1 teaspoon) chilli powder
4 carrots, peeled and diced
3 medium turnips, peeled and diced
1 small swede, peeled and diced
2 medium aubergines, diced
1 small cauliflower, separated into florets
¹/₂ cabbage, chopped
225 g (8 oz) green beans, stringed and cut into 1 cm (¹/₂ inch) pieces
2 parsley sprigs

To serve
450 g (1 lb) cassava grains (*garri*) (see Glossary)

1 Heat the oil in a large pan, add the onions and garlic and fry, stirring, until soft. Add the tomatoes, diluted tomato purée, salt and chilli powder and bring to the boil. Lower the heat and simmer for 5 minutes.

2 Add all the remaining ingredients, mix well, cover the pan and cook gently, stirring occasionally, for 30–45 minutes or until the vegetables are tender and the sauce has thickened.

3 Meanwhile, mix the cassava grains with a little cold water until they form soft granules. Stir in a pinch of salt and serve with the vegetable stew.

sayur lodeh

vegetables in coconut gravy

Coconut milk is the major sauce ingredient throughout western and southern India, Sri Lanka and Malaysia as well as the adjacent lands of Burma, Laos, Kampuchia and Indonesia, where this recipe originates.

Any vegetables in season can be used. The important thing is to cut them into small pieces.

30 ml (2 tablespoons) oil
1 large onion, finely chopped
2 garlic cloves, crushed
1 green chilli, seeded and thinly sliced
1 stalk lemon grass or 2 strips lemon rind or
5 ml (1 teaspoon) powdered lemon grass (*sereh*) (see Glossary)
2 large tomatoes, blanched, peeled and coarsely chopped
600 ml (1 pint) water
300 ml ($^1/_2$ pint) thick coconut milk (see Glossary)
900 g (2 lb) mixed vegetables, cut into small pieces
20–25 ml (4–5 teaspoons) peanut sauce (see *saus kacang* — page 228)
10 ml (2 teaspoons) salt
2.5 ml ($^1/_2$ teaspoon) black pepper

1 Heat the oil in a large saucepan, add the onion and fry, stirring frequently, for 3 minutes. Stir in the garlic and chilli and fry for a further 2 minutes. Add the lemon grass or rind and tomatoes, mix well and cook for 2 minutes. Stir in the water and coconut milk and bring to the boil. Lower the heat, cover the pan and simmer for 15–20 minutes.

2 Now add the vegetables. If you are including carrots or similar vegetables which take a little longer to cook then add them to the pan first and simmer for 4–5 minutes before adding the rest. Cook for 5–7 minutes or until all the vegetables are just tender but still crisp. Remove from the heat, stir in the peanut sauce, salt, pepper and lemon juice and serve.

bgolla

berber mallow and vegetable stew

In the north of the African continent, where the finest and most interesting dishes originate, it is the intermixture of Arab, African, European and above all the Berber influences that are clearly apparent. The Berbers, a people of European stock who have for millennia lived throughout North Africa from Morocco in the west to Libya as well as the Sahara, have created one of the great cuisines of the world.

You can substitute mallow with spinach, but I suggest you try the original, which is freely available (in season) in your garden or on nearby waste ground.

This is a speciality popular throughout Morocco and Algeria.

225 g (8 oz) mallow, thick stems and coarse leaves discarded
150 ml (¹/₄ pint) oil
3 garlic cloves, thinly sliced
1 whole dried chilli (optional)
5 ml (1 teaspoon) paprika
2.5 ml (¹/₂ teaspoon) black pepper
15 ml (1 tablespoon) tomato purée diluted in 60–75 ml (4–5 tablespoons) water
25 g (1 oz) chickpeas, soaked overnight in cold water and drained
25 g (1 oz) haricot beans, soaked overnight in cold water and drained
900 ml (1¹/₂ pints) water
10 ml (2 teaspoons) salt
2 potatoes, peeled and cut into 2.5 cm (1 inch) cubes
1 cardoon washed, stalk and heart separated and cut (optional)
25 g (1 oz) peas
10–12 green olives
15 ml (1 tablespoon) finely chopped fresh coriander or parsley

1 Chop the mallow coarsely and rinse thoroughly under cold running water. Half fill a large saucepan with water and bring to the boil. Add the mallow, blanch for 2–3 minutes and drain in a colander.

2 Heat the oil in a large saucepan, add the garlic, chilli, if using, paprika, black pepper and tomato purée and simmer for 2–3 minutes. Add the chickpeas, beans and water and bring to the boil. Cover the pan, lower the heat and simmer for 60–90 minutes or until the chickpeas are tender. Add a little more boiling water, if necessary.

3 Add the salt, potatoes, cardoon, peas, olives, mallow and coriander or parsley. Stir well and continue to simmer, covered, until the vegetables are tender and the sauce reduced. Carefully remove the whole chilli and serve it separately.

ratatouille and variations

Rata, or ratatouille, is a classic of Provence. It is a stew made with aubergines, courgettes, tomatoes, peppers, herbs and spices and is served hot or cold. There are many versions throughout the Mediterranean coastline but, according to my Tunisian friends, it is of North African origin. '*Chakchouka*', they exclaim in unison. 'It (ratatouille) is nothing but the Frenchified name of our classic Berber dish.' And true enough. On closer study one sees many similarities between the two dishes. But what about the *turlu*-labelled stews of Turkey, or the *guvech* dishes of Romania and Bulgaria? They are all *ratas*. The aubergine came from the Middle East as did the courgette, but then the tomato arrived via America, while their binding ingredient (olive oil) was and is Mediterranean. So what's in a name? Nothing save national pride. Therefore one must tread very carefully and explain that whatever its name a dish made with these vegetables is of Mediterranean origin. The following recipes are all of equally ancient pedigree and fame.

The first then is for a *chakchouka* from Algeria.

chakchouka bil-babendjel
aubergine chakchouka

75–90 ml (5–6 tablespoons) oil
2 large green or red peppers, seeded and thinly sliced
3 large tomatoes, coarsely chopped
3 medium aubergines, peeled, quartered and cut into 2.5 cm (1 inch) slices
2 garlic cloves, chopped
30 ml (2 tablespoons) finely chopped parsley
6 eggs
7.5 ml (1^1/$_2$ teaspoons) salt
2.5 ml (^{1}/$_2$ teaspoon) black pepper

1 Heat the oil in a large frying pan and add the peppers, tomatoes, aubergine slices, garlic and parsley. Mix thoroughly, lower the heat, cover the pan and simmer for 15–20 minutes, stirring occasionally, and adding a little more oil, if necessary.

2 Uncover the pan and break the eggs over the mixture, stirring gently with a fork to break the yolks. Cover the pan again and cook for a further 3–4 minutes or until the eggs are set. Remove from the heat, sprinkle with the salt and pepper and serve immediately.

torsh-e tareh

iranian-style ratatouille

A classic from Iran. Whenever possible use fresh herbs, which is the Iranian way.

60 ml (4 tablespoons) samna or ghee (see Glossary)
1 large onion, thinly sliced
125 g (4 oz) pinto or black-eyed beans, soaked in cold water for 3–4 hours
125 g (4 oz) whole lentils, rinsed
1.7 litres (3 pints) water
2.5 ml ($1/_2$ teaspoon) black pepper
10 ml (2 teaspoons) salt
3 garlic cloves, crushed
50 g (2 oz) dillweed, finely chopped
1 bunch parsley, finely chopped
8–10 mint sprigs, finely chopped
60 ml (4 tablespoons) finely chopped coriander
700 g ($1^1/_2$ lb) spinach, washed thoroughly, drained and coarsely chopped
50 g (2 oz) rice flour
45 ml (3 tablespoons) water
4 eggs, beaten
juice of 1 lime or lemon
75 ml (5 tablespoons) fresh orange juice

1 Melt half the fat in a large saucepan, add the onion and fry until soft. Add the drained beans, lentils, water and pepper, cover and simmer for 1–$1^1/_2$ hours or until the beans are cooked. Add salt.

2 Melt the remaining fat in a frying pan and fry the garlic for 2 minutes. Add the herbs and fry, stirring frequently, for a further 2 minutes. Add this mixture to the saucepan together with the spinach and cook for a further 20 minutes.

3 In a small bowl mix the rice flour and water to a smooth paste. Add a few tablespoons of the hot stock and then add to the saucepan and cook, stirring constantly, until the sauce thickens.

4 Place the eggs in a bowl and stir in the lime or lemon juice and a few tablespoons of the hot stock. Stir this into the saucepan together with the orange juice; cook for a few more minutes, then serve.

ghivechi calugaresti

romanian ratatouille

First created in the monasteries for the gratification of the priesthood from vegetables cultivated in the abbot's patch of paradise — hence the name 'cloister's vegetables'. This is now a popular dish throughout the only land of the Latin-speaking Slav nation.

There are no herbs or spices used in this dish — nothing to stir or tempt the soul or body of the poor monk. I suggest you include a little salt, black pepper, paprika or other herbs or spices.

1 small cauliflower, separated into florets
3 medium tomatoes, quartered
2 medium carrots, peeled and sliced crossways into 2.5 cm (1 inch) pieces
1 leek, washed thoroughly and cut into 2.5 cm (1 inch) pieces
$^1/_2$ cabbage, sliced
2 green peppers, seeded and thinly sliced
1 medium aubergine, cut crossways into 1 cm ($^1/_2$ inch) slices
225 g (8 oz) mangetout or small french beans, stringed and halved
225 g (8 oz) peas
225 g (8 oz) small okra
2 large onions, thinly sliced
150 ml ($^1/_4$ pint) oil

Lightly grease a large ovenproof casserole. Mix all the vegetables together and place in the dish. Season if you wish. Pour the oil over the vegetables and cook in a 180°C (350°F) mark 4 oven for 45–60 minutes or until the vegetables are tender. Serve immediately.

ratatouille

provençal vegetable stew

French housewives sprinkle salt over the sliced aubergines and courgettes and leave to rest in a colander for 30 minutes or more. I leave the choice to you.

2 medium aubergines, cut crossways into 1 cm ($^1/_2$ inch) slices
3 medium courgettes, cut crossways into 1 cm ($^1/_2$ inch) slices
150 ml ($^1/_4$ pint) olive oil
2 large onions, sliced
2 garlic cloves, crushed
2 green peppers, seeded and thinly sliced
450 g (1 lb) tomatoes, blanched, peeled and quartered
10 ml (2 teaspoons) salt
2.5 ml ($^1/_2$ teaspoon) sugar
2.5 ml ($^1/_2$ teaspoon) black pepper
30 ml (2 tablespoons) finely chopped parsley

1 If you have salted the aubergines and courgettes, rinse them and pat dry with kitchen paper.

2 Heat the oil in a large saucepan, add the onions and garlic and fry for 3 minutes, stirring frequently. Add the aubergine slices and fry, stirring regularly until they become soft and change colour. Add the courgettes and green peppers, cover the pan and cook over a low heat for 25 minutes.

3 Add the tomatoes, salt, sugar and pepper and stir thoroughly. Simmer, uncovered, for a further 20–30 minutes. Remove from the heat and stir in the parsley. Serve hot or cold.

tian à la provençale
baked vegetable casserole

Tian is the name of the earthenware dish in which can be prepared any vegetable of your choice.

750 ml (1^1/$_2$ pints) water
10 ml (2 teaspoons) salt
250 g (9 oz) long grain rice, washed thoroughly
under cold running water and drained
90 ml (6 tablespoons) oil
700 g (1^1/$_2$ lb) spinach, coarse leaves discarded, washed
thoroughly and coarsely chopped
2 medium courgettes, cut crossways into 1 cm (^{1}/$_2$ inch) slices
3 garlic cloves, crushed
30 ml (2 tablespoons) finely chopped parsley
175 g (6 oz) cheese, Cheddar or Edam, grated
5 ml (1 teaspoon) salt
2.5 ml (^{1}/$_2$ teaspoon) black pepper
2.5 ml (^{1}/$_2$ teaspoon) basil
2.5 ml (^{1}/$_2$ teaspoon) paprika
3 eggs, beaten
45-60 ml (3-4 tablespoons) fresh breadcrumbs
30-45 ml (2-3 tablespoons) grated Parmesan cheese (optional)

1 Place the water and salt in a saucepan and bring to the boil. Add the rice, lower the heat, cover the pan and simmer until all the water has been absorbed. Set aside.

2 Heat half the oil in a large saucepan, add the spinach and courgettes and fry, stirring gently, for 3-4 minutes or until the vegetables are evenly coated with oil. Add the cooked rice, garlic, parsley, cheese, salt, black pepper, basil and paprika, mix thoroughly, remove from the heat and stir in the beaten eggs.

3 Grease an ovenproof casserole and spoon in the vegetable mixture. Smooth the surface over with the back of a spoon. Sprinkle the breadcrumbs evenly over the top, followed by the Parmesan cheese, if using it. Dribble the remaining oil evenly over the surface and bake in a 180°C (350°F) mark 4 oven for about 40 minutes or until the top is golden and crisp.

chou rouge à la limousine

red cabbage and chestnut casserole

An exquisitely colourful dish from the Limousin region of France. This dish is even more delicious if made a day ahead.

75 g (3 oz) butter
2 medium onions, thinly sliced
900 g (2 lb) red cabbage, finely shredded
450 ml (³/₄ pint) dry red wine
150 ml (¹/₄ pint) water or vegetable stock (see Glossary)
2 bay leaves
3 cloves
1.25 ml (¹/₄ teaspoon) nutmeg
5 ml (1 teaspoon) salt
2.5 ml (¹/₂ teaspoon) black pepper
700 g (1¹/₂ lb) fresh chestnuts, shelled and skinned, or
175 g (6 oz) dried chestnuts, soaked overnight
juice 1 small lemon
15 ml (1 tablespoon) brown sugar

1 Melt the butter in a large saucepan, add the onions and fry, stirring frequently, for 3 minutes. Add the cabbage, a little at a time, stirring constantly, to coat all the cabbage with the butter. Cover the pan and simmer over a low heat for 15 minutes.

2 Spoon the mixture into a large flame-proof casserole and stir in the next 7 ingredients. Bring to the boil, cover and bake in a 160°C (300°F) mark 2 oven for about 2 hours.

3 Remove the casserole, mix in the chestnuts, cover and return to the oven. Cook for a further hour or until the cabbage is very tender and the juices have been reduced.

4 Just before serving, stir in the lemon juice and sugar.

pies, savouries and accompaniments

A Russian adage complains 'the pie is the diner's enemy', for the traditional pies of Russia were heavy, rich and served at the beginning of a dinner. Latvians echo a similar sentiment as they declare 'A big man — a big pie.'

A pie, in its simplest form, is a pastry crust filled with a variety of things, sweet or savoury. Often this type of food preparation is called a tart or flan. The name pie is also sometimes given to dishes made up of layers of vegetables and/or rice.

The finest savoury pies hail from Britain and Russia and they truly can be heavy. However, the all-vegetable pies tend to be lighter.

The most popular vegetable used throughout the world in meatless pies appears to be spinach, followed by the potato, the onion and then mushrooms. Another major ingredient in pies is cheese. There are literally hundreds of cheese-based pies and flans. I have included a few here.

In those recipes which include pastry you should use the specific pastry recipe, if you wish to be really authentic. However, you can, where suitable, substitute wholewheat pastry (see page 269).

Serve all these pies and pastries with salads, pickles and chutneys. They make an excellent lunch or dinner, being so filling and full of goodness that you don't notice the absence of meat.

aginares moussakas

artichoke pie

This recipe is from western Greece. If you wish you can halve the number of artichokes and top the pie with sliced boiled potatoes instead.

4 artichokes, hearts prepared (see Glossary)
175 g (6 oz) long grain rice, washed thoroughly under
cold running water and drained
90 ml (3 fl oz) olive oil
1 medium onion, finely chopped
1 garlic clove, crushed
225 g (8 oz) tomatoes, blanched, peeled and chopped
2.5 ml ($1/2$ teaspoon) basil
2.5 ml ($1/2$ teaspoon) oregano
2.5 ml ($1/2$ teaspoon) paprika
5 ml (1 teaspoon) salt
2.5 ml ($1/2$ teaspoon) black pepper
15 ml (1 tablespoon) ground almonds
75 ml (5 tablespoons) water
600 ml (1 pint) Béchamel sauce (see page 237)
30 ml (2 tablespoons) grated Cheddar or feta cheese (see Glossary)

1 Boil the artichoke hearts in lightly salted water for 10 minutes. Drain and set aside to cool.

2 Meanwhile, half fill a saucepan with lightly salted water and bring to the boil. Add the rice and simmer for 15–20 minutes or until just tender. Pour into a sieve to drain.

3 Heat the oil in a large saucepan, add the onion and garlic and fry for about 5 minutes or until soft. Add the tomatoes, basil, oregano, paprika, salt, black pepper, almonds and water and mix well. Simmer over a medium heat until the liquid has evaporated. Add the cooked rice and mix thoroughly.

4 Grease a large ovenproof casserole. Slice the artichoke hearts crossways and arrange half the slices in a layer over the bottom of the casserole. Top with the rice mixture and smooth over with the back of a spoon. Layer the remaining artichoke slices over the top. Spread the béchamel sauce over them and sprinkle evenly with the cheese. Cook in a 180°C (350°F) mark 4 oven for about 30–40 minutes or until the top is golden.

leek pie

This and similar pies are found throughout Britain, France and the Low Countries. Sometimes bacon rashers are incorporated, but very little else. I like to serve this pie with a rich salad and some chutney.

You can use either home-made or commercial puff pastry or the recipe for Wholewheat Pastry on page 269.

450 g (1 lb) puff pastry

Filling
50 g (2 oz) margarine or butter
1 large onion, thinly sliced
700 g (1¹/₂ lb) leeks, trimmed, thinly sliced and
washed thoroughly under cold running water
120 ml (4 fl oz) double cream
15 ml (2 heaped teaspoons) flour
10 ml (2 teaspoons) salt
2.5 ml (¹/₂ teaspoon) black pepper
1.25 ml (¹/₄ teaspoon) nutmeg

Glaze
1 egg, beaten

1 First prepare the filling. Melt the fat in a large saucepan, add the onion and fry until soft. Add the drained leek slices and fry, stirring frequently, for about 10 minutes or until the leeks have softened. Remove from the heat.

2 In a small bowl, beat together the cream and flour and stir in the spices. Add to the leek mixture and stir thoroughly.

3 Divide the pastry in two equal parts and roll one part out large enough to line a large pie dish about 22.5 cm (9 inches) in diameter and at least 2.5 cm (1 inch) deep. Line the dish and trim off excess pastry. Pile the leek filling into the dish and spread out evenly. Roll out the remaining pastry and place over the filling to completely cover it. Trim the edges, seal with a fork and make 2–3 incisions in the top.

4 Brush the pastry with the beaten egg and bake in a 180°C (350°F) mark 4 oven for about 30 minutes or until golden. Serve hot.

baki sumpoogi moussaka
lent-style aubergine pie

Moussaka, from the Arabic *Muhklabah*, is usually associated with Greece, although the Romanians also claim to have originated it. It was, however, in the days of Harun el-Rashid of the great Arab empire that this Indian-grown vegetable came to the fore in the cuisine of Baghdad and Damascus, where many of the Middle Eastern aubergine dishes were first developed.

This family dish is a regional speciality and comes from that part of southern Turkey which was once an Armenian kingdom. It was created to satisfy the rigid requirements of the Armenian and Greek Orthodox Churches.

2 medium aubergines, cut crossways into 1 cm ($^1/_2$ inch) slices
350 g (12 oz) spaghetti or macaroni
60 ml (4 tablespoons) oil
1 onion, finely chopped
1 garlic clove, crushed
1 green pepper, seeded and finely chopped
2 large tomatoes, blanched, peeled and chopped
30 ml (2 tablespoons) tomato purée
5 ml (1 teaspoon) salt
2.5 ml ($^1/_2$ teaspoon) cinnamon
2.5 ml ($^1/_2$ teaspoon) cayenne pepper
225 g (8 oz) cheese — Cheddar, Gruyère or haloumi (see Glossary)
grated butter

1 Arrange the aubergine slices on a large plate, sprinkle with salt and set aside for 30 minutes. Rinse under cold running water and pat dry with kitchen paper.

2 Meanwhile, half fill a large saucepan with lightly salted water and bring to the boil, add the pasta and simmer for 6–7 minutes. Drain in a colander, rinse under warm water and set aside.

3 Heat the oil in a large saucepan, add the onion and fry, stirring occasionally, until soft. Add the garlic and continue to fry until the onion is golden. Add the aubergine slices and fry for 2–3 minutes until lightly coloured all over. Add the green pepper, tomatoes, tomato purée, salt, cinnamon and cayenne and simmer over a low heat until the aubergines are just tender. Add a little water, if necessary, and turn the aubergine gently so that the slices do not break.

4 Butter a large baking dish and put half of the spaghetti or macaroni over the bottom. Spread the aubergine mixture over the pasta and place the remaining pasta evenly over the aubergine.

5 Sprinkle the cheese evenly over the top and bake in a 190°C (375°F) mark 5 oven for about 30 minutes or until the surface is lightly golden. Remove from the oven, cut into squares and serve warm.

spanakotyropita
spinach pie

Spinach makes an excellent pie filling. Indeed, when mixed with onions, cheese and spices, spinach pies are the very best.

There are many similar dishes throughout the Middle East and the Mediterranean. The finest is this recipe from Greece, although in similar vein the Italian *torta pasqualina* or *rotola di spinaci* make excellent alternatives. In this pie, instead of wholewheat or puff pastry, filo (also phyllo and fillo) pastry is used.

8–10 sheets filo pastry
45–60 ml (3–4 tablespoons) melted butter

Filling
900 g (2 lb) fresh spinach, washed very thoroughly and
with coarse stems and leaves discarded
120 ml (4 fl oz) oil
1 onion, finely chopped
50 g (2 oz) parsley, finely chopped
10 ml (2 teaspoons) fresh dill or
5 ml (1 teaspoon) dried dillweed
10 ml (2 teaspoons) fresh fennel, finely chopped (optional)
1.25 ml ($^1/_4$ teaspoon) nutmeg
175 g (6 oz) cheese, Cheddar, Gruyère or feta
(see Glossary), grated
50 g (2 oz) Parmesan, grated
2 eggs, beaten
5 ml (1 teaspoon) salt
1.25 ml ($^1/_4$ teaspoon) black pepper

1 First prepare the filling. Chop the spinach coarsely, place it in a large saucepan and cook over a low heat for about 10 minutes, stirring occasionally with a fork. When the spinach has wilted, pour it into a colander to drain and, with the back of a large spoon, press hard to remove as much liquid as possible.

2 Heat the oil in a small pan, add the onion and fry for several minutes until soft and turning golden. Place the onion and spinach in a large bowl, add the parsley, dill, fennel, nutmeg, cheese, eggs, salt and pepper and mix thoroughly.

3 Lightly grease a 25 x 30 cm (10 x 12 inch) baking dish or ovenproof casserole. Lay 4 or 5 sheets of the filo pastry in the dish, brushing each one with a little melted butter. Pour the spinach mixture into the dish and spread evenly with the back of a spoon. Lay the remaining sheets of filo over the top, again brushing each one with some of the melted butter. Trim the edges of the pastry. Pour any remaining butter over the top and sprinkle with a little cold water — this should prevent the pastry

curling at the edges.

4 Bake in a 180°C (350°F) mark 4 oven for about 45 minutes or until golden. Remove from the oven, leave to rest a few minutes and then cut into squares and serve.

VARIATION: You can, if you wish, add a small bunch of finely chopped spring onions. Add these to the onion and fry together gently for a few minutes.

gombas lepény
mushroom pie
'Year of mushrooms, year of trouble'
Italian proverb

The favourite Hungarian vegetables are undoubtedly the potato and the capsicum (paprika), but the mushroom comes a close third. This simple peasant dish is one example of the little known but extremely rich and versatile cuisine of the Magyars, who roamed Asia and Europe before finally settling near the Bakony forest and the Matra mountains.

This recipe was given to me by a Hungarian friend who is 'sick and tired' of his country being known as a one-dish nation — namely the ubiquitous *gulyás*.

50 g (2 oz) margarine or butter
450 g (1 lb) mushrooms, wiped clean and thinly sliced
10 ml (2 teaspoons) salt
2.5 ml (1/2 teaspoon) black pepper
2.5 ml (1/2 teaspoon) paprika
30 ml (2 tablespoons) finely chopped parsley
4 thick bread slices, crusts removed
150 ml (1/4 pint) milk
3 eggs, separated
15 ml (1 tablespoon) fresh breadcrumbs

1 Melt the margarine or butter in a large saucepan, add the mushroom slices and fry, stirring frequently, for 3–4 minutes. Add the salt, pepper, paprika and parsley, mix well and simmer over a low heat, stirring occasionally, until all the liquid has evaporated.

2 Meanwhile, soak the bread slices in the milk, squeeze gently to remove excess liquid and then break into small pieces and place in a bowl with the egg yolks. With the back of a fork break up the slices and beat until smooth. Stir in the mushroom mixture.

3 Lightly beat the egg whites and stir into the mushroom mixture. Lightly grease a large ovenproof casserole and sprinkle the breadcrumbs over its base and sides. Pour in the mushroom mixture and spread evenly with the back of a spoon. Bake in a 180°C

(350°F) mark 4 oven for 30–40 minutes or until set.

4 Remove from the oven, cut into squares or wedges and serve.

VARIATION: If they are available, wild mushrooms such as ceps are delicious in this pie, and chopped fresh dill makes a tasty addition to the finely chopped parsley.

tortillas and tacos

These are the *boreks* or *breiks* of Mexico which, in their many shapes, have become part of the North American culture.

Tortillas are flat rounds of unleavened bread. They are traditionally made with masa harina — a specially prepared maize flour which can be bought from many West Indian stores, but you can also use a mixture of medium cornflour and wholewheat flour or just wholewheat flour. The result is not quite the real thing but near enough.

Tacos and enchiladas are filled tortillas which are then fried or baked. Below I give a recipe for tortillas and two suggested fillings.

tortillas

225 g (8 oz) dehydrated masa harina
5 ml (1 teaspoon) salt
240 ml (8 fl oz) warm water

1 Place the flour and salt in a mixing bowl. Gradually add enough of the water, mixing and kneading constantly, to make a firmish dough that does not stick to your fingers. Divide the dough into 12 balls.

2 Taking one ball of dough at a time roll it out between 2 sheets of greaseproof paper until it is about 15 cm (6 inches) in diameter. Repeat with the remaining balls.

3 Heat a large ungreased frying pan over medium heat, add 1 tortilla and cook for about 1–2 minutes on each side or until the dough has small bubbles on the surface. Remove and wrap in a tea towel to keep warm and soft. As you cook each one, stack it on top of the previous one and keep wrapped.

quesadillas

tacos with cheese filling

12 tortillas
oil, for frying

Filling
175 g (6 oz) green chillies, seeded and thinly sliced
450 g (1 lb) cheese — Cheddar, Edam, feta (see Glossary) or pecorino, grated

1 Mix the chillies and cheese together.

2 Take 1 tortilla, place 15 ml (1 tablespoon) of the filling on one half and then fold it over to form a semicircle. Hold shut with 2 or 3 small wooden cocktail sticks. Repeat with remaining tortillas and fillings.

3 Heat a little oil in a large frying pan and fry the tacos, 1 or 2 at a time, depending on the size of the pan, until crisp, turning once or twice. Remove with a slotted spoon, drain and serve.

VARIATIONS: You can, if you like, moisten the filling with a little soured cream; or make it a little less hot by substituting sweet peppers for half of the chillies; or add a little sautéed onion, garlic and mushrooms; or add some cooked, dried potato to the cheese and chilli mixture.

enchilada de legumbres y chilis

enchilada with vegetable filling

Enchiladas are tortillas which are fried, dipped in a spicy sauce
and then filled and baked.

Although this recipe is for a mixed vegetable filling there is no reason why you cannot use just one favourite vegetable or, indeed, any of the fillings suggested for *boreks* (see pages 197-201).

Serve with small bowls of chopped onion, grated cheese, sliced chilli peppers, lemon wedges, etc.

12 tortillas
oil, for frying

Sauce

60 ml (4 tablespoons) vegetable oil
50 g (2 oz) onion, chopped
50 g (2 oz) green pepper, chopped
2 garlic cloves, finely chopped
30 ml (2 level tablespoons) flour
30 ml (2 tablespoons) finely chopped parsley
30 ml (2 tablespoons) paprika
2.5 ml ($^{1}/_{2}$ teaspoon) each of salt, black pepper, cinnamon, cumin, sage and oregano
75 g (3 oz) tomato purée diluted wlth 450 ml ($^{3}/_{4}$ pint) water
30 ml (2 tablespoons) vinegar
2 green chillies, seeded and chopped

Filling

approx 700 g (1$^{1}/_{2}$ lb) cooked vegetables
180 ml (12 tablespoons) grated cheese
4 green chillies, cut into 24 thin strips
180 ml (12 tablespoons) chopped onion

1 To prepare the sauce, heat the oil in a frying pan with a base a little larger than the tortillas. Add the onion, green pepper and garlic and fry until soft. Stir in the flour, parsley and all the seasonings and cook over a gentle heat for 2–3 minutes. Stir in the remaining ingredients and simmer for 5–10 minutes. Keep hot.

2 Set all the filling ingredients out on separate plates.

3 Heat a little oil in a large frying pan. Take one tortilla, dip it into the hot oil for just a few seconds until it begins to blister and becomes limp. Remove and dip immediately into the hot sauce. Lay the tortilla on a plate and spread 30 ml (2 tablespoons) of the cooked vegetables, 15 ml (1 tablespoon) each of the cheese and onion and 2 strips of chilli over one half of it. Roll up and place, opening underneath, in a baking dish. Place in a warm oven. Repeat with remaining ingredients.

4 Pour any remaining hot sauce over the enchiladas making sure the tortillas are coated and do not dry out.

5 Place in a 190°C (375°F) mark 5 oven and bake for about 10–15 minutes to heat through. Serve immediately.

VARIATIONS: Add a little grated Parmesan cheese to the spicy sauce before baking the enchiladas in the oven and bake for 20–25 minutes or until golden brown and bubbling. Serve at once.

The great variety of tortillas, tacos, enchiladas, flautas, quesadillas and chimichangas from Mexico can only be matched by the equally numerous savoury pastries of India. A few are included, but many have been left out due only to shortage of space — I am thinking particularly of samosas, bhajis, dosas and others. However, I hope the two recipes I have chosen will compensate for the omission of the others.

pakoras

vegetable-filled fritters

Pakoras are a favourite tea-time snack all over the Indian subcontinent. They can be prepared with a great variety of vegetables such as cauliflower, potatoes, green chillies and mushrooms. Chicken, cheese and even hard-boiled eggs can be prepared in the same way.

They are easy to prepare, cheap and convenient, for you can part-fry them in advance so that the batter is cooked but not browned, then drain them and set aside until ready to serve, when you can refry them until crisp and golden. Gram flour (*besan*) can be bought at any Indian grocery store.

Batter
175 g (6 oz) gram flour
5 ml (1 teaspoon) baking powder
7.5 ml (1^1/$_2$ teaspoons) salt
2.5 ml (^{1}/$_2$ teaspoon) chilli powder
2.5 ml (^{1}/$_2$ teaspoon) garam masala (see Glossary)
2.5 ml (^{1}/$_2$ teaspoon) dried mint
about 200 ml (^{1}/$_3$ pint) cold water

Filling
about 700 g (1^1/$_2$ lb) mixed vegetables such as potatoes,
onions, cauliflower, aubergines, mushrooms,
prepared as indicated below
oil, for frying

1 First prepare the batter. Sift the gram flour, baking powder and salt into a large mixing bowl. Add the chilli powder and garam masala. Rub the dried mint between your palms and add to the bowl. Mix all the ingredients together well. Slowly add the water, beating constantly until you have a smooth batter. Set aside while you prepare the vegetables.

2 Prepare the vegetables.

POTATOES: peel, cut into 1 cm (^{1}/$_2$ inch) thick slices and soak in cold water until ready to use. Drain and dry with kitchen paper.

ONIONS: peel and cut into 1 cm ($^1/_2$ inch) thick rounds, but do not separate into rings.

CAULIFLOWER: break into florets. If they are thick cut lengthways into halves or they will not cook through.

AUBERGINES: cut into 1 cm ($^1/_2$ inch) rounds and soak in water with the juice of $^1/_2$ lemon until ready to use. Drain and dry with kitchen paper.

MUSHROOMS: wipe clean and peel if you wish.

3 Heat enough oil in a pan to deep-fry.

4 Beat the batter again for a further minute, then dip a few vegetable pieces into the batter to coat thoroughly. Add carefully to the hot oil and fry for 4–5 minutes, turning carefully until golden on all sides. Do not fry too quickly or the vegetables will not be cooked through. Remove with a slotted spoon, drain on kitchen paper and keep hot while you fry the remaining vegetables in the same way.

sangara

indian savoury pastries

This savoury uses a potato filling. It is similar to the better-known samosa pastries, which are traditionally filled with minced meat.

In this recipe *panch phora* is used. This is a mixture of spices that can be bought from all Indian shops and most large food stores. To prepare it place 25 ml (1^1/$_2$ tablespoons) each of black mustard seeds, cumin seeds and black cumin seeds and 7.5 ml (1^1/$_2$ teaspoons) each fenugreek seeds and fennel seeds into a screw-top jar and shut tightly. Store until needed. Shake well before using. You can scale down these quantities if you wish.

Pastry
175 g (6 oz) plain flour
2.5 ml (^{1}/$_2$ teaspoon) salt
15 ml (1 tablespoon) oil
120 ml (4 fl oz) warm water
oil, for frying

Filling
225 g (8 oz) potatoes, boiled and peeled
2.5 ml (^{1}/$_2$ teaspoon) chilli powder
2.5 ml (^{1}/$_2$ teaspoon) *panch phora*
5 ml (1 teaspoon) ground cumin
5 ml (I teaspoon) salt
juice of ^{1}/$_2$ lemon

1 To prepare the pastry, sift the flour and salt into a large bowl. Add the oil and water and mix thoroughly. If the mixture is too dry add a little more water. Transfer to a floured surface and knead for 5–10 minutes or until the dough is smooth and elastic. Cover and set aside while you prepare the filling.

2 When the potatoes are cool dice them into a bowl, add the remaining ingredients and mix well.

3 To prepare the pastries divide the dough into 12 small balls and roll each one out thinly on a floured surface to form saucer-sized circles. Cut each circle in half. Place 5 ml (1 teaspoon) of filling in each half circle. Brush the edges with water, fold the dough over and press the edges together firmly. You now have triangular-shaped pastries. Use up all the dough and filling in this way.

4 Heat sufficient oil in a large pan to deep-fry and, when hot, add a few pastries at a time and fry until golden on both sides. Remove, drain on kitchen paper and keep hot while you fry the remaining pastries in the same way. Serve hot.

boreks

Borek pastries originate in the Middle East and are prepared using filo pastry (see page 198) or special pastry (Borek Hamuru, below). First make the filling of your choice (see pages 198-201), then shape and fill the pastries (see pages 202-204). Either bake, or deep-fry as indicated in Filo Pastry Borek, on the next page.

borek hamuru

homemade borek pastries

This recipe is for very soft flaky pastry traditionally used for making borek.

450 g (1 lb) plain flour
5 ml (1 teaspoon) salt
240 ml (8 fl oz) cold water
5 ml (1 teaspoon) lemon juice
50 g (2 oz) clarified butter or ghee (see Glossary), melted
225 g (8 oz) block margarine or butter, chilled
filling of your choice (see pages 198-201)

1 Sift the flour and salt into a large bowl. Make a well in the centre, add the water and lemon juice and mix thoroughly, using a wooden spoon. Add the melted fat and knead for about 10 minutes or until smooth. Shape the dough into 1 large ball, cover with a damp cloth and leave for 30 minutes.

2 Lightly flour your working surface and roll out the dough until 0.5 cm ($^1/_4$ inch) thick. Put the block of margarine or butter in the middle of the sheet of dough and fold the pastry over the fat so that it is completely enclosed. With a well-floured rolling pin, flatten the dough to a 1 cm ($^1/_2$ inch) thickness. Fold the dough in half and refrigerate for 10 minutes.

3 Roll out the dough again on the floured surface to 0.5 cm ($^1/_4$ inch) thickness. Fold in half and refrigerate for a further 10 minutes.

4 Keeping the work surface well floured roll the dough out once more as thinly as possible. Cut into 7.5-10 cm (3-4 inch) squares or circles,

5 Put 5-10 ml (1-2 teaspoonfuls) of filling in one half of each shape. Dampen the edges with cold water and fold over to make rectangles or semi-circles. Seal the edges with your fingertips or a fork. Arrange on a greased baking tray and brush with a little beaten egg. Bake in a 180°C (350°F) mark 4 oven for 20-30 minutes or until puffed and golden.

filo pastry borek

If you wish to use filo pastry then follow the instructions below. See also Glossary. Commercial filo pastry sheets are usually about 50 X 30 cm (20 X 12 inches). Cut each sheet into 4 pieces measuring 25 X 15 cm (10 X 6 inches), then shape into triangles, fingers or squares (see pages 202-204).

1 packet (450 g/1 lb) filo pastry

125 g (4 oz) butter, melted
filling of your choice (see pages 198-201)

1 When preparing the borek use 1 sheet of pastry at a time and keep the others covered with a damp cloth or they will dry out and go crumbly.

2 For baked borek: Arrange on greased baking sheets and brush the top of each with any remaining melted butter. Bake in a 190°C (375°F) mark 5 oven for about 20 minutes or until golden.

VARIATION: Deep-fry in moderately hot oil until golden and then drain.

cheese filling

450 g (1 lb) cheese: haloumi, feta (see Glossary), Cheddar,
Gruyère or a mixture, grated
2 eggs, beaten
45 ml (3 tablespoons) finely chopped parsley
2.5 ml ($1/2$ teaspoon) black pepper
salt to taste

Mix all the ingredients together, taste and adjust seasoning, if necessary.

spinach filling

450 g (1 lb) fresh spinach, coarse stems and leaves discarded
30 ml (2 tablespoons) oil
1 onion, finely chopped
30 ml (2 tablespoons) pine kernels or chopped walnuts
30 ml (2 tablespoons) raisins
5 ml (1 teaspoon) salt
2.5 ml ($^{1}/_{2}$ teaspoon) black pepper
2.5 ml ($^{1}/_{2}$ teaspoon) allspice

1 Wash the spinach very thoroughly under cold running water and then drain. Chop coarsely, place in a large saucepan and cook over a low heat for about 10 minutes or until it wilts. Drain in a colander and, with the back of a spoon, squeeze out as much of the liquid as possible.

2 Heat the oil in a large saucepan, add the onion and fry for several minutes until soft, stirring occasionally. Add the cooked spinach and all the remaining ingredients and mix thoroughly. Set aside to cool.

VARIATION: Fry the nuts in the oil until golden before adding to the mixture.

courgette filling

450 g (1 lb) courgettes, peeled and grated
2 eggs, beaten
150 g (5 oz) feta (see Glossary), Cheddar or
Gruyère cheese, grated
1.25 ml ($^{1}/_{2}$ teaspoon) black pepper
5 ml (1 teaspoon) dried mint
salt

Place the grated courgettes in a fine sieve and squeeze out as much of the water content as possible. Place the pulp in a bowl, add the remaining ingredients and mix well.

aubergine filling

450 g (1 lb) aubergines, cut into 1 cm ($^1/_2$ inch) cubes
12.5 ml (2$^1/_2$ teaspoons) salt
60 ml (4 tablespoons) oil
2 onions, finely chopped
2 large tomatoes, blanched, peeled and chopped
2.5 ml ($^1/_2$ teaspoon) allspice
2.5 ml ($^1/_2$ teaspoon) black pepper
2.5 ml ($^1/_2$ teaspoon) chilli powder
30 ml (2 tablespoons) finely chopped parsley or fresh mint

1 Place the aubergine cubes in a colander, sprinkle with 10 ml (2 teaspoons) salt and set aside for 30 minutes. Rinse under cold running water, drain and pat dry with kitchen paper.

2 Heat the oil in a large saucepan, add the onions and fry until soft. Add the aubergines and fry, stirring frequently, until soft. Add a little more oil, if necessary. Add all the remaining ingredients, mix well and simmer until the vegetables are very soft. Mash with a fork and set aside to cool. When cold, pour off any excess oil.

onion and tomato filling

30 ml (2 tablespoons) *smen* (see Glossary) or butter
3 large onions, chopped
3 large ripe tomatoes, blanched, peeled and coarsely chopped
5 ml (1 teaspoon) harissa (see page 230)
5 ml (I teaspoon) salt
2.5 ml ($^1/_2$ teaspoon) ground cumin

Heat the *smen* or butter in a saucepan, add the onions and fry, stirring frequently, until soft and transparent. Stir in the remaining ingredients and cook gently for a further 5–10 minutes, stirring occasionally. Set aside to cool.

potato filling

350 g (12 oz) potatoes, peeled and cubed
2 eggs
30 ml (2 tablespoons) oil
1 onion, finely chopped
2-3 garlic cloves, chopped
5 ml (1 teaspoon) salt
1.25 ml (^{1}/$_4$ teaspoon) black pepper
60 ml (4 tablespoons) finely chopped parsley

1 Place the potatoes in a saucepan with 1 of the eggs and cover with boiling water. Simmer until the potatoes are tender. Drain, remove the egg and mash the potatoes.

2 Meanwhile, heat the oil in a frying pan, add the onion and garlic and fry, stirring occasionally, until soft. Stir in the salt, pepper and parsley. Add the mashed potatoes, break in the remaining egg and mix thoroughly.

3 Chop the hard-boiled egg finely and stir into the filling. Set aside until cold.

rice filling

240 ml (8 fl oz) milk
150 ml (^{1}/$_4$ pint) water
75 g (3 oz) long grain rice, washed thoroughly under
cold running water and drained
25 g (1 oz) butter
2.5 ml (^{1}/$_2$ teaspoon) salt
5 ml (1 teaspoon) caster sugar
15 ml (1 tablespoon) orange flower water
30 ml (2 tablespoons) oil
50 g (2 oz) blanched almonds

Garnish
icing sugar and cinnamon

1 Pour the milk and water into a saucepan and bring to the boil. Add the rice, butter and salt, lower the heat and cook, stirring frequently, for 15 minutes. Stir in the sugar and orange flower water and cook, still stirring, for a further 8-10 minutes. Remove from the heat and leave to cool, but stir from time to time.

2 Meanwhile, heat the oil in a small pan, add the almonds and fry until golden. Remove with a slotted spoon and pulverise in a mortar or blender. Add the powdered almonds to the rice mixture and stir well.

3 To prepare and cook follow the instructions for filo pastries (see page 198). When cooked, sprinkle with icing sugar and cinnamon.

shaping borek triangles

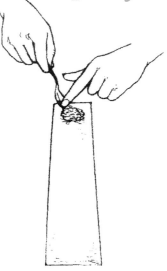

1 Place filling 2.5 cm (1 inch) from edge of pastry

2 Fold pastry diagonally across filling to form triangle. Fold again, keeping apex against outside edge.

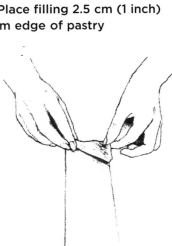

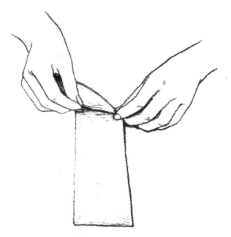

3 Fold apex diagonally to right-hand edge (keeping triangular shape).

4 Repeat folding, keeping triangular shape, until pastry is used up.

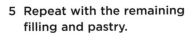

5 Repeat with the remaining filling and pastry.

shaping borek fingers

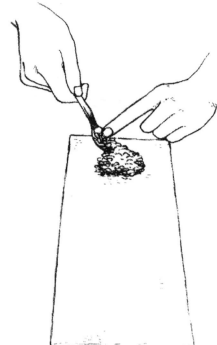

Brush pastry with melted butter, cut in 4 (12.5 x 30 cm/5 x 12 inch) pieces. Put 2 pieces on top of the other 2 to give 2 strips, each of 2 layers.

1 (left) Place 5 ml (1 tsp) filling 2.5 cm (1 inch) from edge nearest you. Spread out in thin strip. Fold pastry over filling.

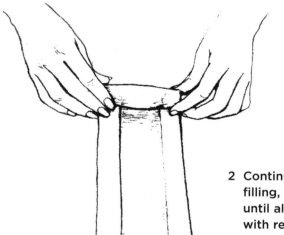

2 Continue folding pastry over filling, rolling tightly and neatly, until all pastry is used up. Repeat with remaining filling and pastry.

shaping borek squares

1 Prepare pastry strips as described on page 202 for borek triangles. Place 5 ml (l tsp) filling about 2.5 cm (1 inch) from the edge nearest you.

2 Fold the pastry over the filling to make a neat square. Make sure the filling is covered with pastry.

3 Repeat folding neatly into squares until all the pastry is used up. Repeat with remaining pastry and filling.

pampoushka

borsch dumplings

Ukrainian by origin, these dumplings are eaten with or in borsch soups and are often coated with a garlic sauce.

15 g (¹/₂ oz) yeast
10 ml (2 teaspoons) sugar
200 ml (¹/₃ pint) warm water
60 ml (4 tablespoons) melted butter or corn oil
450 g (1 lb) plain flour or buckwheat flour
5 ml (1 teaspoon) salt

Garlic sauce
2 garlic cloves, crushed
2.5 ml (¹/₂ teaspoon) salt
15 ml (1 tablespoon) oil
150 ml (¹/₄ pint) warm water or kvass (see Glossary)

1 Place the yeast, sugar and water in a large mixing bowl, stir and leave for a few minutes for the yeast to dissolve. Stir in the butter or oil. Sift in the flour, mix until well blended and then gather up in a ball and knead on a floured surface for about 10 minutes or until smooth and elastic. Place in a clean bowl, cover and set aside in a warm place for 2 hours.

2 Punch down the dough and knead for a minute or two. Keeping your hands damp take walnut-sized lumps, roll into balls and flatten slightly with the palm of your hand. Place on a greased baking tray and cook in a 180°C (350°F) mark 4 oven for 20 minutes.

3 Meanwhile, prepare the sauce by mixing the garlic, salt, oil and warm water or kvass in a small bowl. Serve the hot dumplings coated with the sauce.

fufu and friends

We have potatoes boiled, mashed, chipped, fried, roasted and in and out of their jackets. Other people have rice, cracked wheat or pasta, but in Africa there reigns supreme the *fufu* — a collective name given to stiff puddings which can be made from maize or cassava flour or from boiled yams.

Fufus always accompany soups and stews and are an integral part of the basic diet of millions of people.

The first recipe is from West Africa and is the classic *eba*. It is, in essence, a porridge of cassava grains (*garri*) and is served with soups and stews. *Garri* is sold in 450 g (1 lb) packets in Indian stores and in some whole food stores.

eba

cassava pudding

1.1 litres (2 pints) water
175 g (6 oz) *garri* (see Glossary)

1 Bring the water to the boil in a large saucepan. Stir in the *garri* and remove from the heat. Stir well and rub any lumps against the side of the pan to break them up. Allow the mixture to stand for about 10 minutes to absorb the moisture.

2 Stir thoroughly with a wooden spoon until the pudding is stiff but smooth. Serve at once.

sweet potato and yam fufu

This recipe is from Nigeria.

450 g (1 lb) yam, peeled and cut into small pieces
450 g (1 lb) sweet potatoes, peeled and cut into small pieces

1 Place the yam in a saucepan and add enough water to cover by 5 cm (2 inches). Bring to the boil and cook for about 10 minutes or until the yam begins to soften. Add the sweet potatoes and continue to cook until both vegetables are tender. Drain and pound with a pestle — the traditional method — or process in a blender, adding just enough hot water to soften, if necessary.

2 Transfer to a serving dish and, if you wish, mould the mixture into a smooth mound. Serve with soups and stews.

breadfruit chips

Popular throughout Africa, the West Indies and parts of South America, the breadfruit makes excellent chips, as indeed does the sweet potato and the plantain.

2 firm ripe breadfruit
15 ml (1 tablespoon) salt
oil, for frying

1 Peel the breadfruit and slice thinly as you would potato chips. Sprinkle with the salt and leave to rest for 5 minutes.

2 Heat sufficient oil to deep-fry, add the chips and fry until golden. Remove with a slotted spoon and drain on kitchen paper.

makote chips
plantain chips

Plantains vary in size a great deal. I suggest you allow two average plantains per person.

plantains
oil, for frying

1 Peel the plantains and halve lengthways. Cut crossways into 1 cm (¹/₂ inch) slices. Heat sufficient oil to deep-fry, add the chipped plantains and fry for 4–5 minutes or until soft and light golden.

2 Remove with a slotted spoon, drain on kitchen paper and serve immediately.

couscous

Couscous is a fine semolina made from wheat and is readily available here in packets. It is very simple to prepare.

500 g (1.1 lb) couscous grains
1.2 litres (2 pints) boiling water
75 g (3 oz) butter (preferably unsalted)

1 Spread couscous grains over a tray or baking sheet and pour over a little warm water. Work the couscous grains lightly between your fingers so that each grain is separated and moistened.

2 Drain off excess water, if any, and set aside for 15 to 20 minutes for the grains to swell.

3 Place about 1.2-1.8 litres (2 to 3 pints) of boiling water in the bottom of a steamer or saucepan. Transfer couscous grains to the top half of the steamer or sieve lined with a piece of muslin. Steam for 15 minutes, making sure that no water touches the couscous.

4 Add the butter to the couscous grains and fluff up with a fork so each grain is separate. Transfer couscous into a warm serving bowl and eat hot.

nut and pulse-based dishes

A few decades ago there were lentils (brown or yellow), broad beans, peas and a few other pulses available in our shops. Today, however, the pulse repertoire is so enriched that one is easily mesmerised at the sight of row upon row of those biodegradable cellophane bags filled with small or large, fat or thin, round or flat multicoloured pulses which, to make matters more complicated, often appear to possess several names.

Yet pulses have been around for thousands of years and are some of man's earliest agricultural achievements. They play a very large part in vegetarian and, in particular, vegan diets. Pulses are rich in B vitamins, minerals, protein and carbohydrates. They are often cooked and served with other grains, rice in particular, to make up for the limited amino acids they contain and, of course, for the extra flavour and substance. Pulses are also believed to be somewhat indigestible, hence they are used with all kinds of interesting spices, particularly asafoetida (see Glossary), which counteract the problem of flatulence.

The masters of pulse cooking are undoubtedly the people of South East Asia, particularly those who are vegetarian because of religious beliefs, in India and neighbouring lands. The Eastern Orthodox churches (Coptic, Greek and Armenian) also traditionally relied extensively on pulses during the forty days of Lent. Religion apart, pulses were and are relatively cheap, hence their popularity with the poor peoples of the world.

Nuts such as peanuts, almonds, pistachios, walnuts and other seeds are often used with pulses, thus giving the dishes extra protein, vitamins and texture. Some pulses are ground into a thick paste, made into dumplings and fried, or ground into flour and used to make a batter for frying vegetables or for making into sweetmeats such as the multifarious halvas of the Indo-Pakistani cuisines.

I have refrained, as far as possible, from dishes using rice and pulses together, since grains in general are outside the scope of this book. However, I have included several maize (corn) and pulse recipes, for these are generally little known by us and yet they play a major role in the lives of millions of African and Caribbean people.

For our first recipe we go to Egypt, to a dish that has come down to us unchanged from the days of the Pharaohs.

ta'amia or falafel

egyptian chickpea rissoles

These are served from little stalls on every street corner throughout Egypt's large and small towns. It was and is the food of the people — the fish and chips, the hot-dog or burger of the *fellahine*. It is usually served with slices of tomato and shredded lettuce inside pita bread. *Ta'amia* is also eaten for breakfast, lunch or supper with some *ful medames*, bread, pickles and salads.

Some people substitute dried fava beans for the chickpeas. These are soaked overnight in water, drained and rubbed between the palms to loosen the skin before proceeding with the main preparation.

This recipe is one from my restaurants' and tends to be slightly richer, both in content and flavour, than its Egyptian street corner version.

450 g (1 lb) chickpeas, cooked (see Glossary)
90 ml (3 fl oz) water
1 egg, lightly beaten
5 ml (1 teaspoon) salt
2.5 ml ($^1/_2$ teaspoon) black pepper
2.5 ml ($^1/_2$ teaspoon) turmeric
30 ml (2 tablespoons) chopped fresh coriander leaves
1.25 ml ($^1/_4$ teaspoon) ground cumin
1.25 ml ($^1/_4$ teaspoon) chilli powder
1 garlic clove, crushed
15 ml (1 tablespoon) tahini paste (see Glossary) or olive oil
50 g (2 oz) fresh white breadcrumbs
50 g (2 oz) flour
oil, for frying

1 Put the chickpeas through a mincer twice into a large mixing bowl. Add the water, egg, salt, pepper, turmeric, coriander, cumin, chilli powder, garlic, tahini paste or olive oil and the breadcrumbs. With your hands combine all the ingredients into a soft but firm mixture. Form the mixture into 2.5 cm (1 inch) balls, flatten slightly between your palms and coat with flour.

2 Heat enough oil in a large saucepan to deep-fry and, when hot, add a few of the rissoles and fry for 2–3 minutes or until they are lightly browned. Remove them from the oil with a slotted spoon, and drain on kitchen paper while you fry the remainder. Serve hot.

el-ful (ful medames)
egyptian brown beans

Also from Egypt comes *el-ful* or *ful medames* — a garlicky mixture of brown beans with olive oil, lemon juice and spices. Together with *ta'amia*, *el-ful* has been the food of Egypt for millennia, so much so that Egyptians call themselves 'the children of *el-ful*'. In southern Egypt and the Sudan hard-boiled eggs are included to give this dish added substance.

I recall in my childhood in Syria how, on my way to school every morning, I used to queue for soup made with *ful* beans and a lot of garlic. The cost was a ha'penny and the result a refreshing, awakening feeling which made the rest of the day at school less tiresome and weary — such is the magical effect of *el-ful*.

700 g (1¹/₂ lb) Egyptian brown beans, soaked
overnight in cold water and drained
3 garlic cloves, crushed
30 ml (2 tablespoons) olive oil
juice of 2 lemons
5 ml (1 teaspoon) salt
2.5 ml (¹/₂ teaspoon) black pepper

Garnish
6 hard-boiled eggs, shelled
30 ml (2 tablespoons) finely chopped parsley

1 Put the beans in an ovenproof casserole, cover with water and bring to the boil. Cover the casserole and place in a 120°C (250°F) mark ¹/₂ oven for 4–7 hours, depending on the quality of the beans. At the end of the cooking time the beans should be soft but still whole. Drain the cooking liquid and discard.

2 Stir the garlic, oil, lemon juice, salt and pepper into the beans and then spoon the mixture into soup bowls. Place 1 hard-boiled egg in the centre of each and sprinkle with a little parsley. Serve immediately.

gigantes plaki

butter beans with tomatoes

Still from the Middle East this Greek recipe also appears throughout Turkey, Armenia and the Balkans. It is a very tasty and nourishing dish. Serve with pita bread, pickles and a salad.

What a pleasure.
What a pleasure.
What a delight to me —
As I roast the peas and chestnuts
In the embers all night.
Peace — Aristophanes

450 g (1 lb) butter beans, soaked overnight in cold water and drained
300 ml (1/2 pint) olive oil
2 onions, chopped
450 g (1 lb) ripe tomatoes, blanched, peeled and coarsely chopped
3 carrots, peeled and diced
45 ml (3 tablespoons) finely chopped parsley
7.5 ml (1 1/2 teaspoons) salt
2.5 ml (1/2 teaspoon) black pepper

Garnish
paprika

1 Half fill a large saucepan with water and bring to the boil. Add the drained beans, lower the heat, cover the pan and simmer for 10 minutes. Drain in a colander.

2 Heat the oil in the saucepan, add the onions and fry until soft and golden. Return the beans to the pan and add all the remaining ingredients. Pour in sufficient water to cover and bring to the boil. Lower the heat, cover the pan and simmer gently until the beans are tender and the water has evaporated. Serve warm or cold garnished with a good pinch of paprika.

baghala ba esfanaj

broad beans with spinach

This recipe from Iran is both simple and delicious.

450 g (1 lb) shelled fresh or frozen broad beans
or 225 g (8 oz) dried broad beans, soaked
overnight in cold water and drained
700 g (1½ lb) fresh spinach, Swiss chard or lettuce, washed thoroughly
10–12 small pearl onions, or spring onions, white part only
90 ml (6 tablespoons) finely chopped parsley
15 ml (1 tablespoon) fresh thyme or 5 ml (1 teaspoon) dried thyme
45 ml (3 tablespoons) chopped fresh dill or
15 ml (1 tablespoon) dried dillweed
10–12 dates, sliced
7.5 ml (1½ teaspoons) salt
2.5 ml (½ teaspoon) black pepper
30 ml (2 tablespoons) pistachio nuts, toasted and coarsely chopped
50 g (2 oz) melted butter

1 If using dried beans cook them in a pan of boiling water for about 1½ hours or until tender, adding more boiling water if necessary. Drain and, when cool enough to handle, remove the thin skin from each bean. If using fresh beans remove the transparent skin of each one.

2 Shake excess moisture off the spinach and chop. Place it in a large saucepan with the beans, onions, parsley, thyme, dill, dates, salt and pepper. Mix well, cover the pan and cook over low heat for 20–30 minutes or until the vegetables are tender.

3 Remove from the heat, gently stir in the pistachio nuts and spoon the mixture into a serving dish. It can be eaten hot or cold, but either way pour the melted butter over and toss gently just before serving.

nvig

chickpeas with spinach

Next door to Iran, in Armenia, they prepare this dish during the 40 days of Lent.

175 g (6 oz) chickpeas, soaked overnight in cold water and drained
700 g (1¹/₂ lb) fresh spinach, washed
thoroughly under cold running water
300 ml (¹/₂ pint) water
60 ml (4 tablespoons) tomato purée
50 ml (2 fl oz) oil
10 ml (2 teaspoons) salt
5 ml (1 teaspoon) sugar
2.5 ml (¹/₂ teaspoon) black pepper
15 ml (1 tablespoon) ground cumin

1 Half fill a saucepan with water, bring to the boil and add the chickpeas. Lower the heat and simmer for 1–1¹/₂ hours or until the chickpeas are just tender. Add more boiling water if necessary. Drain and leave until cool enough to handle. Now remove the chickpea skins. The easiest way to do this is to hold a chickpea between thumb and forefinger and squeeze the pea from the skin.

2 Shake excess moisture from the spinach and chop. Place in a large saucepan with the chickpeas and all the remaining ingredients. Mix well and bring to the boil. Lower the heat, cover the pan and simmer for about 30 minutes or until the spinach and chickpeas are really tender and the water has evaporated. Cool and chill before serving.

kulikuli

fried groundnut balls

'It is not for the meat
But for the sport of that we hunt.
If you think we are out for meat
We will go back!
Meat is something you find at home or at the butchers.'
Hausa folk song

If you are a peanut lover, then this recipe is the answer to your dreams (but personally I find it a little too strongly flavoured).

This dish from Nigeria is a traditional speciality of the powerful Hausa tribe. The groundnuts (peanuts) are ground to a powder, formed into balls and fried. For this dish you need roasted peanuts, but not the ones that have been fried in oil and/or salted. You can buy plain roasted peanuts in some shops, but if you cannot find them, then it is easy to roast your own. Put the plain kernels in a 180°C (350°F) mark 4 oven for about 30 minutes, shaking the baking sheet occasionally to turn them. When cool enough to handle, rub off the dark red skins and discard. Alternatively, you can dry-fry them in a frying pan.

Kulikuli are traditionally eaten on their own or with fresh coconut or *garri* (see Glossary). However, a bowl of fresh salad and pickles and yogurt also make excellent accompaniments.

900 g (2 lb) roasted peanuts
about 120 ml (4 fl oz) warm water
5 ml (1 teaspoon) salt
a little groundnut oil, if necessary

1 Put the peanuts in a blender and grind to a powder. Place in a bowl and mould into a ball. By kneading and squeezing extract and reserve as much oil as possible (adding a little warm water from time to time helps to bring the oil out). You may have to knead for at least 30–40 minutes.

2 When you have extracted as much oil as possible, add the salt and a little more water, if necessary, and knead until the mixture is firm, but pliable.

3 Take walnut-sized lumps, roll into balls and then flatten slightly between your palms. Heat extracted oil (add a little more groundnut oil, if necessary), and add a few of the *kulikuli*. Fry until golden. Repeat with the remaining *kulikuli*.

keshewa narial ki dudh

cashew nuts in coconut milk

This recipe from central India needs no apology, it speaks for itself. Although cashew nuts are expensive this is a truly delicious dish which would make a good vegan meal when served with a rice or burghul pilav and a salad. For this recipe use raw cashew nuts and not the salted variety.

5 spring onions or 1 medium onion, thinly sliced
2 garlic cloves, crushed
2.5 cm (1 inch) fresh ginger, peeled and finely chopped
2 green chillies, seeded and thinly sliced
7.5 ml (1^1/$_2$ teaspoons) turmeric
5 cm (2 inch) cinnamon stick
3 cardamom pods
3 bay leaves
10 ml (2 teaspoons) salt
300 ml (^{1}/$_2$ pint) water
450 ml (^{3}/$_4$ pint) coconut milk (see Glossary)
350 g (12 oz) cashew nuts

1 Place all the ingredients except the coconut milk and cashew nuts in a saucepan, cover and simmer over a low heat for 5 minutes. Stir in the coconut milk and cashew nuts, cover and simmer for 15–20 minutes, stirring occasionally.

2 Transfer to a serving dish, discard the bay leaves and cinnamon stick and serve.

moros y cristianos

moors and christians

This is another Cuban speciality which also appears throughout the region. It bears this strangely implicit name. The Moors I assume are the black beans and the Christians are the white rice — quaint but racist.

225 g (8 oz) black beans, soaked overnight
in cold water and drained
60 ml (4 tablespoons) oil
1 large onion, finely chopped
2 garlic cloves, crushed
1 red or green pepper, finely chopped
3 large tomatoes, blanched, peeled and chopped
7.5 ml (1^1/$_2$ teaspoons) salt
2.5 ml (^{1}/$_2$ teaspoon) black pepper
175 g (6 oz) long grain rice, washed thoroughly
under cold water and drained
450 ml (^{3}/$_4$ pint) boiling water

Garnish
6 fried or hard-boiled eggs
plantain or breadfruit chips (see page 207)

1 Half fill a saucepan with water and bring to the boil. Add the beans, lower the heat and simmer for 30–45 minutes or until tender. Drain.

2 Meanwhile, heat the oil in a large saucepan, add the onion and fry, stirring occasionally, until soft. Add the garlic and pepper and fry for a further 2–3 minutes. Stir in the tomatoes, salt and pepper and simmer, covered, until the tomatoes are reduced to a pulp.

3 Stir in the cooked beans, rice and water, cover the pan and simmer for about 20 minutes or until the rice is tender and the water absorbed. Serve hot or cold with garnishes.

Generally, pulses are very poorly represented in Europe. The Scandinavian cuisines are particularly impoverished, while their Slavonic neighbours are satisfied with lentils, which they mix with fried onions and a little salt. Farther south towards the Mediterranean several filling dishes appear which, directly or indirectly, reveal Middle Eastern or North African influences. However, most of the Franco-Spanish pulse dishes are not relevant because of their emphatic reliance on pork or beef.

From this vast pulseless sea there stand, tall and proud, a few remarkable dishes. One such island of simple contentment is *bruna bönor* — a well-loved traditional dish from Sweden.

bruna bönor

brown beans

350 g (12 oz) red kidney beans, soaked overnight in 1.1 litres (2 pints) water
10 ml (2 teaspoons) salt
45 ml (3 tablespoons) wine vinegar
45 ml (3 level tablespoons) black treacle or 75 g (3 oz) dark brown sugar

1 Place the beans and their soaking water in a saucepan and bring to the boil. Lower the heat, cover the pan and simmer for about 1½–2 hours or until just tender.

2 Stir in the salt, vinegar and treacle or sugar, cover and simmer for another hour. Top up with a little more boiling water, if necessary. Serve hot.

In Britain we have the children's (and many grown-ups' too) favourite — baked beans. It is a pleasant enough dish when prepared at home, but cheapened when served straight from the tin.

European immigrants to the Americas took with them their ancestral foods. Two of these were the *bruna bönor* of Scandinavia and baked beans of England. Today they are an integral part of American cookery and pass themselves off as Boston baked beans or Cowboy beans.

Pork appears to have a great affinity to baked bean dishes. There are scores of such recipes where pork or bacon are incorporated in the dish. In Mexico it can safely be said that no meal is complete without beans. Perhaps the most famous Mexican-inspired dish is chilli con carne, which is closely followed by the numerous *frijoles*-based dishes. Now *frijoles* in Mexico (and in Cuba) simply means beans — any kind of beans. They are cooked with onions, garlic, fat and salt until very tender and then either eaten as they are or mashed, topped with crumbled cheese and eaten with tortillas (see page 191)

baked beans

'No more will I eat cold pudding,
No more will I eat hard bread,
No more will I eat that half-baked bean
For I vow, they're killing me dead.'
The Factory Girls — Anon

450 g (1 lb) haricot beans, soaked overnight in cold water
and drained
1 bouquet garni
60 ml (4 tablespoons) oil
450 g (1 lb) onions, chopped
2 garlic cloves, crushed
5 ml (1 teaspoon) paprika
900 g (2 lb) tomatoes, blanched and
peeled or 2 x 400 g (14 oz) cans tomatoes
60 ml (4 tablespoons) tomato purée
450 ml ($^3/_4$ pint) water
15 ml (1 tablespoon) brown sugar
10 ml (2 teaspoons) Worcestershire sauce
7.5 ml ($1^1/_2$ teaspoons) salt
1.25 ml ($^1/_4$ teaspoon) black pepper

1 Half fill a large saucepan with water and bring to the boil. Add the beans and bouquet garni, lower the heat and simmer for about 1 hour or until the beans are just tender. Add a little more boiling water, if necessary.

2 Meanwhile, heat the oil in a large saucepan, add the onion and fry, stirring frequently, until soft. Stir in the garlic and paprika and fry for a further 2 minutes. Add the tomatoes and crush with a wooden spoon. Stir in the remaining ingredients.

3 When the beans are tender drain them, discard the bouquet garni and add to the tomato sauce. Stir well and simmer for about 30 minutes or until the liquid is reduced and the beans coated with the sauce. Adjust seasoning to taste. Serve hot.

frijoles negros pascuales

festive black beans

Cubans have a particular association with beans and bean dishes into which they have poured a great deal of love and imagination. This recipe was traditionally served during Easter and other holidays.

Serve, Cuban style, with a bowl of *Salsa roja para frijoles negros* (page 236).

450 g (1 lb) black beans, soaked
overnight in cold water and drained
300 ml ($^{1}/_{2}$ pint) oil
1 onion, finely chopped
2–3 garlic cloves, crushed
2 small hot chillies, seeded and thinly sliced
2.5 ml ($^{1}/_{2}$ teaspoon) thyme
5 ml (1 teaspoon) ground cumin
2 bay leaves
7.5 ml (1$^{1}/_{2}$ teaspoons) salt
60 ml (4 tablespoons) wine vinegar
2 large red peppers, seeded and cut into 0.5 cm ($^{1}/_{4}$ inch) cubes
15 ml (1 tablespoon) brown sugar

1 Half fill a large saucepan with water and bring to the boil. Add the beans, lower the heat and simmer for 30–45 minutes or until the beans are tender. Drain.

2 Meanwhile, heat the oil in a large saucepan, add the onion and fry, stirring frequently, until soft. Add the garlic, chillies, thyme, cumin, bay leaves and salt and fry for 2–3 more minutes. Add the beans, vinegar, red peppers and sugar and stir gently but thoroughly. Cook over a low heat, stirring occasionally, for 15–20 minutes.

Back in Africa people continued to live and eat as they had done for generations. This recipe for maize, kidney beans and plantains is a good example of that simple but nourishing African cuisine which, unfortunately, is little known outside the continent.

irio

maize with beans and plantains

Corn, as well as other crops, was commercially introduced to Africa by European farmers who saw a great deal of wealth waiting to be exploited in the virgin soil. This Kenyan recipe is typical of many.

900 g (2 lb) sweetcorn kernels, fresh or frozen or 8 corn-on-the cob
450 g (1 lb) French beans, stringed, topped and tailed
and cut into 1 cm ($^1/_2$ inch) pieces
900 g (2 lb) potatoes or sweet potatoes, peeled and
cut into 5 cm (2 inch) cubes
4 plantains, peeled and quartered
1.1 litres (2 pints) water
45 ml (3 tablespoons) margarine
10 ml (2 teaspoons) salt
5 ml (1 teaspoon) paprika
30 ml (2 tablespoons) finely chopped parsley

1 If using corn-on-the-cob first boil them for 20–30 minutes or until tender and then scrape off the kernels and place in a large saucepan. If using frozen corn then simply thaw and place in a large saucepan. Add the beans, potatoes, plantains and water and bring to the boil. Lower the heat, cover the pan and simmer until all the vegetables are very soft and the water has evaporated.

2 Stir in the margarine, salt and paprika and cook over a low heat for 10 more minutes, stirring frequently. Mash the mixture thoroughly with a fork and then spoon into a serving dish.

3 Garnish with the parsley and serve warm with pepper sauce (see page 222) or with *Salsa romesco* (see page 229) or *Salsa roja para frijoles negros* (see page 236).

egbo

cornmeal with hot pepper sauce

Makes no difference what you eat
Whether rice or grains or meat
All the flavah she an los'
Less you got some pepper sauce.
When yo pass by this a-way
Keep alis'nin' to mah call
Pure Jamaica pepper sauce!
Fresh red pepper sauce!
Dats' als!
The Pepper Song
Negro Folk Lore

The song is from the West Indies, the recipe from Nigeria and in between lie
thousands of miles of water and centuries of suffering.

Serve with pickles, bread and salads.

450 g (1 lb) cornmeal soaked overnight in cold water
600 ml (1 pint) water

Pepper sauce
180 ml (6 fl oz) oil
3 medium chillies, finely chopped
6 green peppers, finely chopped
4 large tomatoes, blanched, peeled and chopped
1 large onion, finely chopped
7.5 ml (1 1/2 teaspoons) salt
5 ml (1 teaspoon) chilli powder
3 spring onions, finely chopped

1 Drain and rinse the cornmeal, place in a saucepan with the water and bring to the
boil. Lower the heat, cover the pan and simmer for 5–6 minutes, or until the cornmeal
is soft. Add a little more water if necessary. When cooked stir well with a wooden
spoon and mash as you stir.

2 Meanwhile, prepare the sauce by heating the oil in a saucepan. Add all the
ingredients except the spring onions and cook over a gentle heat for 20–30 minutes
or until soft. Stir in the spring onions for the last 5 minutes.

3 Serve the hot cornmeal with the pepper sauce spooned over it.

porotos granados

lima beans with maize and pumpkin

Serve with bread, sweet potatoes, fried breadfruit or salads.

225 g (8 oz) lima or cannellini beans, soaked overnight
in cold water and drained
50 ml (2 fl oz) oil
1 large onion, finely chopped
30 ml (2 tablespoons) paprika
2 chillies, seeded and finely chopped
225 g (8 oz) sweetcorn kernels
450 g (1 lb) pumpkin, marrow, courgettes or gourd,
cut into 2.5 cm (1 inch) pieces
450 g (1 lb) tomatoes, blanched, peeled and coarsely chopped
2.5 ml (¹/₂ teaspoon) thyme or oregano
10 ml (2 teaspoons) salt
2.5 ml (¹/₂ teaspoon) black pepper

1 Place the beans in a pan half filled with boiling water and simmer, covered, for about 60 minutes or until tender. Drain.

2 Meanwhile, heat the oil in a large pan, add the onion and fry for about 5 minutes or until soft. Stir in all the remaining ingredients and cook over a low heat for about 10 minutes, stirring gently from time to time.

3 Stir in the beans and cook gently for a further 10 minutes. Add a little water if the mixture is too dry.

shiro wot

groundnuts with vegetables

This recipe comes from Ethiopia, which is perhaps the most ancient and unintegrated civilisation within the African continent.

Wot is the national dish of Ethiopia. In essence it is a sauce to which various ingredients are added. The recipe below is for groundnuts (peanuts) with vegetables. There is a definite similarity with the food of India in the clever use of spices and herbs.

The Ethiopian Coptic Church is extremely harsh when it comes to the matter of fasting. On average the Ethiopian fasts for 165 days of the year (the clergy manage 250 days). During fast days no one is permitted to eat meat, butter, eggs or milk, but has to survive on cereals and pulses.

Serve with bread or rice.

50 ml (2 fl oz) groundnut oil
1 large onion, finely chopped
15 ml (1 tablespoon) tomato purée
600 ml (1 pint) water
2 medium aubergines, cut crossways into 2 cm ($^3/_4$ inch) slices
225 g (8 oz) small firm okra, stems trimmed
2.5 ml ($^1/_2$ teaspoon) cayenne pepper
1.25 ml ($^1/_4$ teaspoon) ground fenugreek
5 ml (1 teaspoon) salt
2.5 ml ($^1/_2$ teaspoon) black pepper
225 g (8 oz) groundnuts (peanuts), shelled and ground

1 Heat the oil in a large saucepan, add the onion and fry for about 5 minutes or until soft. Add all the remaining ingredients except the groundnuts, mix well and bring to the boil. Lower the heat, cover the pan and simmer for about 30 minutes or until the vegetables are tender.

2 Carefully stir in the groundnuts and simmer for 10 minutes. Remove from the heat and transfer to a serving dish.

beah yaw

burmese split pea rissoles

Compare this typically Burmese speciality with the Egyptian *Ta'amia* (page 210) and I'm sure you'll agree with two of my basic premises that man is an extremely innovative animal and that the finest things in life are usually the simplest.

Serve with lemon wedges, onion and radish slices, and bread.

225 g (8 oz) split peas, soaked overnight in cold water
2 large onions, finely chopped
3 fresh chillies, seeded and finely chopped
2.5 ml ($^1/_2$ teaspoon) turmeric
5 ml (1 teaspoon) salt
30 ml (2 tablespoons) sesame seeds

Garnish
lemon wedges, onion slices and white radish slices

1 Drain the split peas and grind to a paste in a blender. If necessary add just 15–30 ml (1–2 tablespoons) water to ease the process. Transfer to a bowl and add all the remaining ingredients. Mix thoroughly.

2 Keeping your hands damp take walnut-sized lumps, roll into balls and then flatten between your palms until 1 cm ($^1/_2$ inch) thick.

3 Heat enough oil to deep-fry, add a few of the rissoles and fry for a few minutes until cooked through and golden brown. Remove with a slotted spoon and drain on kitchen paper. Keep warm while you cook the remaining rissoles in the same way.

chanda kidal narjal ki dudh

red lentils in coconut milk

Now we move on to the vast Indo-Pakistani subcontinent, where some of the finest and most extraordinarily imaginative pulse and nut dishes have evolved over the centuries. This is a tasty lentil purée which is served with bread or rice.

75 ml (5 tablespoons) ghee (see Glossary) or oil
3 medium onions, thinly sliced
4 dry red chillies or 10 ml (2 teaspoons) cayenne pepper or to taste
4 garlic cloves
7.5 ml (1^1/$_2$ teaspoons) cumin seeds
350 g (12 oz) red lentils, washed and soaked in cold water for 2–3 hours
600 ml (1 pint) water
10 ml (2 teaspoons) salt
150 ml (^{1}/$_4$ pint) coconut milk (see Glossary)
45 ml (3 tablespoons) malt vinegar
25 ml (1^1/$_2$ tablespoons) brown sugar

1 Heat 60 ml (4 tablespoons) of the ghee or oil in a saucepan and fry the onions, stirring occasionally, for 5–7 minutes or until soft and just beginning to turn golden.

2 Meanwhile, place the dry chillies or cayenne pepper in a mortar with the garlic and cumin seeds and grind with a pestle.

3 When the onions are ready, remove and reserve 15 ml (1 tablespoonful) to use as a garnish. Add the chilli mixture to the pan and fry, stirring frequently, for 3–4 minutes. If it becomes too dry add a little water.

4 Drain the lentils and add to the pan together with the water and salt. Stir well and bring to the boil. Lower the heat, cover the pan and simmer for about 20 minutes or until the lentils are tender. Add a little more water, if necessary.

5 Stir in the coconut milk, cover the pan and simmer for a further 15–20 minutes.

6 Either rub the mixture through a sieve with the back of a wooden spoon or purée in a blender. Return the purée to the pan, stir in the vinegar and sugar and gently reheat.

7 Meanwhile, heat the remaining ghee or oil in a small pan, add the reserved onions and heat through.

8 Spoon the purée into a serving dish and pour the contents of the small pan over it.

dressings, sauces and stocks

'Every cook makes his sauce'
French proverb

John Evelyn, in his *Acetaria*, gives a salad dressing which is very much like the classic French vinaigrette.

He suggests we mix 150 ml (¼ pint) olive oil with 15 ml (1 tablespoon) lemon juice or vinegar, a few slices of horseradish (to marinate in this mixture for a short time) and, of course, salt and pepper to taste. In France they prefer oil mixed with vinegar, in the southern Mediterranean it is oil with lemon juice. In the Indian subcontinent vegetables are dressed with salt and lemon or lime juice; in the Far East soy sauce is mixed with sesame oil; in the Americas all kinds of juices — orange, lemon and tomato — are combined with oil, while in Africa lemon juice is preferred to vinegar.

'To make a good salad dressing it takes a miser to decide the proportion of vinegar, a prodigal that of the oil, a sage to determine the quantity of salt and a mad man to beat up the whole lot together' — in short this Angolan adage implies as little use of vinegar as possible!

The simplest and most popular dressing is vinaigrette. I have also added a few variations worth experimenting with to make your own salads more interesting and tasty.

vinaigrette

french dressing

90 ml (6 tablespoons) olive oil
30 ml (2 tablespoons) wine vinegar
2.5 ml (¹/₂ teaspoon) salt
1.25 ml (¹/₄ teaspoon) black pepper

Place all the ingredients in a screw-top jar and shake vigorously. Makes about 150 ml (¹/₄ pint).

VARIATIONS: Add 1 crushed garlic clove or 15–30 ml (1–2 tablespoons) finely chopped spring onion or finely chopped herbs of your choice such as parsley, chives, tarragon, basil or dill.

saus kacang

peanut sauce

This classic Indonesian sauce appears throughout the cuisine in soups, as a spread on bread and in stews.

45 ml (3 tablespoons) peanut oil
1 onion, finely chopped
1 garlic clove, crushed
125 g (4 oz) peanut butter
1 large dried chilli, finely chopped
juice of ¹/₂ lemon
15 ml (1 tablespoon) soy sauce
5 ml (1 teaspoon) brown sugar
2.5 ml (¹/₂ teaspoon) salt
150 ml (¹/₄ pint) thick coconut milk (see Glossary)

1 Heat the oil in a frying pan, add the onion and garlic and fry, stirring frequently, for 3-4 minutes. Add the peanut butter, chilli, lemon juice, soy sauce, sugar and salt, stir well and cook over a low heat until the peanut butter is well blended.

2 Gradually stir in the coconut milk and cook, stirring constantly, for 2 minutes. Remove from the heat and use as required.

salsa romesco

spanish chilli sauce

A very popular sauce from Tarragona, where the small and excruciatingly hot romesco chillies are grown.

Serve with boiled or fried vegetables.

4 medium tomatoes
3 garlic cloves
about 20 hazelnuts, blanched
4 red dried chillies
5 ml (1 level teaspoon) salt
2.5 ml ($1/_2$ teaspoon) black pepper
250 ml (8 fl oz) olive oil
15 ml (1 tablespoon) dry sherry
30 ml (2 tablespoons) lemon juice

1 Put the tomatoes and garlic on a small baking tray and place in a 180°C (350°F) mark 4 oven for 15 minutes.

2 Meanwhile, roast the hazelnuts under a hot grill until evenly golden.

3 Remove the tomatoes and garlic from the oven and, when cool enough to handle, peel the tomatoes.

4 Place the tomatoes, garlic, hazelnuts and chillies in a blender and process until smooth. Transfer the purée to a bowl, add the remaining ingredients and mix thoroughly until you have a smooth sauce.

concentrated harissa

north african hot sauce

This is the sauce of Tunisia, although it appears throughout North Africa. Concentrated harissa can be bought in small tins from many continental stores.

If you wish to prepare your own here is a simple method.

225 g (8 oz) dried chillies
4 garlic cloves, peeled
45–60 ml (3–4 tablespoons) water
15 ml (1 tablespoon) ground coriander
5 ml (1 teaspoon) ground caraway
15 ml (1 tablespoon) salt

Cut the chillies in half and remove seeds and stalks. Place them in a large bowl of water and leave to soak for 30 minutes. Drain and put in a blender with the garlic and water and process to a purée. Scrape into a bowl and stir in the coriander, caraway and salt. Store in a screw-top jar and use this concentrate as instructed in relevant recipes.

harissa sauce

Harissa sauce is served with all couscous dishes. It is very hot and you will only need 30–45 ml (2–3 tablespoons) per person. However, if you feel you would like more then simply increase proportions accordingly. To make the sauce the concentrate first needs to be diluted.

30 ml (2 tablespoons) oil
1 garlic clove, crushed
15 ml (1 tablespoon) harissa
150 ml (¼ pint) water

Heat the oil in a small saucepan, add the garlic and fry for 1 minute. Add the harissa and fry for a further 1–2 minutes. Stir in the water and bring to the boil.

ebinyebwa

groundnut sauce

This sauce is popular throughout North Africa and is served with steamed or fried plantains, sweet potatoes, yams, cassavas and grains.

It has a unique, rich, earthy flavour.

175 g (6 oz) unsalted peanuts
30 ml (2 tablespoons) margarine
1 onion, finely chopped
1 large tomato, blanched, peeled and chopped
5 ml (1 teaspoon) salt
1.25 ml ($1/4$ teaspoon) black pepper
300 ml ($1/2$ pint) milk
150 ml ($1/4$ pint) water

1 Toast the peanuts under a hot grill until golden all over. Leave to cool for 10 minutes, then grind in a blender.

2 Heat the margarine in a saucepan, add the onion and fry, stirring, for 3 minutes or until soft. Add the tomato and fry for a further 3–4 minutes. Add the ground peanuts, salt and pepper and mix thoroughly.

3 Gradually add the milk, beating vigorously to avoid lumps. Stir in the water and bring to the boil. Cover the pan, lower the heat and simmer, stirring occasionally, for about 30 minutes . Serve as required.

sugo di pomodoro

tomato sauce

Tomato-based sauces and dressings are used extensively in all European, American (North and South), as well as Middle Eastern and North African cuisines.

There are, consequently, many versions. One of the simplest and best is this sauce from Italy. It is used with all types of pastas, vegetable or meat rissoles and with several recipes in this book.

You can use Italian canned tomatoes although blanched fresh tomatoes are preferable.

30 ml (2 tablespoons) oil
1 large onion, finely chopped
1 garlic clove, crushed
450 g (1 lb) tomatoes, blanched, peeled and chopped
10 ml (2 teaspoons) salt
1.25–2.5 ml ($^1/_4$–$^1/_2$ teaspoon) black pepper
2.5 ml ($^1/_2$ teaspoon) dried basil
1.25 ml ($^1/_4$ teaspoon) cinnamon

1 Heat the oil in a saucepan, add the onion and fry, stirring frequently, for 3 minutes. Add the garlic and fry for a further 2 minutes. Stir in the tomatoes and simmer for 3–4 minutes.

2 Remove from the heat and either mash with a fork and then rub through a sieve or, better still, reduce to a purée in a blender. Return the mixture to the pan, season with the remaining ingredients and simmer for 3–4 minutes before using.

VARIATIONS: Neapolitan housewives also add 5 ml (1 teaspoon) oregano and 2.5 ml ($^1/_2$ teaspoon) sugar. Sometimes $^1/_2$ chopped celery stick, 15–30 ml (1–2 tablespoons) chopped parsley and 1 or 2 bay leaves are also added to the sauce.

salsa tat-tadam

tomato and wine sauce

This is a popular tomato sauce from Malta which accompanies all kinds of meat, vegetable, rice and pasta dishes.

Any wine will do, but Marsala is the usual Maltese choice.

I have omitted the chopped ham which often appears in this sauce.

75 ml (5 tablespoons) oil
1 large onion, finely chopped
3 garlic cloves, crushed
900 g (2 lb) tomatoes, blanched, peeled and chopped
5 ml (1 teaspoon) dried basil
2.5 ml ($^1/_2$ teaspoon) oregano
10 ml (2 level teaspoons) sugar
10 ml (2 teaspoons) salt
2.5 ml ($^1/_2$ teaspoon) black pepper
300 ml ($^1/_2$ pint) wine

1 Heat the oil in a saucepan, add the onion and fry, stirring frequently, for 3 minutes. Add the garlic and fry for 2 minutes. Add the tomatoes, basil, oregano, sugar, salt and black pepper and mix thoroughly. Cover the pan, lower the heat and simmer for 20–30 minutes, stirring occasionally.

2 Stir in the wine and simmer, uncovered, for 5–10 minutes. Serve.

molho de tomate castanyas de caju

tomato and cashew nut sauce

A Latin American favourite from Brazil. This delicious, rich and creamy sauce is excellent with all kinds of fried and baked vegetables and all types of poultry.

30 ml (2 tablespoons) butter or margarine
450 g (1 lb) tomatoes, blanched, peeled and chopped
2.5 ml (¹/₂ teaspoon) salt
1.25 ml (¹/₄ teaspoon) black pepper
300 ml (¹/₂ pint) cream
175 g (6 oz) cashew nuts, ground

1 Melt the butter or margarine in a saucepan, add the tomatoes and fry, stirring frequently, for 5 minutes. Season with the salt and pepper.

2 Gradually stir in the cream and ground cashew nuts. Cook over a gentle heat, stirring constantly, for 2–3 minutes. Serve immediately.

sughtorov-madzoun

yogurt and garlic sauce

A popular sauce throughout the Balkans, Caucasus and the Middle East. Simple, tasty and versatile, it can be served with rice, burghul (cracked wheat) pilavs, stuffed vegetables, pastas, fried vegetables and meat.

300 ml (¹/₂ pint) yogurt
1 garlic clove, crushed
1.25 ml (¹/₄ teaspoon) salt
2.5 ml (¹/₂ teaspoon) dried mint
1 spring onion, finely chopped, optional

Pour the yogurt into a bowl. Mix the garlic and salt together, add to the yogurt and mix well. Sprinkle the mint and onion over the top and serve.

garoy salsa
walnut and coriander sauce

This Georgian sauce from the Caucasus (and not its namesake in the southern USA) is served with all types of vegetable dishes as well as with chicken and meat.

175 g (6 oz) shelled walnuts
60 ml (4 tablespoons) finely chopped coriander, tarragon or parsley
3 garlic cloves
5 ml (1 teaspoon) salt
5 ml (1 teaspoon) sumac powder (see Glossary)
90 ml (16 tablespoons) red wine or wine vinegar
450 ml (³/₄ pint) water or vegetable stock (see Glossary)
1 large onion, finely chopped
2 egg yolks, beaten

1 Pound the walnuts, herbs, garlic, salt and sumac to a paste in a mortar or purée in a blender. Transfer the mixture to a saucepan. Stir in the wine, water or vegetable stock and onion and bring to the boil. Lower the heat and simmer, stirring frequently, for 15 minutes.

2 Stir a few tablespoons of the hot stock into the egg yolks and then slowly pour into the pan. Cook for 5 more minutes, stirring constantly, over very low heat, being careful not to let the mixture curdle. Remove from the heat and use as required.

salsa roja para frijoles negros

black bean pepper sauce

A delightful sauce of peppers and tomatoes from Cuba which is usually served with all *frijoles* (bean) dishes, but is equally good with vegetables.

150 ml (¼ pint) oil
450 g (1 lb) tomatoes, blanched, peeled and chopped
2-3 garlic cloves, crushed
2.5 ml (½ teaspoon) cayenne pepper
2.5 ml (½ teaspoon) black pepper
10 ml (2 teaspoons) salt
1.25 ml (¼ teaspoon) thyme
2.5 ml (½ teaspoon) sugar
30 ml (2 level tablespoons) tomato purée
2 red peppers, seeded and finely chopped
45 ml (3 tablespoons) wine vinegar

Heat the oil in a large saucepan, add the tomatoes and fry, stirring, for 5-8 minutes until reduced to a pulp. Add all the remaining ingredients except the vinegar, lower the heat and simmer, stirring occasionally, until the sauce has thickened. Remove from the heat and stir in the vinegar.

béchamel

Reputed to be the creation of Marquis Louis de Béchamel — a financier and the Lord Steward of the Royal Household of Louis XIV.

The quantities below make about 300 ml (¹/₂ pint) sauce.

300 ml (¹/₂ pint) milk
¹/₂ small bay leaf
¹/₂ small onion
bouquet garni
25 g (1 oz) butter
25 g (1 oz) plain flour
salt and black pepper

1 Put the milk in a small saucepan with the bay leaf, onion and bouquet garni and bring slowly to the boil. Remove from the heat, cover the pan and leave the milk to infuse for 15 minutes.

2 In a clean heavy-based pan melt the butter, stir in the flour and cook the roux for 3 minutes.

3 Strain the milk through a fine sieve and gradually blend into the roux. Bring to the boil, stirring constantly, and then simmer for 2–3 minutes. Season to taste with the salt and pepper.

nouri salsa

pomegranate sauce

A Caucasian speciality made with pomegranates and sugar. Concentrated commercial versions of this highly popular sauce can be bought in Middle Eastern shops. I suggest you make your own when the fruit are available. To serve as a sauce add 5 ml (1 teaspoon) sumac powder (see Glossary), a little water to dilute the syrup and, if you wish, garnish with a little chopped spring onion.

Use with all fried vegetables, stews and salads.

juice of 24–30 fresh pomegranates
550 g (1¹/₄ lb) sugar
2 sticks cinnamon

Quarter the pomegranates and squeeze out the juice using a juice extractor. Place the juice in a saucepan and bring to the boil. Add the sugar and stir constantly until it dissolves. Add the cinnamon sticks, lower the heat and simmer for 45–60 minutes until the mixture thickens. Remove from the heat and discard the cinnamon sticks. Leave until completely cold and then bottle, seal and store in a cool place.

carrot and onion stock

25 g (1 oz) butter
450 g (1 lb) carrots, peeled and quartered
450 g (1 lb) onions, quartered
1 celery head, sticks cut into 2.5 cm (1 inch) pieces
4–5 peppercorns
7.5 ml (¹/₂ teaspoons) tomato purée
2.8 litres (5 pints) water
10 ml (2 teaspoons) salt

1 Melt the butter in a large saucepan, add the vegetables and fry, stirring occasionally, until lightly browned. Add the remaining ingredients and bring to the boil. Cover the pan, lower the heat and simmer for 1¹/₂–2 hours.

2 Strain the stock.

chinese vegetable stock

You can omit the monosodium glutamate and use 2.5 ml (¹/₂ teaspoon) sesame oil instead. The mushroom stalks can be (or I should really say 'should be') replaced with dried Chinese winter mushrooms (*Dong gwoo*), or *shitake* in Japanese.

**900 g (2 lb) of any 3 of the following vegetables —
runner beans, french beans, broccoli, cabbage, carrots,
cauliflower, onions, leeks, tomatoes or turnip —
quartered or chopped into smaller pieces
225 g (8 oz) mushroom stalks
1.7 litres (3 pints) water
30 ml (2 tablespoons) soy sauce
2.5 ml (¹/₂ teaspoon) *ve-tsin* or monosodium glutamate
5 ml (1 teaspoon) sugar**

1 Place the vegetables, mushroom stalks and water in a large saucepan and bring to the boil. Lower the heat and simmer for 1 hour.

2 Add the remaining ingredients, simmer for a further 15 minutes and strain.

vegetable stock

Use the outer leaves of cabbages or lettuce, carrot skins, cauliflower stalks, the peels of parsnips, potatoes, turnips, chopped onions, leeks, etc.

900 g (2 lb) mixed vegetable leftovers
50 g (2 oz) butter or margarine
10 ml (2 teaspoons) salt
2.5–3.75 ml ($^1/_2$–$^3/_4$ teaspoon) black pepper
2.8 litres (5 pints) water
mixed herbs, to taste

1 Chop all the vegetable leftovers finely.

2 Heat the butter or margarine in a large saucepan and fry the onions and/or leeks if used. Add all the remaining vegetables and fry for several minutes, turning occasionally. Season with the salt and pepper and add a little of the water. Cover the pan and continue to fry until you get a glaze — this will make the soup clear.

3 Add the remaining water and bring to the boil. Skim and stir in herbs of your choice. Lower the heat and simmer until the vegetables are tender.

4 Strain the stock. You can use it as it is or you can remove and discard the fat when it has cooled and solidified.

pickles, chutneys and sambals

'Preserve to enjoy in March
what you disdained in October'
Russian saying

Our ancestors stored food in times of plenty to supplement provisions when food became scarce in winter months. Initially, man depended solely on Nature's compassion. He ate what was available and starved when Nature had exhausted herself. In time, however, methods of preserving food were discovered.

One such method was drying fruits and vegetables. The vegetables were washed thoroughly, stems were removed, flesh scooped out with specially designed corers, washed again and then threaded on strings and hung up to dry in the sun.

Stuffed with meat, rice and nuts, these vegetables were eaten throughout the winter months. Fruit, too, was treated in this way. In Central Europe and the Far East mushrooms are still dried by the age-old method of stringing them up around the stove like a long necklace. Most suitable for drying are edible boletus. Do not wash them, simply wipe clean, string up and hang in the sun or, as is more often the case, dry in the oven preheated to its lowest temperature. Leave the oven door slightly ajar to ensure a continuous circulation of air. Store in a dry, well-ventilated place.

It is claimed that the art of preserving vegetables in salt originated in ancient China. This may be so as far as the Chinese are concerned, but accounts by Herodotus recall how ancient Egyptians and Lebanese preserved fish and vegetables in salt more than 2,500 years ago. Certainly all the ancient civilisations, Middle Eastern, Indian, Chinese, South American and African, preserved meats and vegetables in salt or brine.

pickles

enginar turşusi

pickled artichokes

This recipe is popular throughout the Balkans, Greece, Turkey and the Caucasus.
Garnish with a little olive oil and chopped parsley before serving.

8–10 artichoke hearts (see Glossary)
8–10 lemons
450 ml (³/₄ pint) water
45 ml (3 tablespoons) sea salt
30 ml (2 tablespoons) wine vinegar
olive oil

1 Cut each artichoke in half and drop into a bowl of acidulated water.

2 Squeeze enough lemons to produce 240 ml (8 fl oz) juice. Strain the juice into a
large bowl. Place any pulp in a sieve and pour the water through it into the bowl.

3 Wash and dry three 600 ml (1 pint) wide-neck jars. Remove the halved artichokes
from the acidulated water and pack tightly into the jars to within 2.5 cm (1 inch) of the
top. Strain the lemon-water into a large jug, discarding any residue. Add the salt and
vinegar and mix well. Pour the brine into each jar to cover the artichokes by 2 cm (³/₄
inch). Reserve any leftover brine. Add a film of olive oil to the top of each jar. Seal the
jars and leave in a cool place for at least 2 weeks. If some of the liquid is absorbed
during this time top up with the reserved brine. Any brine left in the jars can always
be used as a dressing.

sailotyt sienet

pickled mushrooms

Throughout Central Europe and Scandinavia mushrooms are also marinated as a means of preservation. In Finland and adjacent countries they are pickled in the following manner.

Ideally, one should use wild mushrooms for this recipe, but button or oyster mushrooms make adequate substitutes. Good with hot or cold meats and with salads.

900 g (2 lb) mushrooms, wiped clean
About 1.1 litres (2 pints) vinegar
5 cm (2 inch) piece cinnamon stick
2.5 cm (1 inch) piece ginger, bruised
6 cloves
1 blade of mace
175 g (6 oz) sugar

1 Arrange the mushrooms in a large glass jar, cover with vinegar and set aside overnight. You will find it necessary to top up with vinegar after 2–3 hours as the mushrooms will shrink a little.

2 Next day, strain the vinegar into a saucepan. Put the spices in a muslin bag and add with the sugar to the pan. Bring slowly to the boil, stirring until the sugar has dissolved. Leave to simmer for 15 minutes. Allow to cool a little and then pour over the mushrooms. Add the bag of spices to the jar. Cover and set aside for 4 days.

3 On the fifth day, strain the vinegar back into a saucepan, add the spice bag, bring to the boil, lower the heat and simmer for 20 minutes. Leave to cool a little and pour back over the mushrooms, this time discarding the spice bag.

4 When completely cold, cover tightly and store in a cool place. Fills 2 x 450 g (1 lb) jars.

sauerkraut

pickled white cabbage

Cabbage covered in salt makes sauerkraut — well, at least in theory. A theory which was known to the inhabitants of ancient Mesopotamia, Egypt, Crete and Rome. Sauerkraut however has a German twist to it. It is a by-product of centuries of a diet based on cabbage which the people of Germany, Poland and Russia suffered before the introduction of the potato, tomato and even more exotic vegetables from sunnier lands.

3 kg (about 6 lb) white cabbage
50 g (2 oz) sea salt or pure rock salt
15 ml (1 tablespoon) caraway seeds
1 x 4.5 litres (1 gallon) earthenware jar

1 Quarter each cabbage, remove damaged outer leaves and the hard centre stalk. Shred the cabbage very finely.

2 Pack the cabbage and the salt into the jar in layers with the caraway seeds sprinkled through the layers. Cover with a plate that fits into the mouth of the jar making sure that the plate is below the level of the brine — which will be produced by the mixture of cabbage and salt.

3 Skim the brine every other day and put a clean plate on top. See that the top of the jar is always well covered with a cloth. Store the jar for 3–4 weeks in a room with a temperature of about 15°C (60°F). The longer you keep sauerkraut the better.

4 When you use sauerkraut remove some from the jar with a fork or ladle and let the liquid drain back into the jar. Rinse the sauerkraut well, squeezing out the briny juices. Taste and if still salty place in a bowl of tepid water for 15 minutes then taste again. When ready, squeeze out again before using.

sumpoogi titvash

stuffed aubergine pickles

My favourite vegetable pickle of all is this one from Armenia. This is the classic recipe, although there are countless variations throughout the Balkans and Middle East.

1.4 kg (3 lb) very small aubergines
1 small green pepper, seeded and coarsely chopped
1 medium-sized red pepper, seeded and coarsely chopped
1.25 ml ($^1/_4$ teaspoon) chilli powder
60 ml (4 tablespoons) finely chopped parsley
2 garlic cloves, finely chopped
2.5 ml ($^1/_2$ teaspoon) salt
750 ml (1$^1/_4$ pints) white wine vinegar
450 ml ($^3/_4$ pint) water
75 ml (5 tablespoons) sugar
75 ml (5 tablespoons) iodised salt or sea salt

1 Remove stems from the aubergines, wash and place in a large saucepan. Cover with water and bring to the boil. Lower the heat and simmer for 10–15 minutes, then drain and leave to cool.

2 In a bowl, mix together the chopped peppers, chilli powder, parsley, garlic and salt; set this stuffing aside.

3 When the aubergines are cold make a slit on one side of each about 2.5 cm (1 inch) long. Press 5–10 ml (1–2 teaspoons) of the stuffing, depending on the size of the aubergines, into each opening. When all the aubergines are stuffed set them aside for 10 minutes.

4 Meanwhile, in a large saucepan bring the remaining ingredients to the boil. Carefully place the aubergines in the boiling brine, lower the heat and simmer for 3 minutes. Remove the aubergines with a slotted spoon and pack them into 2 x 1.1 litres (2 pint) sterilised jars. Fill the jars with the brine to completely cover the aubergines. Seal tightly and keep for at least 2 weeks.

middle eastern date pickle

Sumac has a sour, lemony taste. It is a reddish brown powder made from the crushed berries of the sumach tree. Both sumac and tamarind can be bought from most continental and Middle Eastern stores. This is an absolutely delightful pickle cum chutney and can be served with all meats. I consider it to be the greatest of all — and it is the pride of Iranian and Iraqi picklers.

75 g (3 oz) sumac
225 g (8 oz) dried tamarind
juice 1 lemon
450 g (1 lb) dates, stoned
2 cloves garlic, crushed
2.5 ml ($^1/_2$ teaspoon) salt
1.25 ml ($^1/_4$ teaspoon) black pepper
1.25 ml ($^1/_4$ teaspoon) cinnamon
1.25 ml ($^1/_4$ teaspoon) nutmeg

1 Soak the sumac in 450 ml ($^3/_4$ pint) water in a bowl overnight. Do the same with the tamarind in another bowl. Then strain both the sumac and the tamarind through muslin or a fine sieve and reserve the liquid.

2 Place the liquids in a saucepan with the lemon juice and boil for 3 minutes.

3 Mince or finely chop the dates and add to the boiling liquids. Add the remaining ingredients, stir well and then pour the mixture into sterilised jars and seal tightly. Use after 1 week.

ogurki-kishone

polish pickled cucumbers

Cucumbers are pickled by almost everyone, but the Central Europeans have refined it into an art form. This recipe is from Poland although, I hasten to add, it was the Franco-Russian cuisine of the nineteenth century which first popularised this pickle throughout the rest of Europe — hence the French term for cucumbers in salt or brine is *agoursi*, which comes from the Russian word for cucumbers, *ougurtsy*.

Use the smallest pickling cucumbers you can find and prepare them whole.

900 g (2 lb) pickling cucumbers
25 ml (1^1/$_2$ tablespoons) dillweed
2 garlic cloves, peeled
1.7 litres (3 pints) warm water
45 ml (3 tablespoons) salt
60 ml (4 tablespoons) white wine vinegar

1 Wash the cucumbers under cold running water and pat dry. Prick the skins of each in several places. Pack the cucumbers loosely into wide-necked jars.

2 Mix all the remaining ingredients together and pour into the jars until filled to the brim. Cover and set aside for 24 hours. Reserve leftover liquid.

3 By the next day some of the liquid will have been absorbed, so top up with some of the reserved liquid. Cover, seal tightly and leave to mature for 2–3 weeks in a cool place.

VARIATION: You can prepare other vegetables such as tomatoes, cauliflower florets, beetroot, cabbage and small onions in this way.

french bean pickle

This is a family recipe given to me by my mother-in-law, who plants, harvests and bottles in Somerset.

10 ml (2 teaspoons) salt
75 g (3 oz) sugar
about 1.1 litres (2 pints) white wine vinegar
2 garlic cloves
2 onions, thinly sliced
6 black peppercorns
10 ml (2 teaspoons) dill seed
900 g (2 lb) french beans — you can also use what are
sometimes called thin beans or Kenyan beans

1 Place half the salt in a saucepan together with the sugar, vinegar, garlic, onions, peppercorns and dill seeds. Bring slowly to the boil, stirring constantly, until the sugar has dissolved. Lower the heat, cover the pan and simmer for 30 minutes.

2 Meanwhile, wash and trim the beans. Half fill a large saucepan with water, add the remaining salt and bring to the boil. Add the beans and simmer for 5 minutes. Drain in a colander.

3 Arrange the beans in an upright position in clean dry preserving jars. I find it easiest to pack them neatly if each jar is held at an angle of 45 degrees.

4 Remove the vinegar mixture from the heat and strain into a jug. Pour over the beans until each jar is filled to the top and the beans are completely covered. Seal and store in a cool place. Fills about 2 x 1 kg (2 lb) jars.

hari mirch ka achar

pickled green chillies

Hot, very, very hot pickles from North India. Use in moderation. Hot green chillies are sold in all Indo-Pakistani and Middle Eastern shops and many greengrocers and large supermarkets.

450 g (1 lb) fresh green chillies, wiped clean
60 ml (4 tablespoons) whole black mustard seeds, ground
30 ml (2 tablespoons) rock salt
15 ml (1 tablespoon) cayenne pepper
15 ml (1 tablespoon) chopped fresh ginger
2.5 ml ($^1/_2$ teaspoon) turmeric
60 ml (4 tablespoons) mustard oil
juice of 2 lemons

1 Trim the stems from the chillies and cut into thin slices crossways. Spread these chilli slices out on a tray and leave to dry in a warm place for 24 hours.

2 When the chillies are dry place them in a large bowl with the ground mustard seeds, salt, cayenne pepper, ginger and turmeric. Mix well.

3 Heat the oil in a small pan over moderate heat for 5 minutes. Remove and leave to cool. Pour the oil over the chilli mixture and mix thoroughly with a wooden spoon. Spoon the mixture into a 1 kg (2 lb) jar or 2 x 450 g (1 lb) jars. Seal and leave in a warm place for 24–36 hours.

4 Open the jars and add the lemon juice, seal and shake the jars thoroughly. Keep in a warm place, preferably in the sun, for 7–10 days before use and then refrigerate.

The cuisines of Korea, Japan and China have many very tasty vegetable pickles. Radishes, cabbages, turnips, cucumbers and garlic are popular choices. Unlike the Western or Middle Eastern tourshi-type pickles these are, in essence, vegetables marinated in brine, vinegar or soy sauce for 24–36 hours and then served.

shoyou daikon

pickled white radish

White radishes can be found in most Indo-Pakistani stores and occasionally now in our large supermarkets. They are smooth skinned and shaped like a carrot, but much larger. One radish will probably weigh anything from 225 g (8 oz) to 900 g (2 lb). The first recipe is from Japan and the second from Korea.

You need not make large quantities of this since it is best when relatively fresh, although it will refrigerate for about 1 week. If possible choose radishes about 15 cm (6 inches) long.

450 g (1 lb) white radish, peeled
150 ml ($^1/_4$ pint) soy sauce

Cut the radishes crossways into 5 cm (2 inch) pieces and place in a shallow bowl. Pour the soy sauce over the radish pieces and turn them in the sauce to coat thoroughly. Cover the bowl and refrigerate for about 36 hours. Turn them every few hours. The radishes are now ready to be served.

kakdooki

korean radish pickle

Koreans adore kimchees and they eat these pickles with any meal from breakfast through to supper. A kimchee is a hot, piquant pickle. The most popular vegetables for such a pickle are radishes, cabbage and cucumbers.

900 g (2 lb) white radishes, peeled and cut into 2 cm ($^1/_2$ inch) cubes
6 spring onions
6 garlic cloves, crushed
15 ml (1 tablespoon) brown sugar
15 ml (1 tablespoon) salt
15 ml (1 tablespoon) cayenne pepper

1 Put all the ingredients into a large bowl and mix thoroughly. Cover the bowl and

leave to rest, stirring occasionally, for 8–10 hours, by which time a considerable amount of liquid will have accumulated.

2 Place a colander over a large bowl and pour the radishes and their liquid into it. Fill 2 x 450 g (1 lb) jars with the radish cubes, packing them quite tightly, and then fill to the brim with the liquid. Seal the jars and leave for 1 week. The pickle is now ready to eat and should be refrigerated.

piccalilli

mixed vegetable pickle

Today piccalilli is as English as Lancashire hotpot, Yorkshire pudding or Cornish pasties, yet its origins lie thousands of miles away in the tropical lands of South East Asia, where Englishmen first tasted spicy, hot food and found that it was good.

2.7 kg (6 lb) vegetables — cauliflower, cucumber, pickling onions, tomatoes
450 g (1 lb) sea salt
1 litre (1³/₄ pints) vinegar
15 ml (1 tablespoon) turmeric
15 ml (1 tablespoon) dry mustard
15 ml (1 tablespoon) ground ginger
2 garlic cloves, crushed
175 g (6 oz) sugar
45 ml (3 tablespoons) cornflour

1 First prepare the vegetables: break the cauliflower into florets, peel the onions, quarter the cucumbers lengthways and cut into 5 cm (2 inch) lengths and cut the tomatoes into wedges. Spread the vegetables out in a large shallow dish and sprinkle with the salt. Set aside for 24 hours and then drain and rinse under cold running water.

2 Place 900 ml (1¹/₂ pints) of the vinegar in a preserving pan or very large saucepan and add the turmeric, mustard, ginger, garlic and sugar. Bring slowly to the boil, stirring constantly, until the sugar has dissolved. Add the vegetables, stir well and simmer for 15 minutes or until they are just tender. Do not overcook — they should still be a little crisp.

3 In a small bowl, blend the cornflour to a smooth paste with the remaining vinegar and stir into the vegetable mixture. Simmer for a further 3 minutes, stirring gently.

4 Remove from the heat and spoon into warm, clean jars. Makes about 2.7 kg (6 lb).

ajar kuning

indonesian mixed pickles

The origins of piccalilli can be found in pickles such as this. Kemiri nuts (also called macadamias) — the nuts of the candlenut tree — are used extensively in Indonesian cooking, but you can use brazil nuts, walnuts or almonds instead.

2.5 ml ($^{1}/_{2}$ teaspoon) sliced, dried lemon grass (see Glossary)
5 ml (1 teaspoon) whole cumin seeds
25 g (1 oz) kemiri (macadamia) nuts, brazil nuts or walnuts, slivered
5 ml (1 teaspoon) turmeric
2.5 ml ($^{1}/_{2}$ teaspoon) cayenne pepper, or more to taste
2.5 cm (1 inch) piece fresh ginger, peeled
2 garlic cloves
2 medium carrots, peeled and cut into julienne strips
1 green pepper, seeded and cut into julienne
50 g (2 oz) mangetout, thinly sliced
50 g (2 oz) shallots, thinly sliced
125 g (4 oz) cauliflower florets, thinly sliced
1 small cucumber, cut into julienne strips
2–3 green tomatoes, halved and thinly sliced
60 ml (4 tablespoons) peanut oil
120 ml (4 fl oz) white wine vinegar
150 ml ($^{1}/_{4}$ pint) water
10 ml (2 teaspoons) salt
2.5 ml ($^{1}/_{2}$ teaspoon) brown sugar

1 Place the lemon grass, cumin seeds, nuts, turmeric, cayenne pepper, ginger and garlic in a blender or mortar and pulverise.

2 Heat the oil in a large saucepan, add the vegetables and stir gently for 1 minute. Add the spice mixture and stir for a further minute. Add the vinegar and water, sprinkle over the salt and sugar, lower the heat and cook, stirring, for 5 minutes.

3 Remove from the heat and serve immediately, or cool and refrigerate in a covered bowl. The pickles will keep for at least 1 week.

marrow pickle

Pickled vegetable marrow is a very English recipe. The vegetable marrow is almost unknown outside the English-speaking world, where courgettes are used instead. This is a pity, for, when mixed with ginger, turmeric, cloves and other spices, the bland marrow acquires a unique flavour of its own. This is well worth preparing.

1 vegetable marrow, about 1.8–2.3 kg (4-5 lb), peeled, seeded and
cut into 2 cm ($^1/_2$ inch) cubes
450 g (1 lb) onions, coarsely chopped
30 ml (2 tablespoons) rock or sea salt
30 ml (2 tablespoons) peeled and finely chopped fresh ginger or
1 tablespoon ground ginger
30 ml (2 tablespoons) turmeric
5 green chillies, halved lengthways and seeded
5 ml (1 teaspoon) cloves
6–8 peppercorns
350 g (12 oz) brown sugar
2.3 litres (4 pints) malt vinegar

1 Since the vegetable marrow contains a large amount of water the first thing is to drain some of it away. To do this, arrange the marrow cubes and chopped onions in layers in a large bowl, sprinkling each layer with a little of the salt. Cover and set aside overnight.

2 The next day, drain off as much excess liquid as possible and set the marrow and onions aside.

3 With a sharp knife, cut the stems off the chillies and then cut them in half lengthways and remove the seeds. (Wash your hands immediately afterwards, for if you touch any part of your face it will burn.)

4 Place the chillies in a large saucepan with the remaining ingredients and bring slowly to the boil, stirring constantly, until the sugar has dissolved. Lower the heat and simmer for 30 minutes.

5 Add the marrow and onions, stir well and bring to the boil. Lower the heat again and simmer uncovered, stirring occasionally, for about 1–1$^1/_2$ hours or until the mixture is thick.

6 Spoon into clean, warm jars, seal and store. Makes about 1.8 kg (4 lb).

titvash

middle eastern mixed vegetable pickles

Popular throughout the Middle East, the Balkans and North Africa, this is the classic way of pickling vegetables. The vegetables may vary, but both quantities (always enormous) and method remain the same.

The recipe is one used in my restaurants and was passed on to me via my great-grandmother.

2 small cauliflowers, separated into florets
8 carrots, peeled, quartered lengthways and cut into 7.5 cm (3 inch) pieces
8 small pickling cucumbers
225 g (8 oz) green beans, trimmed
6 sweet yellow peppers, quartered and seeded
6 small chillies
6 garlic cloves, peeled and halved
6 fresh dill sprigs
1.7 litres (3 pints) water
600 ml (1 pint) white wine vinegar
125 g (4 oz) salt

1 Wash the vegetables thoroughly and pack into 3 large clean jars, distributing them evenly between the jars. Add 2 garlic cloves and 2 dill sprigs to each jar.

2 Put the water, vinegar and salt into a saucepan and bring to the boil. Allow to cool a little and then pour over the vegetables until they are completely covered.

3 Seal tightly and store for at least 4–5 weeks. Makes about 2.3–2.7 kg (5–6 lb).

chutneys

One of the great contributions of the Indian subcontinent to world cookery is the fruit and vegetable preserve called chutney from the Hindi *chatni*. Chutney differs from the Middle Eastern and European pickles in several ways. First, one need not use the very best and freshest fruits or vegetables. Overripe or slightly blemished produce are good enough as they will be finely chopped and cooked well.

Second, preparing chutney need not be a seasonal activity as it can be made from fruits and vegetables available at different times of the year.

Third, unlike pickles, chutneys need long and slow cooking.

The range of chutneys is vast and not all are of Indian origin since, over the centuries, chutneys have evolved all over the world — with a few exceptions such as Africa, South America and most of eastern Europe.

The recipes below are the most popular vegetable-based chutneys. I am well aware that there are equally good fruit-based chutneys, but owing to shortage of space and the fact that this is a vegetable book I have only included a few outstanding ones.

saragwa chatni

drumstick chutney

This is a highly specialised chutney from central India.

Drumsticks are long, 30–40 cm (12–18 inches), vegetables belonging to the pea family. They are seasonal and are available in Indian shops in late spring and early summer.

75 ml (5 tablespoons) oil
1 onion, chopped
450 g (1 lb) drumsticks
225 g (8 oz) karela (bitter melon) see Glossary
450 g (1 lb) tomatoes, blanched, peeled and chopped
10 ml (2 teaspoons) salt
5 ml (1 teaspoon) paprika
5 ml (1 teaspoon) ground cumin
2.5 ml ($^1/_2$ teaspoon) ground allspice
2.5 ml ($^1/_2$ teaspoon) ground fenugreek
125 g (4 oz) sugar
600 ml (1 pint) malt vinegar

1 Heat the oil in a large saucepan, add the onion and fry until soft.

2 Meanwhile, prepare the drumsticks by cutting each one in half lengthways and then scraping off all the flesh with a sharp knife. Reserve the flesh and discard the peel.

3 Prepare the karela by chopping finely. If you think you will not like the bitterness then scrape off the rough skin first.

4 Add the drumstick pulp, chopped karela and tomatoes to the pan and fry for 10 minutes, stirring frequently. Sprinkle in the salt, all the spices and the sugar and cook for a further 2–3 minutes.

5 Pour in the vinegar and bring to the boil. Lower the heat and simmer gently for 30–45 minutes or until the mixture has thickened. Remove from the heat, allow to cool a little and then spoon into warm, clean jars. Seal and store in a cool place. Makes about 900 g (2 lb).

amba chatni

mango chutney

There are over one thousand cultivated varieties of this sweet and exotic fruit which, only a few decades ago, was virtually unknown in Britain.

Today, however, the mango is 'in'. It is eaten as a dessert, made into jam, jellies, ice-cream, fruit drinks and, of course, chutney.

Mango chutney is perhaps the most famed of all Indian relishes. It is easy to make and the fruit is available virtually throughout the year.

Use unripe mangoes.

1.4 kg (3 lb) green mangoes, washed, halved and stoned.
Make sure they are really unripe or
it will be difficult to separate stones from flesh
900 g (2 lb) brown sugar
900 ml (1^1/$_2$ pints) malt vinegar
25 g (1 oz) piece fresh ginger, peeled and finely chopped
^{1}/$_2$ onion, thinly sliced
2 garlic cloves, crushed
50 g (2 oz) salt
2 small green chillies, washed and thinly sliced
225 g (8 oz) sultanas

1 Chop the mango flesh into 3.5 cm (1^1/$_4$ inch) pieces. If possible pull or cut off the hard skin which separates stone from flesh.

2 Place the sugar and vinegar in a large saucepan and bring slowly to the boil, stirring constantly until the sugar has dissolved. Simmer for 5 minutes. Add the mango pieces and all the remaining ingredients. Cook very gently for about 1 hour or until the mango flesh is tender and the chutney has thickened. Stir occasionally.

3 Remove from the heat, allow to cool a little and then spoon into clean, warm jars. Seal and store in a cool place. Makes about 1.4 kg (3 lb).

VARIATION: You can also incorporate 5 ml (1 teaspoon) garam masala (see Glossary) as well as a few chopped fresh or dried apricots or 1–2 chopped apples.

baingan chatni

aubergine and pepper chutney

6 medium aubergines, peeled and cut into 1 cm ($^1/_2$ inch) cubes
2 large red or green peppers, seeded and cut into 1 cm ($^1/_2$ inch) squares
15 ml (1 tablespoon) salt
2.5 ml ($^1/_2$ teaspoon) turmeric
5 ml (1 teaspoon) curry powder
450 ml ($^3/_4$ pint) malt or white wine vinegar
5 cm (2 inch) stick cinnamon
2.5 cm (1 inch) piece fresh ginger, peeled and bruised
75 ml (5 tablespoons) oil
2 garlic cloves, thinly sliced
15 ml (1 tablespoon) brown sugar
15–30 ml (1–2 tablespoons) cayenne pepper,
depending on taste

1 Place the aubergine and pepper in a large bowl, sprinkle with the salt and turmeric and rub in with your fingers. Set aside.

2 Meanwhile, dissolve the curry powder in 30–45 ml (2–3 tablespoons) of the vinegar, add the cinnamon stick and ginger and leave for 15–20 minutes.

3 Heat the oil in a large saucepan, add the vegetables and garlic and cook for 10 minutes, stirring regularly. Add the sugar and mix well. Stir in the curry powder mixture, mix well and cook over a low heat for about 10 minutes, stirring regularly.

4 Pour in the rest of the vinegar, bring to the boil and simmer for 5 minutes. Finally add the cayenne pepper and mix well.

5 Remove the pan from the heat and spoon the chutney into warm, clean jars, discarding the cinnamon stick and piece of ginger. Seal and store in a cool place. Makes about 1.8 kg (4 lb).

pawpaw chutney

A Caribbean speciality, no doubt popularised by people of Indian origin. Makes a delicious chutney.

Use unripe pawpaws for this recipe. The ripe fruit are best used for desserts, drinks and ice-creams.

You can buy pawpaws from most West Indian and Indian grocery stores and from some large supermarkets and greengrocers.

1.4 kg (3 lb) green pawpaws, peeled, halved and with seeds discarded
125 g (4 oz) onion, thinly sliced
450 g (1 lb) sugar
175 g (6 oz) raisins or sultanas
25 g (1 oz) ground ginger
10 ml (2 teaspoons) curry powder
5 ml (1 teaspoon) salt
2.5 ml ($1/_2$ teaspoon) chilli powder
600 ml (1 pint) malt vinegar

1 Cut the pawpaw flesh into 2.5 cm (1 inch) cubes and place in a large pan with all the remaining ingredients. Bring slowly to the boil, stirring constantly until the sugar has dissolved. Lower the heat and simmer gently for about 1 hour or until the mixture has thickened and has a jam-like consistency. Stir occasionally to prevent sticking. Set aside to cool.

2 When completely cold pour into clean jars and seal tightly. Store in a cool place. Makes about 1.4 kg (3 lb).

rubarb ki chatni

rhubarb chutney

A North Indian speciality, this is a delightful chutney which goes well with curries as well as cold meats.

700 g (1¹/₂ lb) rhubarb, washed and trimmed
10 ml (2 teaspoons) chopped fresh ginger
4 garlic cloves
5 ml (1 teaspoon) chilli powder
15 ml (3 teaspoons) mustard seeds
30 ml (2 tablespoons) ground almonds
225 g (8 oz) soft brown sugar
600 ml (1 pint) malt vinegar

1 Cut the rhubarb into 2.5 cm (1 inch) pieces and place in a large saucepan.

2 Crush the ginger and garlic together with a pestle and mortar. Place in the saucepan with all the remaining ingredients and mix well. Bring slowly to the boil, stirring constantly until the sugar has dissolved. Simmer gently for about 1 hour or until the mixture has a thick jam-like consistency. Stir frequently to prevent the mixture sticking and burning. Set aside to cool. Spoon into clean jars, seal and store in a cool place. Makes about 900 g (2 lb).

sambals

Sambal Goreng dishes hail from the Indonesian archipelago. The hundreds of large and small islands have a few things in common and two of them are *santan* and 'chillies'. The former is coconut milk (see Glossary), the latter are small, finger-sized green monsters with a powerful kick.

It is interesting to note how certain fruits and vegetables have become associated with certain groups of people. I am thinking of the cabbage and its love-hate relationship with the people of Central Europe and northern China. Then there is the potato that has been the life source of the British and Irish and yet equally has been the cause of the latter's virtual destruction as a nation. There is, of course, the tomato, which is the love of the Mediterranean people, and finally there are chillies, still little used in Europe but the pride of the Indian subcontinent, East Africa and Mexico.

Chillies and tomatoes together! The green against the red, the bitter with the sweet. How marvellously have the people of South East Asia mastered the use of these two vegetables.

Tomatoes and chillies, either solo or together, make excellent relishes. The most popular tomato relish is, of course, the ubiquitous tomato ketchup with its numerous variations. This recipe shows what a delicious relish tomatoes can make.

sambal goreng tomat

hot tomato relish

60 ml (4 tablespoons) peanut oil
1 large onion, finely chopped
2 garlic cloves, crushed
8–10 small fresh or dried chillies, finely chopped
5 ml (1 teaspoon) brown sugar
5 ml (1 teaspoon) salt
6 medium tomatoes, sliced
15 ml (1 tablespoon) lemon juice
3 bay leaves
450 ml ($^3/_4$ pint) thick coconut milk (see Glossary)

1 Heat the oil in a saucepan, add the onion, garlic, chillies, sugar and salt and fry, stirring frequently, for about 5 minutes. Add the tomatoes and cook, stirring occasionally, for a further 5 minutes. Pour in the lemon juice and simmer for 2 minutes.

2 Add the bay leaves and coconut milk, stir well, lower the heat and simmer for 15–20 minutes or until the mixture has thickened.

3 Serve hot or cold in small side bowls.

VARIATION: Other sambal relishes can be cooked in a similar manner using different vegetables. For SAMBAL GORENG KEMBANG KUBIS — Hot Cauliflower Relish — you will require 1 small cauliflower cut into small pieces. Prepare as for the recipe, above, and add the cauliflower instead of tomatoes.

sambal goreng buntjis

hot bean relish

For this you need 350 g (12 oz) french beans, trimmed and cut into 2.5 cm (1 inch) pieces. Proceed as with the recipe above and add the beans at the same time as the tomatoes.

In Mexico no meal is complete without a sauce-cum-relish called *salsa picante*. It is made with two of Mexico's natural products — tomatoes and peppers. You can use this as a relish, dip or sauce.

salsa picante

mexican chilli relish

1 large onion, finely chopped
4 medium tomatoes (preferably green ones — tomatillos), finely chopped
1 large green pepper, seeded and finely chopped
2–3 jalapeños (use hot red chillies), finely chopped
45 ml (3 tablespoons) cider
2.5 ml ($^1/_2$ teaspoon) salt
5 ml (1 teaspoon) brown sugar or raw cane sugar
15 ml (1 tablespoon) fresh coriander, finely chopped
30 ml (2 tablespoons) oil

Place all ingredients in a large bowl and mix well. Spoon into a clean, dry jar, cover and refrigerate. Use as required. Makes about 900 g (2 lb).

glossary

ACIDULATED WATER

The addition of lemon juice or vinegar to cold water — this prevents discoloration of some vegetables.

To every 300 ml (¹/₂ pint) water add about 5 ml (1 teaspoon) lemon juice or vinegar.

ASAFOETIDA (*FERULA ASAFOETIDA*)

Used in minute quantities in Indian and Middle Eastern cooking to prevent flatulence.

BEAN CURD

Extensively used in Chinese and Japanese cuisines. *Dow foo* or tofu is regarded by many vegetarians as a miracle food. Made from soya beans, bean curds are available fresh and can be refrigerated for 2–3 days — cover them with cold water and change it daily.

There are three types. The one most used in this book is yellow bean curd. The second is dried bean curd, which comes in flat sheets or rounded sticks. Red bean curd is stronger, more pungent and is usually used in sauces. Yellow bean curd is called *Lao dow foo*. Dried bean curd is called *Pai yeh*. Red bean curd is called *Doo foo kan*. Fried bean curd in Japanese is *Aburage*.

BURGHUL, CRACKED WHEAT

This is hulled wheat which is steamed until partly cooked, dried and then ground into three grades:

Large — used for pilavs and stuffings

Medium — for stuffings

Fine — for salads

Sold in most Middle Eastern and Indian shops.

CELLOPHANE NOODLES, (FEN SZE OR FEN P'I)

Sold in a dried form, these are the product of soaked, ground and strained mung beans. Available in Chinese food stores.

CHEESES

FETA is a soft, white cheese made from goat's or ewe's milk. Use Greek or Bulgarian fetas as these are the best. Sometimes sold in brine so tends to be rather salty; soak in cold water for about 1 hour before using, if wished.

HALOUMI — a salty sheep's milk cheese of Syrian origin matured in whey. Often comes flavoured with mint or black cumin.

PANIR — home-made Indian cheese.

PECORINO — a white Italian cheese made from sheep's milk. Comes hard or soft. The hard version, Romano, can be substituted for Parmesan and the soft version for the above Greek and Indian cheeses.

COCONUT MILK

Coconut milk is an important ingredient in the Far Eastern, Polynesian and Caribbean cuisines. It is not the liquid inside the coconut, but the milky liquid extracted from the grated flesh of a mature coconut or desiccated (dried, shredded) coconut. I suggest that for convenience sake you use the latter.

Put 225 g (8 oz) desiccated coconut into a liquidiser with 900 ml (1¹/₂ pints) hot water. Cover and blend for 30 seconds. Strain through a fine sieve (or muslin) squeezing out as much moisture as possible. This is called 'thick' milk. If you need 'thin' milk put the same desiccated coconut back into the liquidiser, add another 900 ml (1¹/₂ pints) hot water and blend again. Strain. If you want a richer milk replace the water with hot pasteurised milk. However, coconut milk is sold in tins in Asian shops and I suggest you use this both for convenience and because the overall consistency is better than that produced at home. Stir well before proceeding with the recipe.

FILO

Paper-thin dough used in the making of pastries and savouries. Sold in Middle Eastern and Greek shops. Each packet weighs 450 g (1 lb) and contains about 20–25 sheets.

TO USE Remove filo from its wrapping. Sprinkle a little flour over a working top and open the sheets out flat. Moisten a tea towel until evenly damp and spread it over top of filo. Remove each sheet as you need it and keep the rest covered with the cloth. Any dough not used should be wrapped carefully and refrigerated.

GARAM MASALA

An important ingredient in Indian cooking. It is a mixture of ground roasted spices, e.g., coriander, cumin, cardamom, cloves, nutmeg and cinnamon, which is usually sold ready mixed.

GARRI

A product of the cassava plant, which is native to the West Indies, Africa and Equatorial America.

It is the staple diet of most Africans, but is deficient in protein and Vitamin B.

Garri cooked in boiling water is made into Eba and Fufu (see page 206), etc.

It is available from many Indian and West Indian shops in 450 g (1 lb) packets.

GHEE OR CLARIFIED BUTTER

Also called *samna* or *smen* in Arabic, ghee or clarified butter is much used in the cuisines of India, Iran, Afghanistan and the Central Asian republics of the Soviet Union. Ghee is readily available in large supermarkets and all Indian stores. It is basically butter that has been clarified so thoroughly that it is totally free of all milk solids and is therefore ideal for frying. It does not need refrigeration.

Ghee has a distinctive nutty flavour and aroma which may not be to everyone's taste, but I suggest you use it whenever mentioned in Indian or Middle Eastern recipes. If you live in parts of the country where there are as yet no Indian grocery stores, try making your own clarified butter. It is very simple. In India the butter is cooked just below simmering point for quite a long time. 225 g (8 oz) butter takes 20–30 minutes; 450 g (1 lb) butter takes 45 minutes.

900 g (2 lb) butter

1 Melt the butter in a large saucepan over a low heat. Skim off the foam with a wooden spoon as it appears on the surface. Remove the pan from the heat and set aside for 10 minutes. Skim off any remaining foam.

2 Spoon the butter into a container, discarding the salty, milky residue at the bottom of the pan. Cover and store. This quantity of butter makes about 550 g (1¹/₄ lb) of clarified butler or ghee.

HARISSA
See chapter on Sauces and Dressings.

HOISIN SAUCE (HOI HSIEN CHIANG)
This is a sweet, reddish-brown, rather spicy sauce made from garlic, soya beans, sugar and spices. Sold in Chinese stores and will keep for a long time.

Often used as a dip for batter-coated, deep-fried vegetables.

KASHA
Is an essential ingredient in all Slavonic cuisines. Kasha is made from cooked grains, such as whole buckwheat, millet or barley. It is sold in most health food shops.

KVASS
A unique traditional Russian alcoholic drink sold from barrels at street corners. This recipe, however, is for kvass for making borsch and is made with rye flour.

450 g (1 lb) rye flour

2.3 litres (4 pints) boiling water

7.5 ml (3 teaspoons) dried yeast

1 Place the flour in a large bowl and pour the boiling water over it, stirring constantly until well blended.

2 In a small bowl dissolve the yeast in a little warm water and add to the flour mixture. Mix well, cover with a towel and leave in a warm place for 24 hours to allow it to ferment.

3 With a slotted spoon remove any foam that has appeared on the surface and discard. Strain the mixture through muslin and pour the liquid into bottles and seal tightly. Store in a cool place and use as suggested.

LEMON GRASS (*CYMBOPOGON CITRATUS*)
An aromatic grass that grows in South East Asia as well as in Australia, Africa and South America. The grass blades are used fresh, dried and powdered. Has a white-coloured slightly bulbous base and is used in curries and other dishes to impart a lemony flavour. Dried lemon grass is found in Indian shops.

As a substitute use 2 strips of thinly peeled lemon rind.

In powdered form it is known as sereh.

MANGO POWDER (*AMCHUR*)
Made from dried, raw green mangoes this sour powder is much used in the Indian cuisine to give a piquant flavour to many dishes.

MIRIN

Sweetened Japanese rice wine (like saké) which, however, is never drunk, but is used exclusively in cooking. It gives Japanese cooking one of its most characteristic flavours. Can be bought from Japanese and some Chinese shops. If not available use dry sherry.

PICKLED LEMONS

Both limes and lemons are preserved in North African cookery in a brine, stored tightly in sterilised jars and kept for 3–4 weeks before using. The preserved fruit is then used in tajines and couscous dishes.

POMEGRANATE JUICE

See page 238, Dressings, Sauces and Stocks.

PREPARED SESAME SEEDS

Although this is now available in Chinese and Japanese shops I suggest you make your own as it is simple to prepare. It is used extensively in Japanese and Korean cooking.

225g (8 oz) sesame seeds
5 ml (1 teaspoon) salt

1 Put the sesame seeds in a heavy frying pan over a moderate heat and brown, stirring constantly. Remove from the heat, stir in the salt and mix.

2 Put the seeds in a blender and pulverise. Store in a tightly lidded jar and use as instructed.

RICE PILAV

250 g (9 oz) long-grain rice
50 g (2 oz) butter
5 ml (1 teaspoon) salt

1 Wash the rice thoroughly; drain.

2 Melt the butter in a saucepan and add the rice. Stirring often, fry the rice for 2–3 minutes until well coated with the butter. Add the salt and 600 ml (1 pint) boiling water. Boil hard for 3 minutes, then cover and simmer over low heat for about 20 minutes or until all the liquid is absorbed and small holes appear in the surface of the rice.

3 Remove from the heat, place a clean tea towel under the lid and leave for 10 minutes. Fluff up the grains with a fork and serve at once.

ROASTED OR TOASTED NUTS

Blanched almonds, sesame seeds, pistachio nuts, etc., can be browned by placing under a hot grill and toasting for 2–3 minutes, turning regularly, until evenly golden. Alternatively, they can be dry-roasted in a heavy frying pan.

SESAME OIL (MA YU)

Used in Chinese, Korean and Japanese cuisines. This oil is prepared from toasted sesame seeds. Darker in colour than the Middle Eastern versions.

Do not use it for cooking — although it is so used in northern China and Mongolia. Treat it merely as a flavouring. Store in the refrigerator to prevent rancidity.

SUMAC

The dried, crushed berries of a species of the sumach tree. Has a sour, lemony taste.

Crush and steep it in water to extract its essence, which can then be used in stews instead of lemon juice.

Is used extensively in Caucasian and Iranian cuisines.

Sold in some Middle Eastern stores.

TAHINI, SESAME PASTE

A nutty-flavoured paste made from toasted and crushed sesame seeds. Not to be confused with the Far Eastern sesame oil (Ma Yu).

Used extensively in Middle Eastern cooking. Can be bought from large supermarkets and most Indian and Middle Eastern stores.

Tahini separates when left standing, so always stir before using.

TAMARIND JUICE

The fruit of the large tropical tree (*Tamarindus indica*) is shaped like a fat broad bean inside of which there are shiny dark seeds covered with brown flesh. Tamarind is dried and sold in packets. It is available in all Indo-Pakistani shops, as indeed is the juice, which comes bottled. However, if it is not available you can prepare your own.

Break 450 g (1 lb) tamarind pulp into smaller pieces and place in a large saucepan with 1.1 litres (2 pints) water. Bring to the boil and simmer for 20 minutes. Stir, strain through muslin and discard all the seeds and fibre. Return the juice to the pan and simmer for 5 more minutes or more depending on taste and desired thickness of the juice. When cold store in a bottle and seal tightly.

WHOLEWHEAT PASTRY

As an alternative to commercially produced puff or shortcrust pastries try this recipe which makes a light, crumbly pastry. It is also, of course, much more wholesome.

225 g (8 oz) self-raising 100% wholewheat flour

2.5 ml ($^1/_2$ teaspoon) salt

50 g (2 oz) margarine

50 g (2 oz) vegetable shortening

30 ml (2 tablespoons) cold water

1 Sift the flour into a bowl and stir in the residue of bran left in the sieve and the salt. Add the margarine and shortening and rub into the flour until the mixture resembles breadcrumbs. Add the water and knead until a dough is formed. Add just a little more water if necessary.

2 Shape the dough into a ball, transfer to a lightly floured surface and knead for a few minutes. Use as required.

VEGETABLES

Further information on some of the vegetables in this book.

ARTICHOKE *CYNARA SCOLYMUS*: Imported globe artichokes are available throughout the year, but the domestic varieties only appear in the summer.

Choose uniformly solid heads with tightly closed leaves. Avoid artichokes with soft, discoloured leaves. Keep in a plastic bag to prevent drying out.

TO PREPARE: wash under cold running water or soak for about 30 minutes in a bowl of cold water to which 30 ml (2 tablespoons) of lemon juice have been added — this helps prevent discoloration and removes insects.

Slice off the stem, lay the artichoke on its side and slice off the top third of the leaves. Rub all cut ends with lemon to prevent discoloration. With kitchen scissors trim 0.5 cm ($^1/_2$ inch) off tops of any remaining leaves with sharp points and rub edges with lemon.

To remove the choke spread out inner leaves, pull out the prickly pink leaves surrounding the choke and then scrape it out with a teaspoon.

Drop the prepared artichoke into acidulated water immediately until ready to use. If using artichoke hearts only: bend back the lower leaves until they snap off and then remove all outer leaves until you reach those bending inwards. Slice off the stalk.

Place the artichoke on its side and cut off remaining leaves just above the white heart.

Trim off the green leaf base by rotating the base of the artichoke against the knife blade — as though peeling a potato. Drop immediately into acidulated water until ready to use. NB Artichoke hearts are also sold in cans.

ASPARAGUS *ASPARAGUS OFFICINALIS*: Imported asparagus is available throughout the year — at a high price. The domestic variety appears in late spring and its season lasts for only 4–6 weeks.

Always make a point of choosing firm, fresh-looking stalks and avoid those that are thin and wrinkled.

The quality has nothing to do with colour — usually green or white. Cook as soon after buying as possible, but if you have to keep asparagus for a day or two then refrigerate in a plastic bag.

TO PREPARE: peel or preferably scrape the stalks very thinly.

Wash carefully and trim to required size.

AUBERGINE (EGGPLANT) *SOLANUM MELONGENA*: Available all the year round. The best come from Kenya, Cyprus and Israel. Originally from the Indian subcontinent, another variety is reputed to have developed in China.

The aubergine is the great vegetable of the Middle East cuisines from where it was passed on to Europe and the Americas.

Choose firm, smooth vegetables with light, shiny skins. Buy small ones for stuffing and larger ones for frying or mashing. Store in a cool and humid place.

TO PREPARE: this is a very versatile vegetable and there are numerous ways of preparing it. I suggest you follow the instructions in the relevant recipes.

It is often recommended that the cut aubergines are sprinkled with salt, set aside for 30 minutes and then rinsed and dried — this is to extract any bitterness.

I must admit that I rarely do this as I have found that in the last few years there has been a great improvement in the quality of imported aubergines. However, if you wish to be on the safe side then do salt them first.

AVOCADO *PERSEA AMERICANA*: Available almost all year round they are imported mainly from Kenya and Israel. They are a round or pear-shaped fruit of dark green or purple colour and native to Central and South America. Buy avocados that are heavy, firm and have a uniform skin with no bruises. These will keep in the refrigerator for several days. Only buy softer ones if you wish to use immediately.

TO PREPARE: cut the fruit in half lengthways, twist halves a little to separate them and then remove the stone.

Rub cut surfaces immediately with lemon to prevent discoloration.

To peel, lay the avocado cut side down and pry off the skin with the back of a teaspoon. Rub peeled surface with lemon.

BAMBOO SHOOTS (CHUK SUN)

There are as many different kinds of shoots as there are bamboo — a conservative estimate is well over 200 but basically there are two categories — winter and spring shoots.

They are used extensively in Far Eastern cuisines. Fresh shoots are difficult to find here, but are readily available in cans. These come ready boiled so they only need to be drained and rinsed before using.

Bamboo shoots have a light sweet flavour and a crunchy texture.

BEANS

There are many varieties of beans. Of the common bean alone there are 200 types and therefore I am only mentioning those that appear in this book.

TO PREPARE: a general rule with dried beans is to wash them under cold running water and then to soak them in cold water for several hours or overnight or place in a saucepan, cover with cold water, bring to the boil and simmer for 3 minutes.

Remove from the heat, cover the pan and leave for 1–1$\frac{1}{2}$ hours. All the beans listed below can be treated in either of these ways unless otherwise stated.

After they have soaked transfer them to a colander and rinse well.

The cooking times given below are approximate and, unless otherwise stated, imply a soaking period first. Remember also that cooking times will depend on the age of the dried beans.

TYPE OF BEAN	COOKING TIME
Adzuki beans	30–40 minutes
Black beans	45 minutes
Black-eyed beans	45 minutes
Broad beans	90 minutes
Butter beans	90 minutes
Cannellini beans	60 minutes
Chickpeas	60–90 minutes
Flageolet beans	60 minutes
Ful beans	60–90 minutes
Haricot beans	60 minutes
Lentils — brown, green, etc.	30 minutes (soaking not necessary)
— red split	15–20 minutes
Lima beans	60 minutes
Peas	45 minutes
Pinto beans	60 minutes
Red kidney beans	60 minutes (boil hard for at least 10 minutes before continuing to cook as usual)
Soya beans	3–4 hours
Split peas	30–45 minutes

BEANS, LONG/DAN GOK
Botanically related to the cowpeas or black-eyed peas. Are used extensively in the Chinese cuisines. Very similar to string beans in taste; however, long beans are more crunchy but less succulent and cook faster, hence ideal for stir-fry recipes. Can be substituted for french green beans.

BEAN SPROUTS
These are the seeds of grains or legumes that have germinated and hence converted their fats and starches into vitamins and proteins.

The two most commonly sprouted beans are the mung bean and soy bean. Available in Chinese groceries all the year round they can now also be found in some greengrocers and large supermarkets. Make sure the sprouts are clean, clear and white from head to tail. They should be eaten absolutely fresh, either raw or cooked. To store keep in water in a covered container in the fridge.

Apart from the two beans mentioned above you can sprout others such as dried peas, adzuki beans or chickpeas. All you need to do is to keep the beans in a damp condition for 3–6 days, rinsing them off in cold water 2 or 3 times a day to remove the toxins produced.

BREADFRUIT *ARTOCARPUS COMMUNIS*
Originally from Polynesia it is now widely distributed in the tropics, particularly in the Caribbean and Pacific islands.

The fruit is round with a thick, warty skin that varies from yellowish-green to brown and with a pale yellow flesh.

Breadfruit has a mild, slightly nutty flavour. It can be boiled, baked, roasted or fried.

Still little known in Britain, it is well worth experimenting with this fascinating fruit-vegetable.

CARDOON *CYNARA CARDUNCULUS*

The cardoon comes from the Mediterranean. It is similar to its relation the globe artichoke, but it has spinier leaves and purple-coloured, thistle-like flowers. Unfortunately it is not easily available in this country, but it is very popular in southern Mediterranean, North African and Iranian cuisines.

Only the inner stalks, which are crisp and succulent, and the firm hearts are eaten.

TO PREPARE: the leaf stalks are blanched for 15 minutes and then peeled and used in soups, salads and stews.

CASSAVA *MANIHOT ESCULENTA; MANIHOT UTILISSIMA*

A native of South America, cassava is a member of the spurge family (genus *Euphorbia*). It is also known as yuca, tapioca plant and manioc. Cassava was introduced into Africa at the beginning of the seventeenth century. It is a valuable source of starch and plays a very important role in African cookery.

There are two types of cassava: poisonous and sweet. The poison is hydrocyanic (prussic) acid. It is removed by first grating the roots, then squeezing them to extract as much of the sap as possible and then heating to remove any still remaining. This process produces a coarse meal known as garri, which is used particularly in Nigerian and Cameroonian dishes.

CELERIAC *APIUM GRAVEOLENS, VAR. RAPACEUM*

Native to the Mediterranean region it was first seriously cultivated in Italy in the sixteenth century. Celeriac is a variety of celery grown not for its stalk and leaves but for its large roots. Not much used in this country, it is a very pleasant white-fleshed vegetable that may be eaten raw in salads or cooked in soups and stews.

Buy small celeriacs with clean roots and avoid those that are soft. To store, remove the top leaves and root fibres. Wrap in a plastic bag and refrigerate.

TO PREPARE: peel and place immediately in a bowl of acidulated water to prevent discoloration.

CHAYOTE *SECHIUM EDULE*

A native of Mexico, this tropical squash appears under several names — choko, xuxu, christophene as well as the French chayote.

It also comes in different colours and textures, white or green, rounded or ridged. It has a single edible seed.

Fresh chayote can sometimes be found in West Indian and Indo-Pakistani shops and I have recently seen it in our large local supermarket under the name chow chow.

They are usually boiled in their skins and then peeled and used in salads, vegetable dishes, chutneys and desserts. They are often served stuffed with other vegetables.

CHESTNUTS, SWEET (*GENUS CASTANEA*)

Edible nuts of several varieties of a tree of the same name. Used extensively in Far Eastern and Mediterranean cuisines.

The European chestnut (*Castanea sativa*) is used in stuffings, mashed or braised. The Chinese variety (*Castanea crenata*) is smaller and sweeter with a distinctive flavour and texture. They are used in cakes and especially in salads.

Use fresh chestnuts when available, although tinned ones are a good substitute. Shelled dried chestnuts can be reconstituted when soaked in water.

It is important to cull the chestnuts to remove any spoiled parts otherwise a dish can easily be ruined.

Soak dried chestnuts overnight in water. Then place in a saucepan, cover with water and simmer, covered, until the chestnuts puff up and are tender. Drain and use as with fresh chestnuts.

CHICORY *CICHORIUM INTYBUS*

Available all the year round. There are three varieties: one used for greens; one for its large roots, which are dried and used in coffee, and one used in salads or braised and served as a hot vegetable, It is the third kind, better known as Witloof or Brussels chicory, that is found in the shops.

Buy firm, crisp, tightly enclosed chicory with creamy-white leaves with yellow-green edges. Avoid those with greenish tips as they tend to be rather bitter in flavour. Use as soon as possible for best results, although chicory will keep for several days if wrapped in plastic and refrigerated.

TO PREPARE: remove wilted leaves, cut off the stem end and then separate the leaves or slice. Wash under cold running water.

CHINESE CABBAGE *BRASSICA CHINENSIS*; *BRASSICA PEKINENSIS*

Cultivated for centuries in East Asia and China these 'cabbages' are now easily available in Europe. There are several varieties:

CHOI SUM — Chinese flowering cabbage

PAK CHOI — white cabbage

WONG NGA BAAK — Peking cabbage

DAAI GAAI CHOI — mustard cabbage

Always choose firm, heavy heads without any blemishes or wilting leaves. The most popular variety is perhaps the Chinese white cabbage with its succulent leaf stalks and tender leaves.

TO PREPARE: separate leaves, soak in water for a few minutes to remove dirt and insects. Drain and proceed with specific recipe instructions.

COLOGASSI

This is a tuber with a dense white flesh. Cyprus is its native habitat and it is much used in the local kitchens.

Very similar to the potato, but it has a turnipy flavour. Can be used in most yam, breadfruit and potato dishes. Is available from November to February in Greek shops.

CORN (MAIZE, MEALIES) *ZEA MAYS*

Corn is not strictly a vegetable although it can, when fresh, be cooked and served as one. A native of the New World it is, after wheat, the most widely cultivated food plant, although most of it is fed to animals.

Cultivated by the Incas and their forebears maize, in reality a grass, was so important to the American Indians that an entire repertoire of folklore, myths and cultural customs was evolved around it.

Corn is today widely used in East European, Middle Eastern and particularly in South American and African cuisines. Maize flour plays an important role in Caribbean and African cooking.

Fresh maize (sweetcorn) is a seasonal vegetable in Britain, but frozen corn is readily available. Always buy fresh green husks with firm, plump kernels.

TO PREPARE: remove husks and silk and wash under cold water.

COURGETTE (ZUCCHINI) *CUCURBITA PEPO*

From the French meaning small gourd, courgette is a variety of marrow. In America courgettes are known as zucchini because they were named after the very first kind of Italian summer squash to be cultivated there.

Courgettes are still relatively little used in Britain, but fortunately along with aubergines and okra they are becoming more commonplace.

Apart from the Italian and French cuisines courgettes are at their best in North African and Middle Eastern cooking.

Always buy medium-sized, well-rounded courgettes. For best results use soon after buying.

TO PREPARE: wash, trim and slice crossways, halve lengthways or core depending on recipe.

FENNEL *FOENICULUM VULGARE*

Fennel is an aromatic plant native to the Mediterranean. Its cultivated variety — var. *dulce* called Florence or French fennel to distinguish it from the herb fennel — is extensively used in salads and as a cooked vegetable. Italians also eat it as a dessert served with fruits.

A bulbous vegetable with broad leaf stalks and bright green leaves, fennel was much admired in medieval Britain not only for its aroma and liquorice-like flavour but also for its many-faceted medicinal qualities. It was believed to be an excellent cure for eye troubles and good for increasing the milk supply of nursing mothers.

Always buy firm, crisp bulbs about 15–20 cm (6–8 inches) in size with 15–20 cm (6–8 inch) long tops which should be pale green in colour.

To keep, put in a plastic bag and refrigerate. Fennel leaves can be used for salads and in stews.

The seeds of the herb are used in sauces, soups and casseroles, and of course in fresh salads.

KARELA (BITTER MELON, GOURD)

Also known as *Foo giva* in Chinese. Is used a great deal in Indian and Chinese cookery. Green, bitter when immature. Turns orange and slightly sweet when ripe. Select fruits when just beginning to change colour.

To remove bitterness of the melon: wash, halve, remove and discard seeds. Drop into boiling water, lower heat, simmer for 2–3 minutes and drain.

KOHLRABI *BRASSICA OLERACEA, VAR. CAULORAPA*

A member of the cabbage family, kohlrabi is derived from the German word for cabbage turnip.

Buy small kohlrabi, about the size of tennis balls. Large heads tend to be tough and tasteless.

Either store in a cool, dry place or refrigerate in a plastic bag.

TO PREPARE: cut off the stalk and wash. Most of the kohlrabi sold in shops have already had their leaves removed. This is a pity as the leaves and stems can be cooked in the same way as spinach.

Peel and slice or dice according to the requirements of the particular recipe.

MUSHROOM

The mushroom is a fungus and not a vegetable although it is regarded and treated as such. There are literally thousands of fungi available, some edible and some poisonous. Many edible mushrooms can be gathered in Britain, but unfortunately we tend to rely on the cultivated mushrooms that are sold in the shops. In Central Europe, in autumn, mushroom gathering has become a national pastime, when millions of people spend days in the forests and fields.

There are three kinds of mushrooms which are available all the year round in our shops. These are button, flat and open mushrooms. Oyster mushrooms are also increasingly available. In recent years 'Chinese' mushrooms have also arrived here. These are straw mushrooms — *tso gwoo* — which are small 2.5 cm (1 inch) long grey and brown walnut-sized fungi, and winter mushrooms — *dang gwoo* — which the Chinese dry and then cook, but the Japanese eat fresh. A third are Jew's ear mushrooms — *wan yee* — which are usually sold in their dried form.

They have the appearance of pieces of black paper. When soaked in hot water for 10–12 minutes they swell into translucent, brown, cloud-shaped ears, hence their other names — cloud ear fungus or jelly mushroom. They have no taste of their own, but add texture to a dish and are cooked in a few minutes.

Button and flat mushrooms are the same variety (*Psalliota campestris*) but are picked at different stages of their growth.

Never soak fresh mushrooms when preparing them. If possible just wipe them clean, but if you prefer to wash them then drop into a bowl of acidulated water, stir, remove and drain. Use immediately.

OKRA (LADY'S FINGER) *HIBISCUS ESCULENTUS*

A little-known vegetable which is rapidly being popularised in Britain due to the efforts of Middle and Far Eastern immigrants.

Okra is a finger-shaped, slightly hairy, green, sticky fruit pod of a tropical plant native to Africa, from where it spread to the Middle East, India and the Mediterranean lands. Understandably okra is at its best in the Arabic-speaking lands, particularly Morocco, Egypt, Lebanon, Syria, Iraq, Turkey and Iran. Always use small, fresh, crisp okra and avoid the large ones as they tend to go soggy when cooked.

When preparing okra trim the stems but take care not to cut into the pod or the juice will escape.

Do not overcook or they become soft and shapeless.

PLANTAIN *MUSA PARADISIACA*

These are green bananas with high starch and low sugar content which are used only for cooking and can be fried, baked or ground into flour.

Plantains are much used in South American, African and West Indian cuisines. The original homeland of this fruit was South East Asia, from where it travelled to the Middle East, Africa and the other tropical parts of the world.

SWEET POTATO *IPOMOEA BATATAS*

This is not a true potato although there are many apparent similarities. Originally from South and Central America, the sweet potato is the edible tuberous root of a vine. It comes in many shapes — round, oblong or beet-shaped with differing skin colours — white, purple and red. It can be as large as 15–30 cm (6–12 inches) long and 5–8 cm (2–3 inches) across.

Sweet potatoes have not, to date, been a great success in Europe or the Mediterranean regions, but they are now appearing in some greengrocers and large supermarkets. They are available all year round in most Indo-Pakistani and West Indian shops. Do not confuse them with yams, although for cooking purposes they are similar. Buy firm, clean tubers with no blemishes and an even colouring. Store in a cool dry place, but not in the refrigerator.

PAWPAW *CARICA PAPAYA*

Pawpaw or papaya is a fruit which is often treated as a vegetable. Originally from the South American tropics it was first brought to Europe by the Spanish from Panama. Pawpaw is now cultivated throughout the tropical regions of the world.

In its unripe form it is usually used in pickles and chutneys. When ripe it is made into desserts and ice-creams.

PEANUT (GROUNDNUT) *ARACHIS HYPOGAEA*

The peanut is a legume not a nut and certainly not a vegetable, but since it plays such a major role in the diet of millions of people in tropical and subtropical regions, mention should be made about a few of its characteristics. Originally from South America the peanut is a major food crop in Africa, South America and the Far East.

Peanuts are extremely nutritious and contain, pound for pound, more 'goodness' than meat or dairy products. They are sold raw, roasted and/or ready salted. Peanuts are also converted into oil and peanut butter.

PEPPERS (THE CAPSICUM FAMILY)

The peppers that Columbus brought back to Europe were new and an instant success. The pepper, or to use its official name *Capsicum annuum*, is now widespread throughout the world and plays a particularly prominent part in Mexican, Indian and Hungarian cuisines. They are relatively new in Britain and little used. Because of their name they are sometimes confused with the product of that aromatic plant of the genus *Piper*, the small berry of which we grind to make black or white pepper. But they are not related.

The word chilli comes from one of the Aztec dialects and is applied to any kind of pepper (of varying degrees of pungency) of the chilli family — *Capsicum frutescens*.

In Britain only a limited number of peppers from a vast range are sold. These are referred to as green peppers, sweet peppers, pimientos or bell peppers. They come in varying colours — green, red, yellow, white and even black.

Paprika is the ground powder of dried red peppers. Cayenne and chilli powder are the ground powder of dried red chillies.

The finest exponents of chilli-based cooking are the Mexicans and the variety of chillies used in Mexico is vast. In recent years a variety of fresh chillies have found their way into Indian shops and some greengrocers, but we still have a long way to go to catch up with the Mexicans.

Peppers will keep for quite a long time if refrigerated unwashed.

PUMPKIN *CUCURBITA PEPO*

Related to the cucumber, squash and melon, the pumpkin is really a berry or fruit, but is treated as a vegetable. Although known and cultivated in Britain since the Middle Ages pumpkin recipes are at their best in Mediterranean, Middle Eastern and Indian cuisines, where they appear in soups, salads, pies, stews and desserts.

British pumpkins tend to be smaller than those from the Mediterranean regions, which can be enormous and often over 15–20 kg (30–40 lb).

Pumpkins are a seasonal vegetable, although, as they become more popular, they are being imported and are, therefore, available for longer periods. Some greengrocers will cut up a pumpkin and sell it in required quantities. In some supermarkets it is sold in prepacked segments.

When buying make sure that the flesh is firm. Store in a dry, well-ventilated place or in the refrigerator.

Pumpkin can be mashed, baked, used in stews or as pie fillings or the fruit can be hollowed out and stuffed with other ingredients. When preparing a pumpkin do not throw away the seeds as they make an excellent snack when roasted called *passotamme* (passing time) in Greek.

Pumpkin also makes excellent desserts and there are some delicious recipes from the Middle East and India.

SALSIFY *TRAGOPOGON PORRIFOLIUS*

Also known as 'vegetable oyster' because of its supposed oyster flavour, salsify is the fleshy, edible root of a member of the daisy family. It is grey-white in colour with white, juicy flesh.

Little known and hence little used, it is now putting in an appearance in some large greengrocers. It is used in all Mediterranean cuisines, but outside of these it is still awaiting wider use.

BLACK SALSIFY — *Scorzonera Hispanica* — belongs to the same family, but as the name suggests its skin is a brownish black. It is very rarely seen in our shops.

TO PREPARE: scrub the roots thoroughly and then cook in simmering water for about 15 minutes or until tender. When cool enough to handle peel and cut the roots into 2 or 3 pieces and follow the recipe as instructed.

VINE LEAVES

You can buy preserved leaves from most Continental stores. They come loose in large containers or in plastic packets. However, if you have access to a vine use the fresh tender young leaves.

To prepare fresh leaves: stack the leaves on top of each other and drop into a large pan of boiling water. Simmer for 5–8 minutes. If the leaves are older cook for a little longer. Drain and leave to cool.

To prepare preserved leaves follow instructions on the packet.

WATER CHESTNUTS *TRAPA BICORNIS*

There are several kinds. The Kashmiri version is triangular in shape with hornlike projections and is deep red in colour. The Chinese version (*Ling gok*) is dark brown, but in taste they are much alike.

I suggest you use the canned versions, although unshelled nuts are sometimes available in Chinese shops.

YAM GENUS *DIOSCOREA*

Popular in African cuisines, the yam is a member of a rich variety of tubers grown in all tropical countries.

Little known to date in Britain although it is always available in Indo-Pakistani and West Indian shops. It is a large vegetable usually weighing 900 g (2 lb) or more. Choose the smallest yams available. By far the most popular is the African yam (white yam).

For cooking it has almost all the properties of the potato and it is treated as such by African housewives. So peel, wash and either boil until tender and mash or bake. Yams can be used in soups, salads, stews and pies.

bibliography

The Unwritten Song — W. R. Trask. Jonathan Cape, London 1969

Poetry in the Dark Ages — trans H. Waddell from *The Mark of the Maker*,
  Constable & Co Ltd, London 1973

First Catch Your Eland — Laurens van der Post. Hogarth Press, London 1977

The Complete Plays of Aristophanes — ed Moses Hadas. Bantam Books Inc, NY 1962

The Oxford Book of American Light Verse — ed William Harmon.
  Oxford University Press 1979

Negro Folklore — ed Langston Hughes and Arna Bontemps.
  Dodd, Mead & Co Inc, NY 1965

Penguin Book of Zen Poetry — ed and trans Lucien Stryk and Takashi Ikemoto.
  Penguin, London 1980

The Complete Asian Cookbook — Charmaine Solomon. Grub Street, London 1995

The Traditional Recipes of Laos — Phia Sing. Prospect Books, London 1981

An Anthology of Moorish Poetry — trans A. J. Arberry.
  Cambridge University Press, 1953

Racial Proverbs — Selwyn Gurney Champion. G. Routledge & Sons, London 1938

An Anthology of the Potato — Robert McKay. Allen Figgis & Co Ltd. Dublin 1901

De Re Coquinaria/Culinaria (translated as *The Roman Cookery Book*,
  by B. Flower and E. Rosenbaum; London, 1958) — Marcus Gabius Apicius

The English Housewife — Gervase Markham 1649

Acetaria, a Discourse of Sallets — John Evelyn 1699

La Physiologie du Goût — Anthelme Brillat-Savarin 1825

index